T. MACCI PLAVTI AVLVLARIA

WITH NOTES CRITICAL AND EXEGETICAL AND AN INTRODUCTION

BY

WILHELM WAGNER

AYER COMPANY, PUBLISHERS, INC.
SALEM, NEW HAMPSHIRE 03079

Editorial Supervision: DIETRICH SNELL

Reprint Edition 1984
AYER Company, Publishers, Inc.

Reprinted from a copy in The University of Illinois Library

LATIN TEXTS AND COMMENTARIES
ISBN for complete set: 0-405-11594-6
See last pages of this volume for titles.

Manufactured in the United States of America

Library of Congress Cataloging in Publication Data

Plautus, Titus Maccius.
    T. Macci Plauti Aulularia.

    (Latin texts and commentaries)
    Reprint of the 1876 ed. published by Deighton Bell,
Cambridge.
    I. Wagner, Wilhelm, 1843-1880. II. Title:
Aulularia. III. Series.
PA6568.A8 1979   872'.01   78-67156
ISBN 0-405-11623-3

T. MACCI PLAVTI
AVLVLARIA

WITH NOTES CRITICAL AND EXEGETICAL
AND AN INTRODUCTION

BY

WILHELM WAGNER, Ph. D.
PROFESSOR AT THE JOHANNEUM, HAMBURG.

SECOND EDITION, RE-WRITTEN.

CAMBRIDGE
DEIGHTON BELL AND CO.
LONDON G. BELL AND SONS
1876.

Cambridge:

PRINTED BY C. J. CLAY, M.A

AT THE UNIVERSITY PRESS.

PREFACE

TO THE FIRST EDITION.

As the present work is intended to supply the wants
of more than one class of readers, I think that on its
completion a few words will not be superfluous in order
to explain its origin and purpose.

In pursuance of my studies on the Aulularia, a first
specimen of which I had given in my dissertation *de
Plauti Aulularia* (Bonn, Marcus, 1864), I had as well
as I could emended the text and collected much ma-
terial towards an exegetical commentary. Easter 1865
I visited London to collate the MS. J in the British
Museum. On my return to Manchester, I went over
the text again, and in this way a critical commentary
was at last produced which appeared to give a clearer
idea of the textual history of this play than could be
had from any former edition. In June, I went again
to London, and there it was that Professor Key kindly
encouraged me to publish my labours. Now, although
I had at first planned nothing more than a critical
edition of the Aulularia, I soon found that my book
would be more useful and perhaps agreeable to a larger
range of readers, if an exegetical commentary should

1—2

be added. It may be that only a few scholars will care
for the critical notes, but surely many students will
desire to have explanatory notes, without which the
edition would to them be quite useless. As it is my
opinion that no Latin author can be advantageously
explained in the same language, I have written my
notes in English, though I am well aware that in so
doing I must rely on the forbearance and kindness of
my readers, who will, I hope, not be very strict in the
case of a foreigner whose acquaintance with the English
language is not of very long standing. I may say that
I have read and studied all the commentaries ever
written on the Aulularia, and there scarcely can be anything of importance in them which would not be found
in my notes. But at the same time, I have tried to
avoid all unnecessary and superfluous erudition which
seemed to have no connexion with the explanation of
the text. On the whole I venture to hope that a student will after the perusal of my notes be sufficiently
prepared for a critical study of the Plautine comedies.
I have not thought my commentary to be a place
wherein to mention the names of former commentators
whenever I am indebted to them for explanations or
quotations; there is indeed a great deal of exegetical
matter running through all commentaries, and well-
known to every scholar; special mention has, however,
been thought necessary in exceptional cases where peculiar honour seemed due to the discovery of difficult
explanations or happy quotations. Whether the original
additions and illustrations given in the present commentary will be thought an improvement or not, I must
leave to my readers to decide.

In the Introduction I have chiefly endeavoured to give a brief, but clear and sufficient summary of the laws of Plautine prosody. This seemed the more necessary as the results of the investigations of Ritschl and other German scholars on this subject are either totally unknown or, at best, but partially known in this country, and are moreover not easily accessible to the English student, they being scattered through Ritschl's Plautus and prooemia, and many volumes of German philological periodicals.

In concluding this preface, it gives me great pleasure publicly to acknowledge the manifold obligations which I owe to Dr Ernest Adams, who has not only kindly touched my English style in many a sore part, but to whose hints and suggestions both the Introduction and notes are greatly indebted.

Thus I dismiss my book, though I feel that it stands in need of much indulgence and forbearance—I venture to say that it would be better if I could have written it at a place more favourable to philological studies than Manchester.

Rusholme, near Manchester,
May, 1866.

The present work will be found to differ from the first edition in not a few respects. In the first place I have omitted the critical commentary which will appear in an amended shape in a critical edition to be published shortly. I have, however, revised the text with much care and have endeavoured to keep pace with the progress of Plautine studies, though I have found it impossible to quote all the treatises and works I have consulted. Let me hope that the re-issue of my Aulularia (which has been out of print for some time) will meet with the same favour as was so largely accorded to the first edition. If the second edition proves to be superior to the first, this should be mainly attributed to the greater facility I enjoy at my present place of residence for procuring more philological works, indispensable to the author of a work like this, than were within my reach at Cottonopolis. By more than one of my countrymen I have been accused of ignoring some treatise or some passage of a grammarian bearing upon the matter I treated of, when in reality the fault lay with the impossibility of procuring certain works at that time. In conclusion I may be allowed to observe that I have endeavoured to preserve calmness of tone and impartiality of judgment in discussing the various theories of Plautine prosody and the multifarious problems of Plautine criticism.

HAMBURG,
Easter, 1876.

INTRODUCTION.

ON LATIN PRONUNCIATION AS SEEN IN THE VERSES OF THE COMIC WRITERS.

ANYONE who undertakes the reading of Plautus and Terence on the sole strength of his acquaintance with the rules of prosody and versification observed by Virgil and Horace, will be sorely puzzled to scan the verses of the two comic poets: he will indeed find it no less difficult than Horace himself whose metrical principles are implied in the line *legitimumque sonum digitis callemus et aure* (A. P. 274). But the ears of those Romans for whom Plautus wrote his plays, were by no means the same as those of the contemporaries of Horace, and it would be more than an anachronism, it would be the greatest injustice to the old poets, if we were to measure their versification by the standard of the refined laws of the Augustan period, or to blame them for not having adapted their prosody to rules unknown to them. The principle which should guide us in our judgment of the verses of the comic poets, is pointed out by Cicero, Orator 55, 184 '*comicorum senarii* propter similitudinem sermonis *sic saepe sunt abiecti*[1], *ut non numquam vix in eis numerus et versus intellegi possit*[2],' and in another passage,

---

[1] This adjective involves no blame at all, being simply an equivalent to *humilis*, see Or. 57, 192 '*ita neque humilem et abiectam orationem nec nimis altam et exaggeratam probat.*'

[2] Priscian, who lived in the sixth century of our era, states in the commencement of his treatise *de metris fabularum Terentii* that some of his contemporaries *vel abnegant esse in*

Or. 20, 67 'apud quos [i.e. comicos*poëtas*], nisi quod versiculi sunt, nihil est aliud quotidiani dissimile sermonis[1].' These two passages should teach us how to deal with Plautine verses and language. Nevertheless, the truth was not found out for nearly two centuries after p. xiv the publication of the first edition of Plautus, and the earlier editors did not hesitate to recognise Greek forms and imitations of Greek constructions in the style of Plautus; and as to metre and prosody, they either had no idea at all of their laws and did not greatly trouble themselves about them, or, at best, their notions were very vague and rather like presentiment than the full possession of truth itself. François Guyet, a French scholar of the 17th century, was the first to study the versification of the comic poets, and though his results were intermixed with a great many errors (as, indeed, it could not be otherwise), his works seem to have given the first impulse to Bentley, if we may argue from the fact that many of Bentley's emendations in Terence are already to be met with in Guyet's *Commentarii*, and that even some of his caprices occur there[2]. It is difficult to

Terentii comoediis metra vel ea quasi arcana quaedam et ab omnibus semota sibi solis esse cognita confirmant (p.418 Hertz). Priscian's own conceptions of the Terentian metres and prosody are, however, far from correct, thus bearing out Cicero's words that even the ancients themselves found it difficult to understand the metrical laws of archaic versification.

[1] Comp. Schuchardt, *vokalismus des vulgärlateins* i 50: *in der komischen poësie spiegeln sich alle freiheiten der vulgären aussprache ab.*—ibid. p. 57: *das alterthümliche latein ist weiter nichts als vulgäres.*

[2] It would seem that Bentley had read Guyet's work and noted down most of his emendations; years afterwards, when he published his own Terence, he appears to have forgotten the real author of a great many of the conjectures he found scattered over the margin of his copy, and as he approved of them, he imagined them to be his own. It would be interesting to possess Guyet's treatise *de prosodia versuum Terentii et Plauti*, which his sudden death did not allow him to finish. Guyet died in April 1655. His *Commentarii in P. Terentii Comoedias* vi were published at Strasburg, a. 1657; the text of his Plautus appeared at Paris 1658, in 4 vols., with the French translation of M. de Marolles.

speak too highly of Bentley's merits with regard to
Plautus and Terence ; but like most of his works, even
his Terence was merely an *extempore* performance and
bears the traces of haste : though for all this, it will continue to be one of the foremost works of classical philology. It would, however, be totally preposterous to
think that Bentley's famous *Schediasma* furnishes the
real key to the full understanding of Plautine prosody
and metres. Gottfried Hermann, whom his excellent
teacher Reiz[1] had early made familiar with Bentley's
Terence, adopted and refined his views both in his
editions of the Trinummus and the Bacchides, and in
his *Elementa doctrinae metricae* (1816), where he has
often occasion to speak of Plautine passages and to emend p. xv
them. F. Ritschl, whose name will always be connected
with that of Plautus, declares in his dedication of the
Prolegomena to the Trinummus, that, next to the great
Bentley, he considers Gottfried Hermann (whose pupil
he was at Leipzig) as his sole guide in the criticism
of Plautus. This admits, however, of many restrictions.
Ritschl does not adhere to the same principles throughout his edition of Plautus. Many facts which he did
not acknowledge in his Prolegomena, were admitted in
the prefaces to the different parts of the second and
third volumes, some even were tacitly given up. After
the appearance of the Mercator (the ninth of the plays
edited by Ritschl), his views underwent so radical a
change that he was obliged to discontinue his work until
further materials had been collected towards the history
of archaic Latin. What he now holds as to Plautine
prosody, etc. is developed in an excellent paper in the
Rheinisches Museum vol. XIV p. 400 ss., and most of the
proofs of his views are contained in the numerous *prooemia*,
which it was his duty to write twice every year while

---

[1] Reiz himself edited the Rudens in accordance with Bentley's principles, Lipsiae 1789 ;
this was reprinted with a critical commentary by C. E. Schnei-
der, Breslau 1824.—Gottfried
Hermann edited the Trinummus, Lipsiae 1800, and the Bacchides, ibid. 1845.

professor at Bonn[1]. In the following sketch, Ritschl's theories have been duly weighed, though not adopted to the exclusion of all others, and proper regard has been paid to the discussions of Corssen, whose elaborate work on Latin pronunciation we have always quoted from the second edition.

But to return to the two passages quoted from Cicero,— we need not dwell upon the fact that for a .full appreciation of Plautine metres and prosody it is indispensable to obtain a just idea of the earliest pronunciation of Latin. A search after this will not fail to throw much light on the earliest history of the Latin language; it will, at the same time, show that many forms now found in the so-called Romance languages were already anticipated in the popular speech of the epoch of Plautus and Terence. This accounts for the otherwise surprising fact that many of the latest forms of the Latin language are either perfectly identical with the earliest forms or must at least be traced back to the working of the same laws. This point is of great importance, but it has been greatly overvalued in the late Prof. Key's paper 'On the metres of Plautus and Terence' appended to his treatise on the Alphabet[2].

[1] In 1865, Ritschl accepted a professorship at the University of Leipzig. His views on Plautine prosody underwent some further change in 1869, when he published his *Neue Plautinische Excurse*, in which he attempts to remove many cases of hiatus in the verses of Plautus by means of the assumption that an ablatival *D* was still employed in the Latin language at the time of the second Punic war. See, for this, Corssen's work on Latin Pronunciation II p. 1005 sqq. and the Preface to my second edition of the Trinummus. In 1871, Ritschl published a second edition of the Trinummus, but without the Prolegomena of the first, which are now out of print and have become rather a scarce book.—*C. F. W. Müller's* work on Plautine Prosody (Berlin 1869, with an appendix —*Nachträge*—1871) is valuable on account of the materials collected with great industry: but Ritschl himself (in his new ed. of the Trinummus) speaks rather contemptuously of the author's critical sagacity, though Müller adheres mainly to the views set forth in Ritschl's own Prolegomena. See my pref. to the Trin., p. IV.

[2] Prof. Key's system of pro-

A. ARCHAIC LONG VOWELS.

In its most remote period, the Latin language abounded p. xvi in long and heavy vowels, while at a later period many of the endings which were originally long became weakened and were shortened. Some of these endings or suffixes are occasionally found long even in later writers, but a great many of these long quantities are still met with in Plautus and his contemporaries. They are, however, of rare occurrence in Terence, nay, some of them seem to have been shortened in the period dividing Plautus from Terence. In the following pages instances are given of those suffixes which are used by Plautus in their original long quantity : but the reader should bear in mind that Plautus is by no means consistent in attaching to these suffixes always the same (and no other) quantity ; on the contrary, he allows himself considerable licence in treating them just as it suits his verse. This is, of course, very con-

nouncing Latin verse may be called a *contractive* one, since he makes use of a contracted pronunciation of certain words even where metrical reasons (at least those generally accepted) would well admit of the uncontracted forms. E. g. Prof. Key tells us to read *poëta cúmprim* *ám adscríbend áppulit'* ('Alphabet' p. 146), there being no metrical reason at all, why we should not admit a dactyl $-\breve{}\breve{}$ (*prim áni*) instead of the spondee *prim ám*. I am afraid that a general application of this system would reduce Plautine lines to a monotony quite detrimental to the charm of conversational vivacity we find in the comic writers. In his work on 'Language: its Origin and Development,' Prof. Key has stated his views at greater length, and we have occasion-

ally referred to some of his arguments, though we have found it impossible to enter into a full discussion of his views, which do not seem to be shared by any other scholar.—-It is scarcely necessary to add that Prof. Key's theories of 'scansion' are quite at variance with the precepts of the ancient grammarians, whose authority is unduly set aside by him. We may here quote the *locus classicus* in Marius Victorinus II p. 80 sq. ed. Keil: *similiter apud comicos laxius spatium versibus datum est...ita dum cotidianum sermonem imitari nituntur, metra vitiant studio, non imperitia, quod frequentius apud nostros . quam Graecos invenies.* See also the extracts from Juba in Rufinus *de metris comicis* p. 2711 P. = p. 562 Keil.

venient to the poet himself, but often proves a source of
embarrassment to his reader. But then again, Plautus
composed his dramas for oral recitation, and not for
perusal in the student's closet.

1. In *declension* we find the following deviations from
the common usage of the Augustan period:

a in the nom. and voc. sing. of the first declension
was originally long in old Latin, as it is indeed in Sanskrit
and in many cases in Greek. That it must have been
so, might, even in default of other proofs, have been concluded from the simple fact that the genitive *āi* would be
left unaccounted for, but for the length of the nom. *a*
(Ritschl, Rhein. Mus. xiv 400). But we actually find it
long in three lines of the old inscriptions on the sepulchres
of the Scipios.

> honós *famá* virtúsque glória átque ingénium
> *terrá* Publí prognátum Públió Cornéli.
> quoieí *vitá* defécit, nón honós honóre[1].

(Ritschl, *ibid.*) Nay, Bücheler shows (*jahrbücher für clas-
sische philologie* 1863 p. 336 s.) that in all the Saturnians
which have come down to us, the nom. and voc. *a* is con-
p. xvii stantly long. We find it long again in some lines of Livius
Andronicus, Naevius and Ennius (Ann. 148. 484. 319.
433. 305 *ed. Vahlen*), and in a hexameter in the sepulchral inscription which Plautus is said to have composed
for himself:

> scaénast désertá: dein Risus Ludu' Iocusque.

It is therefore by no means surprising to find that Plautus
uses the same quantity in several passages of his comedies. This fact had already been acknowledged by Lindemann in Trin. 251[2], and in about a dozen passages by

---

[1] See also Corssen ii 449.
The fourth instance of a long *a*
in the nom. sing. quoted by
Corssen from the epitaphs of the
Scipios is very doubtful. I
should scan it
> mors pérfecít tua ut éssent |
> ómniá brévia.

See also Wordsworth, 'Spec. of
Early Latin,' p. 31.

[2] *De prosodia Plauti* p. x in
his second edition of the Captivi, Miles gloriosus and Trinummus, Lipsiae 1844. The
last editor of the Trinummus,
Prof. J. Brix, gives the passage

Weise[1], but it was again rejected by Ritschl. Nevertheless, Prof. Key was right not to be daunted in stating the fact, Lat. Gram. § 88 p. 13 (5th ed). Corssen gives three instances of it in Plautus in the first edition of his work on Pronunciation I p. 330: Fleckeisen has as many as eighteen in his excellent paper on this subject, but there probably remain more to be discovered[2].

us in the nom. of the second declension is occasionally found long in Naevius :

> dein póllếns sagíttis ínclutús arquítenens
> sanctús Delphís prognátus Pútiús Apóllo[3].

There are, however, no trustworthy instances of this quantity to be met with in Plautus; but he uses sometimes

būs (dat. and abl. plur.) as a long syllable : see Merc. 900. 919. Most. (842?) 1118. Men. 842. Rud. 975.[4]

in question in accordance with Lindemann, though he seems unaware of this precedence. The instance which Prof. J. Brix quotes from Ter. Hec. prol. 2 is very doubtful.

[1] See his index in his edition of Plautus, Quedlinburg 1838.

[2] See Fleckeisen, Krit. Misc. (Leipzig 1864) p. 11—23 and Corssen II 451—454. The results of Fleckeisen's and Bücheler's investigations have been attacked by C. F. W. Müller, Prosody p. 3—10; see also Ussing's Prolegomena to Plautus (Havniae, 1875), p. 195: '*A casus recti primae declinationis et neutri pluralis ceterarum nisi vitiose a Plauto produci non potuisse Müllero credo; unum exceperim; nam in masculinis nominibus primae declinationis a finale interdum productum videtur, ut Sosiā Amph. 434, 435, Antidamā* Poen. 958: nam *Antidamas* (quod codices praebent) Plautina forma non vide-

tur. *Leonidā* Asin. 733 vocativus est.' The most trustworthy instances of the long quantity of the *a* of the nom. sing. are as follows —

ne epístulā quidem úlla sit in aédibus Asin. 762.

potuít: plus iam sum líbera quinquénnium Epid. III 4, 62.

inéptiā stultítiaque adeo et témeritas Merc. 26.

haec mi hóspitalis téssdrā cum illó fuit Poen. v 2, 92.

and *Palaestrāne* Rud. 237 (comp. Lachm. on Lucr. p. 406), *Canthārā* Epid. IV 1, 40.—It would be perverse to change the text in these passages, though Müller does so.—The passages in which *a* of the neuter plural would seem to be used long, are less clear: see Müller, Pros. p. 11—13.

[3] See *Naevi de bello punico reliquiae*, ed. *Vahlen*, p. 14.

[4] It should be understood that the above references al-

This quantity admits of an easy explanation. The Latin
suffix *bus* corresponds to the Sanskr. *bhyas*, and would
appear to have been long by way of contraction; and
indeed the long quantity remained for ever in *nobīs* and
vobīs, in which *bīs* is the same suffix as *bus* (Corssen I
169. II 49, and chiefly p. 498 sq., where the Plautine
instances are discussed). Virgil, Aen. IV 64, has *pec-
toribūs inhians*, in seeming imitation of the archaic prosody : see Nettleship in Conington's Virgil III p. 468.

The ending *or* in nouns of the third declension is
frequently long. That it was originally long, might
readily be concluded from the genitive *ōris* and from a
comparison with the Greek ωρ. Thus we have *sorōr*
Poen. I 2, 29. 151. 194. IV 2, 73. Epid. v 1, 50. Bacch.
p. xviii 1140. *uxōr* Stich. 140. As. 927. The same is the case
with the comparatives *stultiōr* Bacch. 123, *auctiōr* Capt.
782, *longiōr* Amph. 548, *vorsutiōr* Epid. III 2, 35[1]. It
seems, therefore, but natural that we should find the
neuter *longiūs* Men. 327, on which passages Brix's note
may be compared. C. F. W. Müller, Pros. p. 55—57,
alters the passage quoted in support of this quantity :
wrongly, as we think. Comp. also Bücheler's treatise on
Latin Declension, p. 4. Corssen II 500. 507.

er would seem to be long in *pater* Aul. 772. Trin. 645[2].
Poen. v 5, 15. It has the same quantity in three passages
in Virgil, Aen. v 521. XI 469. XII 14. (Nettleship ap.
Conington, III 467.) The fact is accounted for by Prof.
Key, Lat. Gram. p. 437. Phil. Essays p. 86. But I have
now yielded to Corssen's objections II 502 sq. and corrected
these two passages.

ēi. Originally the *e* in the gen. and dat. sing. of the
fifth declension was always long[3]. Thus we have *fidēi*
Aul. 575. It may be added that the datives *mihi tibi*

ways apply to the readings of
the mss., which are however
generally altered by Ritschl.
[1] Ritschl, Proll. Trin. CLXXV.
Müller, Pros. p. 42—44. This
peculiarity of archaic prosody
was likewise imitated by Virgil;

see Nettleship, as quoted before, p. 466 sq.
[2] According to the reading of
the Ambrosian ms.
[3] See Key, L. G. § 147, and
Lachmann on Lucr. p. 151.

sibi are used both as iambs (which is their original quantity) and pyrrhichs. Ritschl had originally doubted the possibility of employing them as iambs in iambic and trochaic metre, but his theories have been refuted by A. Spengel, Plautus p. 55 sqq.

2. I will now proceed to enumerate those terminations in *conjugation* which sometimes preserve their original long quantity contrary to the general usage of the Augustan period.

In Plautus' prosody all those endings may be long in which an original vowel is contracted with the root-vowel of the verb. Thus Plautus has not only

$$\bar{a}s \; \bar{e}s \; \bar{\imath}s = ais \; eis \; iis$$

which even later times did not deviate from, but we find in his verses the third persons analogously long :

$$\bar{a}t \; \bar{e}t \; \bar{\imath}t = ait \; eit \; iit.$$

This is admitted on all sides ; see Key, Lat. Gram. p. 428, who quotes Ritschl's Proll. Trin. CLXXXIII. Prof. Key justly adds : ' There are not wanting similar examples in Virgil and Horace ; but editors and teachers complacently get over the difficulty by attributing the unusual length to the so-called principle of caesura, or to poetical licence.' We may notice the same error in Parry's Introduction to Terence p. LV, where the subjunctive *augeāt* (Ter. Ad. *prol.* 25) is attributed to the influence of '*ictus :*' but the ending *at*, just as well as *bāt* in the imperf., was originally long, as will be seen from the second persons *ās bās* and the plural *āmus ātis*, and appears therefore in its real p. xix quantity in the passage alluded to. Thus we have *fuāt* and *sciāt* in Plautus, and *soleāt* in Horace (Serm. I 5, 90). It is the same with the imperfects *ponēbāt* (Enn. Ann. 314), *amittebāt* (Virg. Aen. v 853)[1], and *erāt* (Hor. Serm. II 2, 47). It is the same with the ending *et* of the sub-

---

[1] Lucian Müller thinks that the passages from Virgil should be corrected according to the authority of some mss. See his observations on the whole subject of lengthened endings, *de re metr.* p. 326—333. See also Nettleship, l. c. p. 468.

junctive (both present and imperfect)[1]. The ending *et*
of the future belongs, of course, to the same series[2].
Nay, even the suffix *it* in the present of the so-called
third conjugation was originally long, e. g. Plautus has *per-
cipīt* Men. 921, and Ennius *ponīt* (Ann. 484). Hence we
should not be surprised to find similar unusual long vowels
in Horace (*agīt* Serm. II 3, 260. *figīt* Od. III 24, 5. *defendīt*
Serm. I 4, 82) and in Virgil (*sinīt* Aen. X 433. *facīt* Ecl.
VII 23. *petīt* Aen. IX 9). An explanation of this quantity
is given by Corssen, II 492 : it will at once be understood
by comparing the Latin and Greek forms of λέγω and
lego :

λέγω *legō*
λέγεις *legīs* or *legeis* [*ei* = *ī*][3]
λέγει(τ) *legīt* or *legeit.*

We find the same quantity again in the third pers. sing.
perf. Once, it is even expressed by the spelling *ei* = *ī*[4]
Merc. 530, where the ms. A gives *redieit*, and it is well
established by many instances in Plautus and Terence[5], to
which we have to add about eight different examples
from Virgil[6], Horace and Ovid.—The same remark applies to the subjunctive ending *erīt*, the fut. perf., *īt* in

[1] I may quote an instance of
this quantity from thePseudulus,
v. 58:
cum eó simul me mítterēt. ei
reí dies.
In this line, Ritschl and Fleckeisen insert *leno* after *me* and
consider *simul* to be monosyllabic. This word seems however not indispensably necessary, and I am inclined to read
the words in accordance with
the mss. Prof. Sauppe proposes
to read: *cum eó simitu mitterer*
(ind. schol., Gott. 18⅘ p. 4).

[2] Most of these originally long
syllables were first pointed out
by Fleckeisen, *neue jahrbücher*
LXI 18 ss.

[3] Compare *scribis* Hor. Serm.
II 3, 1.

[4] For inscriptions see E. Hüb-
ner's Index in the C.I.L. I p.
601.

[5] Corssen II 493 sq. gives a
sufficient number.

[6] See Nettleship, l. c., p. 469.
Wherever archaic quantities
occur in the later poets, they
should be considered as the result of imitation of the earlier
writers. We may add that the
original long quantities are admitted by the later poets quite
exclusively *in arsi*, i. e. when
the metrical accent falls upon
the ending in question.

sĭt velĭt mavelĭt, nay even to the simple future *erĭt* ('he will be') Capt. 208 and *bĭt* in *vaenibĭt* Most. 1160[1].

In the passive, the shortening propensities of the Latin language displayed themselves chiefly in the first person of the singular. In Plautus we find sometimes the original quantities *ōr ār²*, nay *ferār* is met with as late as Ovid (Met. vii 61). Analogously, the endings *er* and *rer* in the subj. were originally long.

It may finally be remarked that *es* ('thou art') is invariably long in the prosody of the comic poets.

B. IRREGULAR SHORTENING OF LONG FINAL VOWELS.

All these long vowels are, however, of but occasional occurrence in Plautus and Terence—they are, indeed, nothing more than a few scattered remnants of a period of the language, which was rapidly waning and dying away. The *general character* of the language in the time of Plautus was quite different. A destructive element had already commenced its powerful influence upon the language, and had already deeply affected and altered the original quantity of many endings and even of many root-vowels of Latin words.

The accent in Latin never falls on the last syllable, and its tendency was to destroy the length of this last syllable[3], especially in case the word was disyllabic and had a short penult.

---

[1] See Corssen, i 496. C. F. W. Müller, Pros. p. 705, is against Corssen, whose work he styles 'the most impure source of Plautine prosody.'

[2] Corssen, i 501. See Aul. 214, 230.

[3] 'The latter part of a word is naturally liable to a less careful pronunciation.' Key, *Trans. of the Phil. Soc.* 1857 p. 295. Benary (Röm. Lautl. p. 1) considers as one of the most cha-

racteristic features of the Latin language 'die schwächung des auslautes, dem consonantismus wie dem vocalismus nach.' Comp. Quintilian, Inst. Or. xi 3, 33: *dilucida vero erit pronuntiatio, si verba tota exierint, quorum pars devorari, pars destitui solet, plerisque extremas syllabas non perferentibus, dum priorum sono indulgent.* We need not remind the reader that the same cause has by its powerful opera-

We find, therefore, in Plautus a greater number of instances in which the above-mentioned archaic long vowels have been shortened than where they still retain their original quantity—and of this phenomenon we should attribute the main cause to the influence of the accent. But the development, having once commenced, did not stop there ; on the contrary, many short quantities are to be found in the comic poets which were either entirely rejected or but exceptionally admitted by later poets.

p. xxi   I shall first speak of the final vowels occasionally shortened in the rapid pronunciation of the times between the second and third Punic wars.

It will be observed that all the instances which we are about to produce represent disyllabic words which are used as *pyrrhichs*, instead of their original *iambic* prosody. This could never have taken place, had they been pronounced with the accent on the last syllable.

The long *a* of the first declension was not only shortened in the nom. and voc. (as it remained indeed ever afterwards), but even in the ablative, e. g.

pró mală víta fámam extolles, pró bonă partam glóriam.
Ennius ed. Vahlen p. 94.

The same happened to the *o* of the dat. and abl. sing. of the second declension, e. g. the abl. *domo* stands as a pyirhich in the following two instances :

unde éxit? : : unde nísi domō : : domŏ? : : mé vide : : etsi vídeo.
Mil. gl. 376[1].
domŏ quém profugiens dóminum apstulerat, véndidit.
Capt. prol. 18.

In the abl. *ioco* the final *o* is shortened Bacch. 75, where the reading of the mss. is as follows :

símulato me amáre : : utrum ego istuc iócŏn adsimulem an sério?

tion destroyed the inflexional endings of the English language, which shares the peculiarity of the Latin with regard to the slurred pronunciation of unac-cented last syllables.
[1] See Ritschl, praef. Stich. xvii. But see also Brix's note in his recent edition of the Miles gl., p. 138.

and so Fleckeisen gives the line, while Ritschl writes

> utrum ego iocón id simulem an sério.

ero (dat. of *erus,* master) stands as a pyrrhich Aul. 584 and Most. 948. *bonŏ* is another example of the same kind :

> haéc erít bonŏ génere nata, níl scit nisi verúm loqui.
> Persa 645 [1].

malŏ falls under the same head :

> malŏ máxumo suo hercle ílico, ubi tántulum peccássit.
> Cas. IV 4, 6.

> sét etiam unum hoc éx ingenio málŏ malum inveniúnt suo.
> Bacch. 546.

> cavĕ sís malŏ. quíd tu málum nam mé [anapæstic].
> Rud. IV 3, 12.

In the last passage, Fleckeisen alters the metre by inserting *nunc* after *nam*.

The abl. *modŏ* (which should not be confounded with p. xxii the particle) stands as a pyrrhich Aul. 589 :

> eōdem módŏ servóm ratem esse amánti ero aequom cénseo,

and Pseud. 569, where the mss. read as follows [2]:

> novŏ módŏ, novom aliquid íuventum adferre áddecet.

In this case, the words *novo modo* should be taken as a proceleusmatic, a foot which is very frequent in the first place of a senarius (see Ritschl, Proll. Trin. CCLXXXIX). With the same quantity we have in the Trinummus 602

> quó modŏ tu istuc, Stásime, dixti, nóstrum erilem fílium.

Lachmann (on Lucretius p. 116) calls the short quantity of this *o* ‘ mirabile :' Prof. Key, to avoid recognising a fact like this, proposes the monosyllabic pronunciation

---

[1] In this passage, Ritschl gives *bono* without the mark of ecthlipsis (Proll. CXLIV), i. e. he considers the final *o* to be shortened.

[2] Ritschl omits *inventum* and thus restores *modo* to its usual measure. I am glad to see that Fleckeisen does not follow his example.

mo, and to corroborate this conjecture, he appeals to the
Roman way of abbreviating the word : *mō* ('Alphabet'
p. 141). But I may observe, that by abbreviating the
orthographical representation of a word, nothing is *prima
facie* insinuated as to its pronunciation[1]. Prof. Key's
other argument is drawn from the Romance languages,
where *quomodo* appears in the shape of *como come comme:*
it would, no doubt, prove that *quomodo* really sounded
like *quomo* (*como*) in the latest period of the Latin
language, but would it explain the real nature of the
general law whose slow but steady working at last degraded full words and endings to poor cripples ? We
recognise in Plautine prosody the beginnings and the
first germs of a depravation of the Latin language, which
attained its final development in the Romance languages.
We need not, therefore, hesitate to explain Romance
forms from such shortened endings as are found in
Plautus, but great caution should be used in remodelling
the pronunciation of Plautine forms upon the analogy of
Romance corruptions. The spirit of modern philology
requires that the order of time should be observed and
forbids us to blend the peculiarities of the different
p. xxiii periods of any language[2]. If, however, any further proof

---

[1] If e. g. we were to take the
copy-books of German students
as the indication of their pronunciation, we should arrive at a
great many surprising discoveries in German pronunciation;
but unfortunately, they would
all be repudiated by the actual
pronunciation of those students
themselves.

[2] The sense of these words is
borrowed from Prof. Key himself ('*On the so-called A priva-
tiuum*' p. 8).— The list of contracted words, given by Prof.
Key ('Alphabet' p. 146—148),
would require a great many additional observations, if the
present writer really intended

to examine each separate instance. But he has no intention to criticise all his predeces-
sors, nor does he think it necessary always to state when he
deviates from the views of other
scholars. He would, however,
ask his readers not to think
him unacquainted with really
excellent labours in the same
field, even when he does not
expressly quote them; but taking notice of everything would
too much increase this Introduction, which the author first
thought he could entirely dispense with. He may, however,
state that almost the same
views as those given here, will

should be required that in *modo* the final *o* was actually shortened, the word *not* being contracted to a monosyllable, it suffices to quote Horace, Serm. I 9, 43 :

cúm victóre sequór.   Maecénas quó modŏ técum?

In this case, the monosyllabic pronunciation *quómo* would violate the metre.   And if we find the *o* shortened by so nice a judge of Latin prosody as Horace, we shall certainly not hesitate to acknowledge the same fact in the conversational language of Plautus[1].

A whole class of words belongs to the same category as the ablatives just mentioned : viz. prepositions and adverbs, in which the final *a* and *o* were originally ablative-endings.   Thus we have *contra*, which is read with

be found in Brix's Introduction to his edition of the Trinummus (Leipzig, 1864), and that he is frequently indebted to Prof. Brix for the instances quoted, though the order and arrangement in Brix's book differ totally from the present sketch. The chapters of Ritschl's Prolegomena which deal with the same matters, are still very useful for furnishing examples of all kinds, but as to the doctrine itself propounded in them, there is not one page where Ritschl himself could now dispense with many alterations. We should not, however, forget that it is due to Ritschl himself that we now possess sounder theories than in the year 1848.

[1] In his work on 'Language: its Origin and Development' (published 1874), Prof. Key has repeated his theory of the pronunciation of *quomodo* as *quomo*, 'notwithstanding the dissent of Dr Wagner' (p. 131), but without replying anything to the argument I had deduced from Horace. I may, therefore, be excused for maintaining my own theory, as my arguments would seem to be no less valid now than they appeared to me ten years ago. I may add that Schuchardt has dealt with the Romance forms in his work on Vulgar Latin, II 393 ; but while Prof. Key treats *mo* as 'an instance of a silent *d*,' Schuchardt proves from the Corsican *cumed* and the Lombard *comòd* (which is also contracted into *cmòd*), that *mo* owes its origin not to contraction (*modo moo mo*) but to apocope (*mod mo*). The disappearance of the final syllable (*o*) is in agreement with the general law, according to which a long vowel first becomes short, being attacked as it were by a kind of consumption, which terminates in death, when it falls off altogether. The final stage is that of the Romance languages, the middle stage is traceable in Plautus and the Augustan poets.

a short *a* in Prudentius and Ausonius[1], though it preserves its legitimate quantity in Plautus and the classic poets. In *frustra* the *a* is shortened by Prudentius and Martial[2], and the same quantity has been established for Plautus by Brix[3] in five instances, where Ritschl and Fleckeisen had, however, removed it by somewhat violent alterations.—All adverbs in *e* were originally ablatives[4], and their final *e* was therefore long; it became, however, short in many cases; it remained so ever afterwards

p. xxiv in *bene* and *male*[5], while it was common in *fere;* but in Plautus we find *probĕ* with the same short quantity (Poen. v 5, 1. Pseud. 603. Persa 650)[6]. The adverb *cito* had its final *o* common in all periods of Latin poetry[7].

The ablative-ending *e* of the third declension was originally long, e. g. in the following line from the sepulchral inscription of Scipio Barbatus :

Gnaivód patrē prognátus, fórtis vír sapiénsque.

---

[1] See Luc. Müller, de re metr. p. 341.

[2] L. Müller, *ibid.*

[3] See his Introduction to the Trinummus, p. 18. Müller, Pros. p. 13 sq. Corssen ii 454.

[4] See Corssen, i 200.

[5] See Key, L. G. § 770.

[6] M. Crain, Plaut. Stud. p. 10. In the line from the Persa Ritschl expressly acknowledges the short final *e*. See also Corssen ii 470.

[7] For Plautus see Ritschl, Proll. Trin. p. clxix; for later poets L. Müller, de re metr. p. 335, and on the whole point Key, L. G. § 772 with note. Corssen ii 480.

Ritschl and Fleckeisen admit even *prospere* in an anapaestic line, Pseud. 574. It is, however, highly probable that this line should be read as a trochaic octonarius :

pró Iovis, ut mihi quídquid ago
   lepide ómnia prosperéque
   eveniunt.

The mss. give *Iuppiter:* I have followed Bücheler's emendation (Rhein. Mus. xv p. 445).—In another anapaestic line, Mil. gl. 1024, Ritschl reads with the mss.

age, age, út tibi máxumĕ cóncinnumst,

M. Haupt proposes to transpose the words as follows

age máxume utí tibi cóncinnumst.

It is difficult to decide how far a licence would extend in the so-called 'free' metres; yet in the first instance we are entitled to remove it because trochaic metre follows; in the second I should not admit Haupt's conjecture.

In the comic poets, however, this ending is, generally speaking, short[1].

i in the ablative of the third declension appears shortened in the anapaestic line from Plautus' Bacchides 1108

igitúr parī fortuna, aétate ut sumus, útimŭr :: sic est. séd tu.

This is the reading of the mss. adopted by Fleckeisen.

The *i* of the dative is shortened in *canĭ :*

cánī quoque etiam adémptumst nomen...
Epid. II 2, 50.

The *i* of the nom. plur. appears short in *merĭ :*

merī béllatores gígnuntur, quas híc praegnatis fécit.
Mil. gl. 1077.

u of the fourth is shortened in *manŭ* Trin. 288. It is the same with the *e* of the fifth, which is occasionally found short, e. g. Poen. IV 2, 68 *Fĭdĕ non melius créditur.* So also Mil. gl. 1369, *fĭdĕ nulla ésse te.*

In the datives *mihi tibi sibi* the final *i* was originally p. xxv long and is still found so in Plautus and Terence, though both have it also short. Even the usage of the later poets was never constant, and the *i* in these words was always common[2]. We have noticed this point in a previous place.

In the same way we find the genitive-ending *i* of the second declension shortened in the words *eri* (=*domini*) Mil. gl. 362. *virĭ* Ter. Phorm. v 3, 4. *bonĭ* Truc. II 4, 78 (= 428 G.), and *novĭ* ibid. II 4, 32 (= 382 G.). *pretĭ* Mil. gl. 1061. *modĭ* Poen. v 4, 103.—*malĭ* (nom. plur.) occurs Pseud. 142 (Fleck.)—the *i* of the locative appears short-

---

[1] See Corssen, II 462, who has reproduced the instances of a long *ē* in the ablative sing. collected by Bücheler and myself (Rh. Mus. XXII 114 sq.), some of which are, however, extremely doubtful. See also Ussing, Proll. p. 195, who says 'his in locis si quis editor constantiae causa aut *i* aut *ei* [the old termination of the abl.] scribat, vituperari vix possit.' This is pretty much in agreement with C. F. W. Müller, Pros. p. 15—18.

[2] See L. Müller, de re metr. p. l. p. 334.

ened in *domĭ* (Mil. gl. 194. Most. 281. Trin. 841. Aul. 73. Pompon. Ribb. com. p. 201)[1]. It may finally be added that in many cases *homo* and in most cases *ego* stand as pyrrhichs[2] (Ritschl, Proll. CLXVI. CLXIX).

I shall now enumerate the verbal endings in which the prosody of the comic poets allows short final vowels contrary to the general usage of the Augustan period. Here again we may notice that the short quantities are limited to disyllabic words of original iambic prosody.

The final *a* of the imperative of the first conjugation[3] appears short in *rogă*:

> quándo vir bonus és, responde, quód rogó. :: rogă quód lubet.
> Curc. v 3, 30.

> úbi lubét, rogă : réspondebo, níl reticebo quód sciam.
> Men. 1106.

p. xxvi   satis sí futurumst :: rógă me vigintí minas.
> Pseud. 114.

> rógă velitne an nón uxórem...
> Ter. Hec. IV 1, 43 (= 558 Fl.).

> rogă círcumducat : heús tu :: at hic sunt múlieres.
> Most. 680.

> rogă, númquid opus sit :: tú qui zonam nón habes.
> Poen. v 2, 48.

amă stands with this quantity Curc. I 1, 38

> iuvĕntúte et pueris líberis, amă quód lubet.

The same short quantities are found in the following imperatives of the second conjugation:

cavĕ[4]:

> Hégio, fit quod tíbi ego dixi : glíscit rabies : cávĕ tibi.
> Capt. III 4, 26.

---

[1] Even the nom. plur. *ae* is shortened in a line of the Bacchides (1139), if we credit Ritschl's text. The line is however better divided into two separate parts, and the words *stultae ac malae videntur* are to be considered as an iambic dim. catal. See Spengel, *de vers.* *cret. usu Plautino* p. 24.

[2] *egō* Aul. 454. 562 (?).

[3] Faërnus observes on Ter. Hec. IV 1, 43 that Martial has *pută*: see L. Müller, de re metr. p. 340.

[4] See Hor. Serm. II 3, 38. 177. 5, 75. Ep. I 13, 19. Prop. I 10, 21.

atque aúdin :: quid vis? :: cávĕ siris cum fília.
Epid. iii 3, 19.

cavĕ praéterbitas úllas aedis quín roges.
Epid. iii 4, 1.

omítte, Lude, ac cávĕ malo :: quid, cávĕ malo?
Bacch. 147.

The same quantity will be found in the Aulularia (v. 90. 600. 610. 652). It is, however, very probable that the final *e* of *cave* was at a very early time entirely dropped, *au* being pronounced as a diphthong. This view rests on Cicero de div. ii 40 : *cum M. Crassus exercitum Brundisi imponeret, quidam in portu caricas Cauno advectas vendens 'cauneas' clamitabat, dicamus, si placet, monitum ab eo Crassum, ' caveret ne iret.'* (The same anecdote is related by Pliny, N. H. xv 19.) But even the entire dropping of the final *e* presupposes a former shortening of the vowel, at least if we may trust the laws laid down by the science of comparative philology. We find the same process in other forms derived from *cave-*, e.g. *cau*(i)*tum cau*(i)*tor cau*(i)*tio :* it is the same with *fau*(i)*tum fau*(i)*tor :* but in all these words there is reason[1] to assume that Plautus still used the full forms p.xxvii *cavitum cavitor* etc., as shown by Fleckeisen, ep. crit. xxi[2]. In Plautus' time, we find the shortening process in its full vigour and working ; in later times (and we should not forget that there are more than 100 years between Plautus and Cicero) the dropping of those shortened vowels seems to have set in already. The conjecture that after a consonantal *u* vowels first began to

---

[1] *cavitum* occurs twice in the lex agraria a. 643 : C. I. L. i 200, 6. 7.

[2] We may add that even *caveto* would seem to follow this analogy in two lines in Plautus:

móx quom Saureám imitabor,
cávĕto ne suscénseas.
Asin. ii 2, 105.

átque horunc verbórum causa
cávĕto mi iratús fuas.
Capt. ii 3, 71.

These passages are, however, very doubtful and have justly been altered by Fleckeisen, who writes *cave tu* instead of *caveto.*

be dropped, the ambiguous nature of this *u* giving rise to a diphthong, does not seem without foundation[1].

Another instance of a shortened *e* in an imperative of the second conjugation is *tacĕ* Aul. 325. Similarly we find *tenĕ*:

ádimit animam mi aégritudo : Stásime, ténë me :: vísne aquam?
Trin. 1091.

sín secus, patiémur animis aéquis. ténë sortém tibi.
Cas. II 6, 25.

v. 412 of the Aulularia furnishes us with a good example of the variable quantity of such imperatives, since we should there pronounce the first *tene* as a pyrrhich, but the second as an iamb. A somewhat analogous instance occurs in Ovid's line ' *valē valĕ inquit et Echo* ' (see L. Müller, de re m. p. 308)[2]. We may further enumerate *docĕ* Aul. 431. *vidĕ* Trin. 763. Cas. II 6, 26, and *iubĕ* (see Ritschl, Proll. CLXV). It may be useful to add that the same quantity of the imperative -*e* of the sec. conj. occasionally reappears in the Augustan period, e.g. Ovid has *favĕ* (am. II 13, 21) and *havĕ* (am. II 6, 62), Persius (I 108) and Phaedrus (III 6, 3) have *vidĕ*. We may also p.xxviii quote Luc. Müller's words (de re m. p. 340) ' etiam hanc licentiam intendere christiani, apud quos inveniuntur attenuata finali *time dimove praecave arce extorque percense*.'

The imperatives of the fourth conjugation show the same shortening propensity. Thus we have *venĭ* (Persa 30) *abĭ* (Most. 66) *redĭ* (Aul. 81. 441. Truc. I 2, 106 = 210 Geppert).

It is not difficult to collect more instances of all the cases mentioned, but I think those given will suffice to convince even the most incredulous of the existence of

[1] Compare Juvenal IX 120, where the ms. reading *causis* has been changed to *cavĕ sis* by Lachmann.

[2] A hexameter in a late sepulchral inscription in Burmann's Anthology gives the same prosody (II p. 154): semper perpetuo valĕ, mi carissime coniux.
See Jo. Schrader's Emendationes, p. 218.

shortened final vowels in the prosody of the comic poets.
I have not quoted any instances from Terence, but may
be allowed to refer the reader to my Introduction to the
Cambridge edition of 1869, p. 15 sq. I may also add
that Prof. Key accounts for the apparent shortening of
the imperatives and other suffixes by treating these
words as monosyllables by way of contraction; see his
'Language, etc.' p. 470—473.

We shall now briefly enumerate other verbal endings
which appear short in Plautine prosody contrary to the
usage of the Augustan period.

An originally long *i* was shortened in the passive
infinitive[1], e.g. *darĭ* (Plaut. Rud. 960. Ter. Ad. 311.
Phorm. 261), *patĭ* (Aul. 719), *loquĭ* (Bacch. 1104): see
Ritschl, Proll. CLXVIII. So also *emĭ* Epid. II 2, 116—a
line which is read in Geppert's edition in a sadly cor-
rupted state[2]. The same took place in the perf. act. *dedĭ*
bibĭ stetĭ, and even in *adtulĭ* (Aul. 430) and *occidĭ* (ib.
705)[3].—*o* was shortened in the first persons *eŏ agŏ volŏ*
sciŏ[4] *sinŏ negŏ dabŏ erŏ cedŏ :* in the same way we have
iusserŏ Aul. 439, which may be compared to *dixerŏ* Hor.
Serm. I 4, 104. *oderŏ* Ov. am. III 11, 35. Other instances
of a shortened final *o* from later poets are given by

---

[1] Comp. *fruĭ* Anth. Lat. Mey.
1164, 2.

[2] Thus we have *vehĭ* and
sequĭ in the 'sortes Praenes-
tinae,' a number of hexameters composed in the popular
prosody: see Ritschl, Rh. Mus.
xv p. 396. As the *i* (or *ei*) became short, it could easily pass
into a simple *e*: thus we have
fiere in Ennius Ann. 15, a form
also given by the cod. Put. of
Livy xxvi 3, 13 in a solemn in-
terrogation of the plebs: see
H. A. Koch, Rh. Mus. xvi 120.

[3] These are examples derived
from the so-called 'free' metres.
Compare *vicĭ* Anth. Lat. Mey.

1157, 7. *fecĭ* ibid. 9. It is cu-
rious that the editor of the Anthology denies the short quantity of the final *i* in the perf. in
another instance, 1165, 5 *finibus Ítaliaé monuméntum vidĭVo-
bérnae*. A pentameter ends *vixĭ
dies* 1203, 13. But shortenings
like *vicĭ fecĭ vixĭ* would be inadmissible in Plautine prosody,
as the original prosody of these
words is not *iambic*.

[4] The ancient grammarians
pronounced *sco* ('*elisa i littera*')
in Virgil's line *nunc scio quid
sit amor:* see Marius Vict. I p.
2472 P.

L. Müller, de re metr. p. 336. The imperative *dato*
stands as a pyrrhich Bacch. 84, and it seems to have the
p. xxix same quantity in a line of Lucilius, if Lachmann's conjecture be right (L. Müller, l. c.). In Juvenal we have
estŏ (VII 79) and in Martial *respondetŏ* (III 4, 7).

C. DROPPING OF FINAL CONSONANTS.

A careful reader of the Plautine comedies will soon
find out that, for scanning these verses, he must very
often free himself from the observance of the rules commonly taught under the head of *positio*. But at the
same time he cannot fail to observe that an absolute
negation of the laws of position in Plautus would render
the case even worse, for then we should be at a loss how
to explain many instances of naturally short vowels
lengthened by *position*. Most of the cases in question
will be explained by the following remarks.

*The metres of Plautus and Terence testify a general
tendency of the Latin language of their time to drop the
final consonants of many words.* This tendency was not,
however, confined to Latin; on the contrary, we trace it
in most of the dialects of ancient Italy. Thus, to give a
few examples, we have *vestikatu = vestigium, frehtu =
frictum, facia = faciat* in Umbrian[1].

[1] I may add that the same
process has taken place in many
modern languages. E. g. a modern Greek is at liberty to say
πόδι or πόδιν (=πόδιον, foot),
χέριν or χέρι, χάρι or χάρις, etc.,
nay in modern Greek popular
poetry final consonants are very
often cut off where they ought
to stand, and even added where
they have no grammatical title
to appear.—The history of the
English language furnishes a-
bundant instances of all the
same processes enumerated in
this sketch of Plautine prosody:
viz. the shortening of originally
long vowels, the dropping of
final consonants, the entire loss
of whole inflexions. The English language is, in this respect,
more instructive than many
others, because, though flowing
from a richly inflected language,
it has now lost almost all its
inflexions. It will, in general,
be found that all the laws detailed in our Introduction are by
no means arbitrarily assumed
for a certain stage of the Latin
language, but are in reality
only special applications of the

It may be useful to premise that in many cases the
Latin language, when first employed for literary pur- p. xxx
poses, had already lost many final consonants : e.g. from
the original genitives

| mensa-is | servo-is | re-is |

we have after the loss of the final *s*

| mensai | servoi | rei |
| mensae | servi | (rē) |

The formation of the abl. sing. gives us another instance.
Originally this case ended in *d* : *mensad servod patred
manud red:* this *d* was however dropped there as well as
in the adverbs *faciled* etc., which were originally ablatives.
These losses are previous to Plautus' time, and in his
language we find but obscure traces of them left[1]. We
read in a few instances a nom. plur. of the sec. decl. in
is[2], and the forms *med* and *ted* are still used by Plautus,
not by Terence. (See note on v. 120.) We may now
proceed to enumerate those instances where final consonants are dropped (i. e. do not count with regard to versification) in Plautus and Terence, contrary to the usage of
the later or classical language.

m. We learn from Priscian I 38 (Hertz) '*m obscurum
in extremitate dictionum sonat,*' and Quintilian states the
same IX 4, 40 '(m) *parum exprimitur...neque enim eximi-
tur, sed obscuratur.*' On account of its weak sound, a
final *m* was often neglected in writing both in nouns and
verbs, as will be seen in numerous instances collected
from the oldest inscriptions by Corssen I 267 sqq. This
disregard of a final *m* seems to have been quite familiar
to all the popular dialects of Latin throughout its different
periods, and hence we should explain hexameters ending
ardéntĕm lŭcérnam, iuvenílĕm figúram (quoted from
Meyer's Anthology 1223, 1. and 1171, 4 by Ritschl, Rhein.

general laws which govern the
growth and decay of all forms
of human speech.

[1] See also above, p. 10.

[2] See Ritschl, Rheinisches
Museum IX 158 = Opusc. II 646
—652.

Mus. xiv 379)[1]. We shall not therefore be surprised to find numerous instances in which a final *m* is entirely discarded in Plautine prosody, e.g. *domum* is to be pronounced as *domu* Aul. 148 etc. We shall not here give any special instances of this fact, but it will be useful to p. xxxi draw the particular attention of our readers to the two words *quidem* and *enim*, which should frequently be pronounced as *quide* and *eni*[2] (Aul. 209. 496 etc.).

Even in later poetry, a final *m* was entirely disregarded in all cases where the next word began with a vowel, this being the last trace of a licence which had formerly extended over a larger territory.

As to *s*, we have a very memorable passage in Cicero's Orator 48, 161 '*quin etiam quod iam subrusticum videtur, olim autem politius, eorum verborum quorum eaedem erant postremae duae litterae quae sunt in* '*optumus*' *postremam litteram detrahebant, nisi vocalis insequebatur. ita non erat ea offensio in versibus quam nunc fugiunt poëtae novi. ita enim loquebamur* '*qui est omnibu*' *princeps,*' *non* '*omnibus princeps*' *et* '*vita illa dignu*' *locoque,*' *non* '*dignus*[3].'

---

[1] A pentameter ends with the words *úndecïm post* Anthol. 1203, 12: the final *m* should of course be dropt. As Ritschl observes, we need not assume the construction of *post* with an ablative in such a line as *cunctorum haec soboli sedem post morte reliquit* (Anthol. iv 394 Burm.). On Plaut. Bacch. 404 *Pátrĕm sodalis ét magistrum hinc añscultabo quám rem agat* Ritschl observes—'Plautus sprach ohne zweifel und schrieb *sehr mögiicher weise* pátre sodalis' (ib. p. 398).

[2] Prof. Key ('Alphabet' p. 142), Ritschl (Proll. p. cxl. cliii) and Bergk (*zeitschrift für die alterthumswissenschaft* 1848 p. 1130) assume a monosyllabic

pronunciation of *quidem* and *enim*. It would be preposterous to deny the possibility of such a fact,—and indeed some arguments, especially one alleged for *enim* by Bergk, seem strongly to point to it. But as it cannot be concluded on the evidence of the Plautine metres, we think it safer to follow a general theory which affords an equally satisfactory explanation, instead of assuming an exceptional pronunciation which would after all not be supported by entirely undoubted arguments. See also Key's 'Language' p. 132. 139.

[3] The truth of Cicero's observation '*quam nunc fugiunt poëtae novi*' may be exemplified

This licence is known to every reader of Lucretius, and its extension may be shown by a line from Ennius' Annales (601 Vahlen)

tum lateralis dolor, certissimus nuntius mortis.

Corssen (i 286. 599) gives lengthy lists of names from inscriptions, many of which are as old as the Punic wars, and in which a final *s* is entirely omitted, and the same fact occurs again in inscriptions of the decline of the Roman empire[1]. It would, therefore, be very surprising if no traces of it were found in the prosody of the comic writers. As instances of it will be frequently met with in Plautus, we shall confine ourselves to some examples from the Aulularia. Thus we should pronounce

> *minus = minu* prol. 18. 19.
> *nimisque = nimique* 61.
> *nimis = nimi* 493.
> *prius = priu* 206.
> *latus = latu* 415.
> *magis = magi* 419.
> *ullus = ullu* 419.
> *venimus = venimu* 426.
> *moribus = moribu* 500.

p. xxxii

We shall now easily understand such endings of iambics as the following, all of which are taken from Terence's Hecyra: *aúctŭs sit* 334. *deféssŭs sum* 443. *incértŭs sum* 450. *expértus sum* 489. *núllŭs sum* 653. *úsŭs sit* 878. Comp. *occidístĭs me* Bacch. 313.

r was, in many instances, merely a substitute for an earlier *s*, and we should therefore be prepared to find that

by comparing two lines of Ennius and Virgil. Aen. xii 115 we read *Solis equi lucemque elatis naribus efflant*, on which words Servius has the following note '*Ennianus versus est ordine commutato: funduntque elatis naribu' lucem.*' (See Ennius ed. Vahlen p. 85 and the passage quoted there from Marius Victorinus.) The reason which induced Virgil to change the order of the words appears at once.

[1] See Schuchardt, on Vulgar Latin, ii p. 445.

occasionally a final *r* is dropped. Thus we should pronounce *soro* (=*soror*) in a line from the Poenulus (i 2, 84)

> Sátis nunc lepide ornátam credo, sóror, te tibi vidérier.

and in two short anapaestic lines from the Stichus (18 and 20):

> haec rés | vitae | me, sóror, | saturant—
> ne lácru|ma, sóror, | neu túo id | animo—

Another line in the same play furnishes a fourth example of the same pronunciation (v. 68):

> quíd agimús, soror, si óffirmabit páter advorsum nós :: pati—

In Terence we have the same, Eun. i 2, 77

> soror díctast : cupio abdúcere ut reddám suis.

This is the reading of the Bembine ms., and the prosody of -*soro dict*- is rightly explained by Faërnus in his note on the passage[1].

p.xxxiii   The word *color* should be pronounced *colo* in the following line :

> color vérus, corpus sólidum et suci plénum.
> Ter. Eun. ii 3, 27.

and *amor* loses its final *r* in Ter. *Andr.* i 5, 26

> amor, misericordia huíus, nuptiárum sollicitátio.

pater follows the same analogy, e. g.

> né tibi aegritúdinem, pater, párerem, parsi sédulo.
> Trin. 316.

---

[1] Liber Bembinus quocum hic consentiunt omnes fere libri recentes—nec versus repugnat, si abicias *r* ex *soror*, ut primus pes sit anapaestus. FAERNVS. —If we adopt Corssen's views (*krit. beitr. zur lat. formenlehre*, *p.* 399 *s.*), we should have to acknowledge the possible dropping of a final *r* only in those words where it had supplanted an original *s*. The sole exception to this law would be *pater*, and this instance has been neglected by Corssen.—Comp. also the Italian *suora frate moglie.* Schuchardt i p. 35 shows that the popular pronunciation *dolo* instead of *dolor* gave rise to a confusion between *dolor* and *dolus* in the later stages of Latin.

quid ego agam? pater iam híc me offendet míserum adve-
niens ćbrium.

Most. 378 (according to the mss.)

pater vénit, sed quid pértimui autem, bélua.
Ter. Phorm. 601.

In these cases Prof. Key adopts a monosyllabic pronunciation = Fr. *père*. The possibility of such a pronunciation is
questioned by Ritschl (Proll. Trin. CLV) whose words are
as follows: 'In quibus (*i.e.* monosyllabis) si etiam *pater*
habitum est, eius rei et rationem et documenta desidero.
et omnium minime ex eo argumentandum esse quod, ut e
soror monosyllabum *soeur*, ita e *pater* similiter factum
esse *père* dicunt, vel hinc intelligitur quod, etsi *frère*
quoque et *mère* e *frater* et *mater* contracta sunt, tamen
haec latina nec contendit quisquam nec poterit contendere
unquam monosyllaba fuisse.' This is, indeed, the best
argument[1] which can be alleged against Prof. Key's way
of pronouncing and contracting Latin words according to
the analogy of the corresponding French forms ; but has
it been understood and appreciated by Mr Parry? This

---

[1] I have left this passage exactly as it was written ten years
ago. In his work on 'Language,'
p. 133, Mr Key alludes to the
above as follows—' In *parricida*
for *patricida* we see already that
change which led to the Fr.
père from *pater ;* and here again
when *pater* appears in Latin
comedy, as it sometimes does, to
need a shortened pronunciation,
it seems simpler to drop the *t*
than to drop the *r*, as Dr Wagner proposes. Of course *mäter*
and *fräter*, with their long pen-
ults, were better able for a
time to resist such compression,
so that Ritschl's contention has
I think little weight.' This is a
remarkable instance of perverse
argumentation. Mr Key apparently assumes a form somewhat resembling *paer*, to be

pronounced like the Fr. *père*.
But *père* is not, as he thinks,
descended from *pater*, but from
patrem, comp. the Italian *padre*,
and see e. g. Brachet, Dict.
étym. de la langue franç. p. 404.
It is evident that *père = patre(m)*
cannot represent *pater*. But
what weight shall we attribute
to the assertion of a modern
writer of the 19th century that
he considers this or that pronunciation to be 'simpler,'
when this is quite contrary to
the very evidence of the inscriptions and earliest mss.?
See the instances collected by
Schuchardt, On Vulgar Latin
II 390 sq., where both *pate* and
soro are quoted from ancient
testimony.—See also Corssen II
656.

W. P.   3

scholar accuses Ritschl of 'losing sight of the difference
in quantity' between *frater mater* and *pater*[1]. But
Ritschl's argument is entirely based on this very same
difference. He means that, if we once begin to re-
model the old pronunciation of Latin upon that of the
French of the nineteenth century, we must be prepared
to find a contracted pronunciation of *mater* and *frater*
just as well as of *pater*, all these words being treated
alike in French as *mère frère père*. But we never meet
in Plautus and Terence with *mater* or *frater* as monosyllables, *on account of their different quantity*, and this
fact proves that, as we cannot draw a correct inference
from *mère* and *frère* as to *mater* and *frater*, we cannot

p. xxxiv.   consequently rely upon the comparison of *père* and *pater*.
And indeed in Plautus or other poets, we never find *mate*
and *frate* = *mater* and *frater*, though in a Faliscan inscription we actually read MATEHECUPA, i.e. *mater
hic cubat*[2]. But this is of course a low dialectic corruption[3].

The same theory accounts for the loss of a final *t* and
d. An old form *hau* (instead of *haud*) owes its existence
to this process (see note on v. 170): it remained in use
until the time of Tacitus, if we may trust the authority
of the Medicean ms. In the Aulularia we have *apu*
(= *aput* or *apud*)[4] in several instances (v. 83. 340. 736.),
in the same we should pronounce

> *caput* = *capu* 422. 423.
> *erat* = *era* 421.
> *ut* = *u* 320.
> *decet* = *dece* 136. (See M. Crain, Plaut. Stud. p. 10)[5].

---

[1] Parry's Introd. to Terence,
XLVI.
[2] See Ritschl, Corp. Inscr.
Lat. I 89, or Rh. Mus. XVI 603.
[3] We need not add how dangerous, nay how fallacious, it
is to draw inferences from
French with regard to the pronunciation of Latin. I do not
hesitate to accede to Ritschl's

assertion 'omnino tam esse lu-
bricum hoc genus compara-
tionis arbitror, nihil ut inde
proficias.' (Proll., l. l.)
[4] For *ape* = *apud* see Schuchardt, On Vulgar Latin I p.
123.
[5] See also the instances given
by Corssen II 650.

Thus we find *dedit* written as *dede* in three very old inscriptions, C. I. L. i 62ᵇ. 169. 180.

The preposition *ad* is thus often degraded to a simple *ă*, e.g.

> séd ăd postrémum. Poen. iv 2, 22.
> quís ăd forés est? Amph. iv 2, 1.
> et ăd pórtitóres. Phorm. i 2, 100.
> ut ăd paúca rédeam. Phorm. iv 3, 43.

But it would be superfluous to accumulate more instances of this fact: we shall only add that even *nt* was entirely dispensed with in the rapid pronunciation of the time of Plautus. Bentley has quoted in his Schediasma (p. xv ed. Lips.) the following instances:

> *solent ésse = solĕt ésse.*
> *student fácere = studĕ fácere.*
> *habent déspicatu = habĕ déspicatu.*

To these we might easily add other instances from Plautus, but to prove the existence of such forms as we assume p. xxxv. here in the metres of the comic poets, we mention the form *dedro*, which in an inscription from Pesaro (C. I. L. i 177) stands as an equivalent to *dederunt*. This form is an unmistakable precursor of the corresponding Italian form *diedero*[1].

But precisely the same kind of form as is assumed exists in *emeru = emerunt* C. I. L. i 1148, in an inscription later than the second Punic war, but earlier than the Lex Julia de civitate sociis danda. This *emeru* forms the stepping-stone from *emerunt* to the secondary form *emere*.

The final letters *m s r t d* are more frequently dropped than two others which we have yet to mention. The first is *l*, which is sometimes cut off in the word *semol* (*simul*), e.g. Aul. 617. Mil. gl. 1137. Ter. Eun. ii 2, 10. Haut. tim. iv 5, 55[2]: the second *n*, which is dropped in the word

---

[1] See Corssen, i 186 sqq., where further materials are produced from the Inscriptions.

[2] These instances are taken from Corssen ii¹, 96 (ii 643). Corssen contends (i¹, 79) that a final *l* was never dropped on account of its marked pronun-

tamen in such passages as Mil. gl. 585. Ter. Hec. v 4, 32. Ad. I 2, 65. Eun. v 2, 50. These two cases are, however, not generally acknowledged[1]. Sometimes the final *n* is dropped in such forms as *rogan viden iuben* etc., which stand in the place of the original forms *rogasne* etc.

It may finally be observed that all monosyllabic prepositions occasionally drop their final letters, e. g. *in* should be pronounced as *ĭ* Capt. IV 2, 97. Poen. IV 2, 82. 2, 13. 5, and oftener; *ab* as *ă*, and in the same way we might explain the short quantity of *ex* (e.g. Stich. 716. Merc. 176), though in many cases it suffices to assume the soft pronunciation of $x = s$[2]. This would explain the short quantity of *senĕx* in such lines as Aul. 293 :

<blockquote>senĕx óbsonari fíliaï núptiis,</blockquote>

ciation (I 219). He assumes therefore what he calls an 'irrational' pronunciation of the vowel of the first syllable. I do not hesitate to adopt Guyet's view as given in his note on Ter. Eun. II 2, 10 'τὸ *l* in *simul* eliditur, ut ultima syllaba corripiatur. idem factum Hecyrae IV 1......idem et in senario illo Turpilii apud Nonium Marcellum [Ribb. Com. p. 94, v. 194] *simul circum spectat: úbi praeter se néminem.* apud Plautum Capt. III 4, 19 [551 Fl.] ibidem τὸ *l* in *procul* eadem causa elisum est in septenario: *proin tu ab istoc prócul recedas....*' This is the reading in *BJ*, which Fleckeisen would certainly keep now, if he were to revise his first volume. At present he gives *apscedas* instead of *recedas.* Surely, Corssen would not say that the *o* in *procul* was 'irrational.' [He maintains that the *u* was 'irrational,' II 666 : he would, therefore, pronounce *procl.*]

[1] The dropping of the final *n* in *tamen* may be inferred from the passages given above (we are indebted for them to Corssen, II 642) and receives an important support from the various readings in Stich. 44, where all our mss. read *tamen* with the sole exception of the Ambrosian palimpsest, in which we find *tam;* but not from Festus p. 360 'antiqui *tam* etiam pro *tamen* usi sunt,' since Corssen shows (*krit. beitr. zur lat. formenl.* p. 273—279) that the passages quoted by Festus do not prove that *tam* was ever used as an equivalent for *tamen.*—In the Umbrian dialect we find *nome* for *nomen* (Aufrecht u. Kirchhoff, *umbrische sprachdenkmäler*, II 407). Compare the Italian forms *lume nome nume volume*, etc.

[2] See Corssen, I 276. Schuchardt, I 132. See also Corssen, II 665, whose explanation is in agreement with the one adopted above. For curiosity's sake, I may quote Mr Key, 'Language,' p. 473, who says 'the pronunciation *s'nex* has been erroneously ascribed to myself, for I

but we should entirely drop the *x* in such lines as Rud. prol. 35:

senĕ*x* qui hûc Athenis éxsul venit, haû malus.

D. SHORTENING OF OTHER LONG ENDINGS.   p. xxxvi.

We have hitherto always observed that final syllables in which the vowel was long by nature were not short-ened by the sole influence of the accent, unless the words to which they belonged were originally iambs[1]. We have yet to mention that the same shortening process affected even such endings as would seem to oppose the strongest resistance to every attempt to shorten them : *ās ōs ēs īs ūs*; nay, sometimes not only the vowels of these endings are shortened, but even the final consonants dropped. Some instances will serve to exemplify this observation.

1. Thus the ending *ās* appears shortened in *bonas foras*[2] *negas* :

have long held that it would be better to read it as *sĕn*, i.e. as representing that old lost nomi-native whence the oblique cases were deduced, in other words the simpler noun of which the *sen-ec* is a diminutive.' It is the pervading tendency of Mr Key's theories on Latin versifi-cation to reduce Latin disylla-bles and trisyllables to mono-syllables. Such a proceeding is indeed very much in the style of that language which has suc-ceeded in contracting the noble ἐλεημοσύνη into a convenient mo-nosyllabic *alms*, but it may be doubted whether these violent contractions suit the genius of the Latin language.

[1] Exceptions to this rule would be *adtulĭ occidĭ* and *iusserŏ*. But the first may be explained from *tulĭ*, and *iusserŏ*

follows the analogy of the short *o* of the present. *occidĭ* occurs in an anapaestic line, i.e. in so-called 'free' metre. *frustră* (p. 22) is quite isolated.— With regard to the dropping of final consonants, we have to modify our statement. *s* and *m* were indeed so frequently dropped that the prosody of the antepenult cannot be considered to limit the extension of this license. But in all other cases the law given above would ap-ply to the dropping of final consonants just as well. See our remarks on *pater* and *mater* p. 33 sq.

[2] Comp. the same shorten-ing in the Doric dialect, e.g. Theocr. I 83 πάσᾰς ἀνὰ κράνας, IV 3 πάσᾰς ἀμέλγες, I 134 ὄχνᾰς ἐνείκαι — though we find also the original prosody in θύρας

bónăs ut aecumst fácere, facitis.
　　　　Stich. 99.

fórăs, forăs, lumbrice...
　　　　Aul. 620[1].

quíd, forăs? forŭs hércle uero.
　　　　Stich. 597.

ípse abiít forăs, me reliquit.
　　　　Poen. v 5, 4.

tén negăs Tyndarum ésse? : : nego ínquam : : tún te Philo-
cratem ésse ais?
　　　　Capt. iii 4, 39.

síc sine igitur, sí tuom negăs me ésse, abire líberum.
　　　　Men. 1028.

In the last two instances, we give the reading of the
mss., which has been altered by Ritschl, Proll. Trin.
CXLVIII. In the line from the Captivi the accentuation

ₚ. xxxvii. *Tyndárum*, which in accordance with Ritschl is adopted
in Fleckeisen's edition, seems to be against the general
habit of Plautus, the metre running much smoother, if
read according to the accentuation given by us[2].

2. In the same way we find *ŏs* in *novos viros dolos*[3]:

vírŏs nostros quibus tú nos voluisti.
　　　　Stich. 98.

mágnificé volo mé summós virŏs áccipere...
　　　　Pseud. 167 (according to the mss.).

dúplicis triplicis dólŏs perfidias, út ubi cum hostibús con-
grediar.
　　　　Pseud. 580 (according to the mss.).

sempér datores nóvŏs oportet quaérere.
　　　　Truc. ii 1, 33 (= 245 G.)[4].

ii 6, alongside of περὶ τὰς θύρᾰς
ὅσσος ὅμιλος xv 65.
　[1] I quote Taubmann's note
on this passage, simply to show
that his view of the fact in question was quite correct. 'Cri-
tici posteriores non admisere,
quod ignorarent *foras* utranque
syllabam habere brevem : ut
liquet vel ex Poen. v 5, 4.

Stich. iv 2, 1 & iv 4, 55.'
　[2] For the reappearance of
such quantities as *vidĕs putăs*,
etc. in later Latin see also Corssen ii 941.
　[3] Comp. in Doric τὰς παρθένος,
Theocr. i 90.
　[4] *novos* may possibly have
been one of the first words to
admit a monosyllabic (or con-

novŏs ómnis mores hábeo, veteres pérdidi.
Truc. iii 2, 9 (=665 G.).

Another example (Trin. 78) does not belong to this head, and will be mentioned hereafter.

3. Analogously we have *ŭs* (acc. plur.) :

mánŭs ferát ăd papíllas, aut labra á labris numquam aúferat.
Bacch. 480.

This is the reading of the mss. adopted by Ritschl, while Fleckeisen follows Brix's transposition: *ád papillas mánŭs ferat* and considers *manus* to be a monosyllable (*mnus*).

Another instance of the same prosody occurs Mil. gl. 325.

túm mihi sunt manŭs ínquinatae—

a reading justly maintained in Brix's recent edition[1].

4. It is the same with *ĕs* (*ĭs*) :

ovīs ín crumina hac húc in urbem détuli.
Truc. iii 1, 11 (=644 G.).

ovĕs and *bovĕs* are commonly explained by admitting a monosyllabic pronunciation, see Ritschl's Proll. L. For *bovĕs* see Aul. 232. Pseud. 812.

avĕs falls under the same head, Asin. 216 (according to the mss.).

fórīs pultabo. ad nóstras aedis.
Trin. 868.

somnóne operam datis? éxperiar, forēs án cubiti ac pedés
plús valeant.
Stich. 311.

te hás emisse. nón tu vidēs hunc vóltu ut tristi sít senex?
Most. 811.

non vídēs referre me úvidum reté sine squamosó pecu?
Rud. 942.

tracted) pronunciation, owing to the ambiguous nature of the semivowel *u*. But see also

Corssen ii 654, note **.
    [1] See also Bücheler, On Latin Declension, p. 15.

Archínam : : mala tu fémina's : : olĕs únde es disciplínam.
Truc. ɪ 2, 29 (=133 G.).

intús produci iúbĕs : haec ergo est fídicina.
Epid. ɪɪɪ 4, 41 (according to Geppert).

aut té piari iúbĕs, homo insanissume?
Men. 517 (according to the mss.).

p. xxxviii.   sí tu ad legioném bellator clúĕs, at in culína ego.
Truc. ɪɪ 7, 54 (=604 G.).

Another instance of the same kind is *habĕs* Aul. 185
and Pseud. 161, which prosody will also be found in the
ms. reading of a passage greatly altered by Ritschl,
Persa 227.

5. In the same way the ending ĭs in the dative and
ablative plural of nouns and in the present of verbs is
occasionally shortened :

ex graécis bónĭs latínas fecit nón bonas.
Ter. Eun. prol. 9.

quós penes mei fuit potestas, bónĭs meis quíd foret ét meae
vitae.
Trin. 822[1].

bonĭs ésse oportet déntibus lenám probam : adridére.
Truc. ɪ, 14 (=226 G.).

satĭn sí quis amat, nequit quín nili sit ätque ímprobĭs árti-
bus se éxpoliat.
Truc. ɪɪ 7, 2 (=549 G.) [anapæstic].

vírĭs cum summis, ínclutae amicae—
Pseud. 174.

múltis súm modĭs círcumventus . . . .
Ennius (ed. Vahlen p. 96. Ribb. Trag. p. 15).

is mé scelus auro usque áttondit dolĭs dóctis indoctum út
lubitumst.
Bacch. 1095[2].

at pól ego abs te concéssero : : iamne ábĭs? bene ambuláto.
Persa 50.

peregré quoniam advenĭs, céna datur.
Truc. ɪ 2, 28 (=129 G.) [anapæstic].

[1] *meis* and *meae* should be
pronounced as monosyllables.
[2] This is the reading of the

mss. restored in Fleckeisen's
edition.

The last instance should be explained from the analogy of the simple form *venis*, which would, of course, fall under the general rule.

A very strong instance of a shortened final syllable occurs in the Bacchides (48) :

póteris agere : atque ís dum veniat, sédëns ibi opperíbere.

For even if we readily grant that an *n* before an *s* disappears in many instances, the long quantity of the *e* would still remain unaltered : but for all that we must here admit a short pronunciation of the syllable *ens*. Ritschl changes the reading of the mss. by transposing *atque ibi sedens, dum is veniat, opperibere.* Fleckeisen adheres to the authority of the mss.

All these short quantities are, of course, of but occasional occurrence ; but they suffice to prove the large extension of a very dangerous propensity of the Latin language in Plautus' time, which was fast making its way and has left permanent traces. p. xxxix. I do not forget that such strong violations of natural prosody as those given above, cannot be otherwise than shocking to an ear accustomed to Augustan prosody, and I am fully aware that many scholars will therefore treat them with obstinate incredulity : but an impartial consideration of the matter would show that there is at least no *rational* difference between the shortening of *āt ēt ūt* and of *ās ēs ís ōs :* only the first we accept, because we imbibed the notion of the short quantity of the suffixes of the third pers. sing. at the time of our first acquaintance with Latin prosody ; the latter appears strange to us, because the literary language of the so-called classical epoch preserved the original long quantity. To be brief, most people readily acknowledge the *fait accompli*, while they obstinately close their eyes to the traces left by a destructive and revolutionary power in the popular speech of a certain period, because the same tendencies were afterwards theoretically checked and resisted and could not, therefore, manifest themselves in the literary dialect of a more cultivated period. But for such as are determined not to acknowledge any difference between literary and popular dialects, these pages are not destined [1].

The shortened quantities of these syllables were once doubted by Ritschl, who in his edition of Plautus gets rid of them partly by very extravagant alterations of the ms. readings, partly by assuming the extrusion of the radical vowels of the words in question. I propose to give a brief criticism of the latter point, in translating a passage from M. Crain's excellent paper 'Plautinische Studien,' p. 12 :

"G. Hermann (*el. d. m.* p. 65) considers *domi boni mali malum* as monosyllables in many passages, though he has never produced his arguments for the possibility of putting together such thoroughly different cases. In accordance with G. Hermann's views Ritschl assumes monosyllabic pronunciation for *enim aput quidem fores manus senex simul,* on which he remarks '*quae quis tam pravo iudicio est ut correptis potius ultimis syllabis quam pronuntiando elisis primis dicta esse contendat?*' (Proll. Trin. cxl. s.) But where are the proofs for the possibility of extruding a radical vowel [in Iambic words], to preserve which in its integrity must always be considered to be the tendency of language? It is true, Ritschl says '*quid? quod ne usu recepta quidem monosyllaba scriptura alius vocis cuiusdam de vera ratione admonuit? nam quid est quo a monosyllaba* bonas *vel* senem *forma* mnas *differat pro* minas *scribi solitum?*' (p. cxliv). I intentionally give this passage without the least omission, as it would otherwise be incredible that Ritschl could have written such things. It is easy to understand that Ritschl actually compares matters of a very different character. We want the proofs for the extrusion of a radical vowel in *Latin*

p. xl.

---

[1] It may be of interest to add a passage relating to the pronunciation of the comic stage at Rome. Quintilian says II 10, 13 : *quod faciunt actores comici, qui nec ita prorsus, ut nos vulgo loquimur, pronuntiant, quod esset sine arte, nec procul tamen a natura recedunt, quo vitio periret imitatio, sed morem communis huius sermonis decore quodam scenico exornant.* See also Corssen II 619 sq.

[Iambic] words, and Ritschl alleges the *Greek* μνᾶ, which the Romans (to whom the joint consonants *mn* in the beginning of a syllable are unfamiliar) transformed into *mina* by inserting a short *i*: but of course the Greek form could equally well remain in use. That a Roman could not say *snex* instead of *senex*, *mnus* for *manus*, *qu'dem* for *quidem*, seems, in the absence of any satisfactory evidence to the contrary, pretty clear; and indeed such forms as *am'r* and *en'm* (Proll. Trin. CLXVII) may be good enough for Etruscan or Polish, but they are not Latin."

The same arguments as those alleged in this extract, are brought forward by Corssen II 623 [1]. Ritschl has now himself entirely altered his theories, and I should not even have mentioned his former views, had it not been for the presumption that most of the current information about Plautine prosody in this country is derived from Ritschl's Prolegomena, which, it must be repeated, are in this respect entirely antiquated.

I may add that, in accordance with the short quantities of *vidēs abĭs* etc. we find *vidĕn rogăn iubĕn adĭn redĭn* etc., forms which stand for *videsne rogasne iubesne adisne redisne:* see Corssen, II 642.

E. FURTHER INFLUENCE OF THE ACCENT. p. xli.

In all the instances which we considered in the preceding pages, we confined ourselves to the quantity of the final syllable, and it appeared that all the changes in question were limited to a certain number of iambic words. We may express this rule in the formula—

[1] 'Qui primam particularum *enim* et *quidem* vocalem syncope haustam putarunt (*'nim q'dem*), ii mihi videntur pronuntiandi rationem nimis obscuram minimeque credibilem statuisse.' Ussing, Proll. p. 195. — 'Vt *s'mul* pronuntiatum esse credam, non adducor.' Id. p. 202. — 'Talia qui per syncopen prioris syllabae explicare student, miram necesse est habeant linguae facilitatem, quid autem faciant, ubi vox a vocali incipiat, ut, "erus," omnino non intelligo.' Id. p. 207.

⌣ – = ⌣ ⌣. We shall now consider the accent in its influence on the un-accented syllables of polysyllabic words.

It was the general tendency of the Latin language
of these times *to hurry over the un-accented parts of
longer words, or of metrical complexes of words, in order
to lay all the stress on that syllable which was rendered
prominent by the accent.* But even here a long syllable
could not be shortened unless preceded by another short
syllable, i. e. only original iambs were changed into
pyrrhichs.

In a formula this may be expressed as follows
⌣ – ⌣ = ⌣ ⌣ ⌣. This will be examined in detail and exemplified in the following remarks.

We first propose to consider such cases as actually
fall under this head, though the shortening process was
probably assisted by some secondary circumstances.

Many seeming violations of prosody will be explained
by the fact that *doubled consonants were unknown in
Plautus' time, they being first introduced into the Latin
language by Ennius*[1]. Thus we find that in many
instances *ll* does not affect the quantity of the preceding
vowel, e. g.

> supelléctile opus est : ópus est sumptu ad núptias.
> Ter. Phorm. 666.
>
> tace átque parce múliebri supĕlléctili.
> Poen. v 3, 26.
>
> íd conexum in úmero laevo, éxpapíllato brácchio.
> Mil. gl. 1180[2].

According to a passage of Pliny, preserved by Priscian ɪ 38 '*l* exilem sonum habet, quando geminatur
secundo loco posita, ut *ille, Metellus.*' This was the
reason why in many names ending in *lius* the *l* was

---

[1] Festus v. *solitaurilia* p.
293. — 'Geminatio consonanti-
um nulla ante Ennium, ferme
ex aequo fluctuans ab a. circiter
580 ad 620, praevalens ab a.
620 ad 640, fere constans ab a.
circiter 670.' RITSCHL, priscae

lat. mon. epigr. p. 123.
[2] See Brix's note in his recent edition. Corssen ɪɪ 664
would seem to agree with Ritschl
and C. F. W. Müller (Pros. p.
264) in considering the word
expapillato as a corruption.

frequently doubled[1], there being almost no difference p. xlii.
between the pronunciation of a single or a double l[2],
Plautus, who wrote *ile*, had therefore unlimited license
to lengthen the i (i. e. to assume a slower and weightier
pronunciation of the l as ll) wherever sense or metre
seemed to require it, or to shorten it, whenever the word
did not appear to be of much importance. In fact, the
short pronunciation of the i in *ille* occurs in Plautus in
more passages[3] than that quantity which this word
retained ever since the prosody of the Latin language
was entirely reformed and fixed by Ennius' dactylic
poetry.

The superlative *simillumae* has a startling quantity
in a line in the Asinaria (241),

> pórtitorum símillumae sunt iánuae lenóniae.

But when seen under this point of view, we understand
this seeming irregularity at once. Plautus himself who
wrote *similumae* was at entire liberty either to say
simillumae, or in drawing the accent back on the first
syllable to shorten the second, which was the less ob-
jectionable, because ll (according to the latter spelling)
had indeed a very weak sound[4].

---

[1] See the instances collected
by Corssen, I 227. For *Polio
Pollio, Popilius Popillius*, see
Ritschl's note on the life of
Terence by Suetonius, in Reifferscheid's edition of the fragments of Suetonius, p. 512.

[2] In the name *Achilles* the i
appears short in the first line
of the prologue to the Poenulus :

Achílem Aristárchi míhi com-
mentarí lubet.

The spelling *Achilem* stands
thus in *BC* and the short quantity of the i may be defended
by a line from Plautus' Mercator (488) *'Achíllem orabo, ut
aúrum mihi det; Héctor qui ex-
pensús fuit.* For this line see

Bücheler, Rhein. Mus. xv 435,
and on the whole question M.
Crain, Plaut. Stud. p. 13. We
may add the line Mil. gl. 1219,
in which the mss. warrant the
following reading

mittó iam ut occidi 'Achílles
civis pássus est.

Bothe justly wrote *Achíles*.
Plautus himself spelt this name
Aciles, a spelling actually found
in an ancient inscription on a
cista discovered at Praeneste:
C. I. L. I 1500 (p. 553). We
may compare the two forms
Ἀχιλλεύς and Ἀχιλεύς as found
in Homer.

[3] Abundant examples will be
found in Corssen, II 624 sq.

[4] For this, and the following

In the same way, the word *satellites* should be read
sátĕlites in a line of the Trinummus (833).

p. xliii. *mm* does not lengthen the first syllable in the word
immo, which Plautus himself would have spelt *imo:*
see Merc. 737, Caec. Ribb. com. p. 47, Ter. Phorm. 936,
Hec. 437. 726. 877[1].

mn fall under the same rule, as the following instance
shows :

> per ännónam caram díxit me natúm pater.
> Stich. 179.

This is the reading of all the mss., including the old
Ambrosian ; Ritschl has *per caram annonam*, in accordance with a conjecture of Bothe[2].—As there was in the
original pronunciation of the Romans no difference
between *mn* and *nn*[3], we find the first syllable in *omnis*
treated as short in several passages in Plautus[4].

pp does not differ prosodiacally from a single *p* in
the word *Philippus*, which in Plautus almost invariably
appears with the Greek accentuation Φίλιππος *Philĭpus*[5].

instance, see Corssen, ii 663 sq.
—Brix compares (ed. of the
Trin. nachtr. p. 113) the spelling *facilumed* in the SC. de
Bacanalibus.—All those scholars who believe in an entire
harmony between the natural
and metrical accent in the versification of the comic poets cannot of course credit the short
quantity of the second syllable
in *simillumae*. They will consequently save the long quantity by pronouncing *smillumae*.
We believe, on the contrary,
that in this one passage the
syllable in question was rhythm-
ically shortened, and we may
compare the analogous case of
ságita, which will be mentioned
hereafter.
¹ See O. Ribbeck, Com. fragm.
Coroll. ed. sec. p. xxiv. So far
as our mss. are concerned, the
spelling *immo* is generally supported by better authorities than
imo.
² See also Müller, Pros. p.
289.
³ Comp. *solennis* and *sollem-
nis*, and the Italian forms *alun-
no colonna dannare = alumnus
columna damnare;* in Italian
ogni stands for *omni*.
⁴ See Aul. 598. Trin. 78.
Other examples are found in
Ritschl's Proll. cxxxii. ss.
⁵ Ritschl, Proll. lxxxix.
cxxiii. Scaliger's statement on
the quantity of *Philippus* 'et
numquam aliter invenies apud
Plautum quin mediam corri-
puerit' is not accurate. The
Plautine spelling of this name
was *Pilipus*, just as we find it
on a coin of the year 620 : see
C. I. L. i 354.

Probably, the short quantity of the second syllable is to be attributed to the influence of the Greek accentuation: see Scaliger, Auson. Lect. lib. II 21 (p. 147 ed. 1588). See also my note on Aul. 86.

ss has the metrical value of a single *s* in the verb *esse*, which must often be read *ĕse*[1]. The same reason explains the prosody of *dĕdisse* Amph. II 2, 130[2], and *vicissatim* Stich. 532[3].

tt has the metrical value of a single *t* in *sagita* = *sa-* p. xliv. *gitta*, Persa 25 and Aul. 393[4]. This prosody was first pointed out by Kampmann, and after having been rejected by Ritschl (Proll. Trin. CXXIII), has lately been revived by Fleckeisen (Krit. Miscellen, p. 39—42).

cc = *c* in *ŏecasio* (Persa 268) *ŏcculto* (c.g. Trin. 712) *ăccumbe* (Most. 308) and *ăccepisti* (e.g. Trin. 964[5]). In the words *eccum eccam eccos eccas* the first syllable is frequently shortened.

dd would seem to be equal to a single *d* in *ădde* (Trin. 385) and *rĕdde* (Stich. 786)[6].

---

[1] For instances see Corssen II 646.

[2] Corssen II 647. The same prosody occurs Cist. I 3, 24. Pseud. 893. Ritschl corrects the passage o. the Amphitruo in his Prolegomena p. cxxv. The line of the Pseudulus should be read: *nómen est* : : *scio iám tibi me récte dĕdisse epístulam*, for this is the reading of the mss., the Ambrosian palimpsest not being trustworthy in this passage. I am glad to see that Fleckeisen does not adopt Ritschl's conjectures in these two passages.

[3] *nós potius onerémus nosmet vicíssatim volúptátibus.* 'This is the reading of the mss., recommended by the alliteration ; it will no doubt be acknowledged by Ritschl in a second edition ; Fleckeisen has

it in the text.' BUCHELER, *jahrb. für class. phil.* 1863 p. 336. See also Corssen II 665.

[4] 'Anapaestum ars vetuit binorum vocabulorum consociatione fieri, quorum prius in media anacrusi finiretur : eaque elegantiae observatio, quantum intellexi, constans est apud hunc poëtam.' RITSCHL, praef. Mil. glor. XXII. We cannot therefore read *confi | ge sagit | tis*.

[5] *oculto* (with only one *c*) is the spelling of the Decurtatus Trin. 712. The famous SC. de Bacanalibus gives INOQVOLTOD, i.e. *inocultod (qu=c)*. Ritschl, Proll. Trin. CCXXIV. Comp. also OQVPATVM C. I. L. I 200, 25.— *ăcceptrici* occurs Truc. II 7, 18 (= 566 G.).

[6] These two instances have been corrected by Ritschl and

An *n* before another consonant was, in Latin, very weakly sounded and was, therefore, apt to fall out entirely[1]. We find it thus at times quite neglected in the hurried pronunciation of the days of Plautus, i. e. *n* followed by another consonant does not influence the quantity of the preceding vowel. Thus Plautus has the quantities

ferĕntárium esse amícum. Trin. 456.

sedĕntárii sutóres. Aul. 508.

qui ovís Tarĕntínas. Truc. iii 1, 5 (=638 G.).

talĕntúm Philíppum huic opus aúrist. Mil. gl. 1061 [anapæstic].

quo némo adaeque iúvĕntute. Most. 30.

iuvĕntúte et pueris líberis. Curc. i 1, 38.

cólere iúvĕntutem átticam. Pseud. 202.

si íd mea volŭntate fáctumst. Trin. 1166.

néc volŭntate id fácere meminit. Stich. 59.

tuá volŭntáte. Pseud. 537.

quód ïntellexi. Eun. iv 5, 11.

p. xlv.

égo ïnterim. Most. 1094.

séd ïnterim. Haut. tim. 882.

tibi ïntérpellatio. Trin. 709.

neque ïntélleges. Phorm. 806.

ego ïntérea. Hec. prol. ii 34.

quíd ïnterest. Eun. 233.

ut ïncéʒit. Aul. 47.

sine invídia. Andr. 66.

et ïnvídia. Aul. 478.

fore ïnvíto. Poen. v 4, 35.

bonum ïngénium. Andr. 466.

tíbi ïnde. Persa iii 1, 96.

quíd ïnde. Rud. iv 3, 20[2].

Fleckeisen, and it is indeed very difficult to accept them as authentic.

[1] See Schuchardt, On Vulgar Latin i 104 sqq.; he says that 'verdunkelung des N vor dentalen und gutturalen' is one of the characteristic features of the first period of vulgar Latin.

Bücheler, *jahrb. für class. phil.* 1863 p. 342. *toties* and *totiens*, *decies* and *deciens*, *vicesimus* and *vicensimus* are equivalent forms generally known. *commostraret* (as γ has, Aul. 12) would be a perfectly correct form (comp. Mostellaria).

[2] There neither exists a form

Brix has collected the following instances of *ĭnde*: Amph. I 1, 4. Capt. I 2, 19. Aul. II 7, 4. Poen. prol. 2. IV 2, 80. v 3, 39. *ŭnde* occurs as a pyrrhich in the following passages which we likewise borrow from Brix: Trin. 218. Capt. I 1, 41. Cist. II 3, 19. Persa IV 3, 23. Mil. gl. III 1, 93. Eun. II 3, 14. For *ĭntro* see my note on Aul. 448.

Even the first syllable in *inquam* is shortened Capt. III 4, 39 (see p. 38), a passage where Ritschl boldly substitutes *ego* for *inquam*.

To these examples we may add the short quantity of the first syllable in *ĭgnave* Eun. IV 7, 7[1]. So also *ĭgnorabitur* Men. 468 according to the mss.

As it is our intention to consider all such instances as admit of a different explanation from that afforded by the sole influence of the accent, before mentioning those examples which compel us to find the ultimate cause of the change of quantity in the power of the accent, we may add here some examples of words in which *x* does not lengthen a preceding vowel, e. g.

> sed ŭxór scelesta. Rud. IV 1, 4.
> sibi ŭxórem. Aul. prol. 32.
> ad ŭxorem. Merc. II 1, 20.
> in ĕxércitum. Amph. prol. 101, 125.
> ab ĕxércitu. Amph. prol. 140.
> ad ĕxércitum. Amph. I 3, 6.
> mage ĕxígere. Trin. 1052[2].

In these cases we might explain the violation of quantity by assuming the soft pronunciation of the *x* as *s*; but this would not help us to explain such instances as the following:

> ego ĕxclúdor. Eun. I 1, 79.
> ibi ĕxtémplo. Poen. III 4, 23.

p. xlvi.

ti instead of *tibi*, nor is it possible to pronounce *qu' inde*. See Ritschl, Proll. Trin. CLIX.

[1] Comp. the spelling *inavia* found in the Medicean ms. of

Virgil, Aen. XI 733. See my Introduction to Terence, p. 20. Add also Corssen II 938.

[2] See also Corssen II 665.

But a host of other instances still remains unexplained and will be unaccounted for, unless we really admit the truth of the general law laid down at the head of the present section. We cannot of course promise to give all, or nearly all, the instances which should hence be explained, but it will be useful to mention some prominent examples, were it only as a brief exemplification of our law. By carefully studying the Plautine plays, a rhythmical ear will soon become familiar with these licenses of prosody, and when once accustomed to them, no reader can fail to discover the wonderful vivacity and elasticity of the comic versification of the Romans, a fact which would have been perfectly impossible, had the Latin language always been bound by the prosodiacal fetters which, since Ennius' time, restrained its youthful agility and turned it into a slow, but majestic and pompous array. These words are not, however, intended to depreciate Ennius' merits : for it was he who preserved the language from premature decay and dilapidation.

We may first draw the reader's particular attention to two little pronouns which, on account of their frequent occurrence, were liable to an uncertain mode of pronunciation. We mean *ipse* and *iste :* and both occasionally being enclitics, it was, of course, left to the free choice of the speaker, which place to assign to them in his sentence, i.e. either to run over them by connecting them with the preceding word, or to give them more importance by fully pronouncing their first syllable. In the first case these pronouns would be pyrrhichs[1], in the latter trochees, and accordingly they appear in Plautus and Terence in both shapes : *iste* has even a secondary form *ste*, which was first discovered by Lachmann, on Lucr. p. 197[2]: in the same way we may

---

[1] 'Cum antiquitus *ipse* pyrrichium aequasset *p* littera sic ut in *voluptate* correpta, post adsimilantes *isse* pronuntiabant vulgo' Bücheler on Petron. p. 74, 20 (ed. mai.), whose entire note should be read as a specimen of a neat contribution to Latin philology. Comp. also Schuchardt, On Vulgar Latin i 148.

[2] See note on Aul. 261.

fairly presume the existence of an analogous form *pse*, though there are no historical documents for it [1].

The second class of our instances of violated quantity p. xlvii. will be divided into two sections : 1, violation of quantity in vowels naturally long; 2, violation of quantity in vowels long by position.

1. Under this head we have to mention some very strong cases ; but it may be premised that, in almost every separate instance, some critic has attempted to remove such offensive violations of regular quantity either by transposition or some kind of alteration of the text, i.e. by admitting a kind of criticism which may have its justification if the case in question should be quite isolated, but which must be entirely discarded if the multitude of analogous instances defies correction. We simply put some instances together and let them plead for themselves.

The *e* in an imperfect of the second conjugation is shortened in the following line :

> quid ád me ibatis? rídiculum verĕbámini.
> Ter. Phorm. 902 [2].

Bentley might well call this an *indigna et turpis licentia*, because he was not aware of the general law which accounts for the shortened *e*.

In Plautus the word *Acheruns* generally occurs with a long *a*, and therefore, as Ritschl observes, *non produci brevis syllaba dicenda est in* Acheruns *per Plautinas fabulas novem, sed longa corripi in Poenulo* (Proll. Trin. CLXXI). The passages alluded to by Ritschl are :

> ipse ábiit ád Acherúntem sine viático.   Poen. prol. 71.

<hr/>

[1] We may add to these two pronouns some particles which share their ambiguous prosody. *ĕrgo* occurs frequently (Poen. IV 2, 59. Pers. II 2, 3. Mil. gl. IV 2, 17. Haut. tim. V 2, 40. Merc. V 4, 10. .Poen. IV 2, 71 etc.). *hĕrcle* stands Trin. 58.

559. Most. I 3, 72, and *nĕmpe* is found in an overpowering multitude of passages (e.g. Aul. 292); see, above all, Trin. 328 with our note.

[2] *veremini* Bentley, see M. Crain, Plaut. Stud. p. 13. Luc. Müller, de re metr. p. l. p. 365.

quó die Orcus áb Ăcherunte mórtuos amíserit.
Ibid. ɪ 2, 131.

quódvis genus ibi hóminum videas, quási Ăcheruntem
véneris.   Ibid. ɪv 2, 9.

to which Crain (Plaut. Stud. p. 16) adds a line from the
Mostellaria (509):

vivóm me accersunt ád Ăcheruntem mórtui.

We have here four instances of a rhythmical shortening of a vowel which is in all other instances long. That
this same vowel is always short in the usage of later
poets, is no doubt due to the adoption of the quantity of
the Greek word[1].

p. xviii. The two genitives *eius* and *huius* are occasionally
shortened in their first syllable, when standing after a
short accented syllable[2]:

ut síbi ĕius faciat cópiam.   illa enim sé negat.
                              Ter. Phorm. 113.

si quíd hŭius simile fórte aliquando evénerit.
                              Ter. Haut. tim. 551.

Mr Parry gives in the first instance *sibi ut eius*, while
he preserves the reading of the mss. in the second passage, where it would have been just as easy to transpose
si huius quid. But there is no note on either passage
to enlighten the reader about such a surprising incon-
sistency.

To this shortened quantity in the genitive we may
add an instance in which the dative *huic* has the metrical
value of a short syllable: Ter. Ad. ɪv 5, 4 (= 638 Fl.):

quid huic híc negotist? túne has pepulistí foris?

This is, as far as I can see, the reading of all mss.
and editions, but no editor has a note on the shortened
quantity of *huic*. Guyet alone (Comm. p. 244) proposes
to write *quid híc huic*.

---

[1] The above passages are corrected by A. Spengel, T. Maccius Plautus, p. 69 s.

[2] See Lachmann on Lucr. p.
161.

The word *aut* appears shortened Bacch. 491, where Fleckeisen reads in accordance with all the mss. as follows :

> sátin ut quem tu habeás fidelem tíbi aŭt quoi credas néscias ?

Ritschl admits a hiatus, omits *tu* and transposes *tibi fidelem.*

Even the shortening of the first syllable in *audivi* would have to be assumed, if the reading of a line in the Truculentus (I 2, 92 = 126 G.) were safely established. In this passage the mss. give

> peperísse eam aŭdívi :: ah, óbsecro, tacĕ Díniarche :: quid iam.

But, according to Geppert's and Studemund's testimony, the Ambrosian palimpsest omits *eam*, so that the line would be unobjectionable. It is, however, not impossible that the omission of *eam* is due to the metrical correction of some ancient grammarian whose authority was followed by the scribe of the ms.

Another instance is Epid. v 1, 15 according to the Ambrosian palimpsest—

> híc danista, haec íllast autém quam égo ĕmi de praeda :: haécinest.

Comp. also the quantity of *Surăcúsas* Men. 37.

2. We shall now mention some instances where the usual rules of *position* have to yield to the rhythmical influence of the accent. Thus we find the following p. xlix. combinations of letters without any influence on the prosodiacal value of the preceding vowels :

a. pt.

> mércimonium. aéqua dicis. séd ŏptume eccum ipse ádvenit.
> Persa 544.

> nunc ádeo ibo illuc, séd ŏptume gnatúm meum.
> Merc. 329.

This is the reading of the mss. in both passages which Ritschl alters somewhat arbitrarily; it is, however, defended by M. Crain, Plaut. Stud. p. 16. Geppert adds a third instance of the same quantity, Most. 410:

nam cuívis homini, vél ŏptumo vel péssumo,

but this line is considered spurious by Ritschl and A. O. F. Lorenz.

néque dum exarui éx amoenis rébus et volŭptáriis.
Mil. gl. 642.

volŭptábilem mihi núntium tuo ádventu adtulísti.
Epid. i 1, 19.

volŭptátem inesse tántam....Rud. 459.

The same quantity *volŭptatem* in the beginning of a line occurs Ter. Haut. tim. i 2, 10 and Afran. Ribb. Com. p. 179. In the same way we have *volŭptati* Ter. Haut. tim. i 1, 19. Andr. v 4, 41. *volŭptatis* [acc. plur.] Plaut. Stich. 657. The short pronunciation of *volŭptas* itself is very frequent, e. g. Truc. ii 4, 75. ii 6, 59. 65. iv 4, 7. Most. i 3, 92. 136. In all these cases *mea* follows and the two words conclude the line[1].

p. l.

β. st.

quasi mágĭstratum sibi álterive ambíverint.
Amph. prol. 74.

iámiam hercle apud omnís magĭstratus fáxo erit nomén
tuom.   Truc. iv 2, 48 (=749 G.).

magĭstrátus quóm ibi adésset, occeptást agi.
Ter. Eun. prol. 22.

ubi sínt magĭstratus quós curare opórteat.
Persa 76.

---

[1] Perhaps we should also acknowledge a short vowel before *pt* in the following line from the Pseudulus (597),

sĕptumás esse aedis á porta...

This is the reading of the mss. kept by Fleckeisen. Ritschl gives trochees from v. 595 to 603, but not without the most violent alterations and deviations from the mss. Fleckeisen gives anapaests and is thus enabled to be more conservative. In this one instance Ritschl reads *séptumas esse á porta aedis.* We venture to ask whether it would not be better to read *septúmas,* the last syllable being shortened in consequence of the accent being thrown on the penult.—See also Corssen i 657.

magĭstrátus, si quis me hánc habere víderit.
Rud. 477.

atque út magĭstratus públice quando aúspicant.
Caecilius Ribb. com. p. 56[1].

parvís magnisque mĭnĭsteriis praefúlcior.
Pseud. 772[2].

nósmet inter nós minĭstremus...
Stich. 689.

túte tabulas cónsignato : híc minĭstrabit, dúm ego edam.
Curc. 369.

quae hic ádminĭstraret ád rem divinám tibi.
Epid. iii 3, 37[3].

In the Oscan dialect, the i disappeared entirely, and
we therefore find in it the forms *minstrois* and even *mis-
treis :* see Corssen, ii 659.

vetŭstáte vino edéntulo aetatem ínriges.
Poen. iii 3, 97.

hic ómnes volŭptátes, omnés venŭstatés sunt.
Pseud. 1257.

quís me est fortunátior, venŭstátisque adeo plénior?
Ter. Hec. 848.

neque fénĕstra nisi clatráta...
Mil. gl. 379.

inlústriores fécit, fenëstrasque índidit.
Rud. 88.

A contracted form *festra* is mentioned by Festus,
p. 91[4].

quam huc scélĕstus leno véniat nosque hic ópprimat.　　p. li.
Rud. ii 4, 35.

scelëstae haé sunt aedes, ímpiast habitátio.
Most. 504.

---

[1] See also Key, 'Language,
etc.' p. 130 sq.

[2] In a Saturnian line of Naevius (32) we have *éxta minĭstratores* (not *minĭstratores*, as
Vahlen's edition has it, see
Bücheler, *jahrb. für class. phil.*
1863 p. 335).

[3] See Key, l.c., p. 135.

[4] Fleckeisen gives *fenstras* in
both passages, and analogously
has *minstrabit* and *minstremus*
Curc. 369. Stich. 689. See also
Corssen ii 659. Bentley on
Ter. Haut. iii 1, 72.

Both instances have been altered by Fleckeisen and Ritschl, but the reading of the mss. is defended by Geppert, lat. ausspr. p. 93 (Corssen, II 660).

ego ŏsténderem :: certó scio :: quo pácto :: parce sódes.
Ter. Phorm. 793.

dedĭstíne hoc facto ei gládium qui se occíderet.
Trin. 129[1].

Prof. Key, in his 'Miscellaneous Remarks on Ritschl's Plautus,' p. 195, justly observes that this pronunciation of *dedisti* (*dedsti, desti*), *dedistis* and other derivations gave rise to the contracted forms of this verb which we find in Italian (*desti deste diero*), Spanish (*diste distes dièron dièra dièsse*), and Portuguese (*déste déstes déra désse*). Still, I must differ from Prof. Key when he applies the same contracted pronunciation to the verses of the ancient comic poets themselves: it may here be repeated for the last time that the application of late and modern forms to an entirely distant period seems to violate the laws of historical philology; we are, therefore, entitled to recognise the working power and the first germs of Romance forms in the shortened forms of Plautine prosody, but we should not use the final stage of any historical development as an explanation of the remote cause which first originated it. What would be the result if we were to explain Anglo-Saxon forms from modern English corruptions[2]?

γ. *rn.*

cum nóvo ŏrnatu speciéque simul.
Trin. 840.

---

[1] Fleckeisen gives Stich. 731 in accordance with the mss. as follows:

áge tibicen, quándo bíbĭsti, réfer ad labeas tíbias.

Ritschl has in his text *quóm bibisti*. The ms. reading is also found in Nonius, p. 210. Ritschl adds '*fortasse igitur fuit* quando biberis.'

[2] See now also Key, 'Language, etc.' p. 157. I may well leave others to judge between Mr Key's views and my own.

Hílurica faciés videtur hóminis, éo örnatu ádvenit.
                    Trin. 852.

male pérditus péssume örnátus eo.   p. lii.
                    Aul. 713.

mé despoliat, méa örnamenta clam ád meretrices dégerit.
                    Men. 804.

lepidé factumst': iam ex sérmone hoc gubërnábunt doctius
    pórro.   Mil. gl. 1091.

cássidem in capút—dormibo pérplacide in tabërnáculo.
                    Trin. 726.

So also *gubërnabunt* Mil. gl. 1091 and *gubërnátor*
Caecil. 110 in Ribbeck's second edition.

δ. *bs* (*ps*)[1]:

égo öpsonabo. nám id flagitium sít mea te grátia.
                    Bacch. 972[2].

scio äbsúrde dictum hoc dérisores dícere.
                    Capt. ɪ 1, 3 (=71 Fl.)[3].

and even in such a word as *abstulisti* the first syllable
appears shortened Aul. 637[4]. (Comp. also *abscessi* Epid.
ɪɪ 2 53 = 229 G.) It is very difficult now to find these
instances in Ritschl's text[5], since most have been eliminated

---

[1] Comp. also Schuchardt, ɪ
148.

[2] This is the reading of all
the mss., and Fleckeisen's edition gives the line in accordance with it. Ritschl however transposes *ópsonabo ego*.

[3] Fleckeisen (ep. crit. xxɪ)
was inclined to transpose *dictum apsurde*. He would not do
so now.

[4] A Saturnian line of Livius
Andronicus seems to attest the
short quantity of the syllable
-ups- in *Calupsonem:*

apúd númfam Atlántis fíliám
    Calúpsónem.

This is at least Bücheler's
opinion, *jahrb. für class. phil.*
1863 p. 322.

[5] As regards Fleckeisen's text,
we must draw the reader's attention to the great difference
between his first and second
volumes. In the first he is almost entirely guided by Ritschl's
principles, while in the second
he is more conservative in consequence of the metrical and
rhythmical discoveries made by
him in his article on Ritschl's
Plautus. In his first volume
he did not admit *öbsecras* (Mil.
gl. 542): but in his second he
kept *öpsonabo* (Bacch. 97).

by means of conjectures sometimes very arbitrary, e.g.
Mil. gl. 542 s.; the mss. (*ABC*) would give us the following text:

> perqué tua genua : quíd óbsecras me? :: inscítiae
> meae ét stultitiae ignóscas. nunc demúm scio.

In this case *quid obsecras me* would be a very natural
and convenient question, the slave having said two lines
before *te obsecro*. Ritschl gives, however, as follows:

> perqué tua genua :: quíd iam? :: meae ut inscítiae
> et meaé stultitiae ignóscas. nunc demúm scio.

p. liii. Every student of the Plautine plays cannot but agree
with the opinion of Prof. Key, who calls Ritschl's text
'in not a few instances untrustworthy,' because it differs
'what with omissions, insertions, changes and transposi-
tions of words, and not unfrequently of lines, from what
the mss. sanction, by a very considerable percentage.'
But then again, the mss. are not our sole and exclusive
guides, and it would be even more strange to be ruled by
them in all instances.

ε. rg.

> quód ărgentum, quas tú mihi tricas nárras?...
> Curc. v 2, 15 (613 Fl.).
> néc pueri suppósitio, nec ărgénti circumdúctio.
> Capt. v 5, 3 (1031 Fl.).
> séd sine ărgénto frustra 's...
> Pseud. 378.

(This is the reading of the mss. given by Fleckeisen,
while Ritschl has *sine nummo*. In the Prolegomena,
p. CXLVIII, he thinks of pronouncing *s'n'argento*. In the
passage from the Captivi Fleckeisen writes *aut argenti*
against the authority of the mss.)

> éum ărgentúm sumpsísse apud Thebas...
> Epid. II 2, 67 (according to the mss.).
> áge iam cupio, sí modo ărgentum réddat.
> Ter. Ad. 202.

(This is the reading of the mss.; Guyet, Bentley and Fleckeisen *modo si*[1].)

But we shall stop here, though it would be easy to accumulate more examples of similar 'violations of prosody.' We use this expression, although it is quite erroneous when applied to Plautus or other comic writers. For them that prosody which prevails in Horace and Virgil did not exist, and they could not therefore ' violate ' it. Their sole guide in prosodiacal matters was their ear, and in many cases, they obeyed the dictates of the rhythmical, rather than of the quantitative, laws of the language. This proves the influence which the accent exercised on the *quantity* of many syllables; but this should not be confounded with another question : *did the ancient Roman poets purposely attempt to make the metrical stress of their verses agree with the prosaic accentuation of everyday life ?*

The theory that the natural accent of the Latin was, p. liv. in the earliest period of Latin poetry, an important factor in versification, which decided its whole character, was first established by Bentley in his ' Schediasma.' Nevertheless, Bentley could not carry out his theory without allowing a difference between natural and metrical accent in the first and last dipodies, because without this liberty it would have been a mere impossibility to adapt Greek metres and versification to the Latin language. Bentley was, of course, obliged to correct a great many passages in Terence which were at variance with his theory, and correct them he did undauntedly. His theory was adopted by G. Hermann (*el. d. m.* p. 141), though with the admission, that the poets to whom it applied did not seem to follow it consistently[2]; and the same theory is the groundwork of Ritschl's views as developed in the xvth and xvith chapters of the Prolegomena. In the versification of the comic writers, Ritschl discovers a struggle between a

---

[1] See also Corssen ii 662.

[2] 'Non enim amant Latini voces in ultima syllaba ictu notare, nisi in primis et postre- mis senarii pedibus, *etsi ne in hac quidem re ubique sibi constant.*'

merely quantitative metrical accentuation and the real accent of everyday life. According to his theory, the natural accent of the language still exercised great influence upon the versification of Plautus and his contemporaries, while it was entirely disregarded in the Augustan period, when a merely quantitative system of versification became dominant.

An accurate examination of this theory is due to the joint labours of Franz Ritter, A. Böckh, Weil and Benloew, and Corssen.

In the first place it may be observed that the Latin language is, on the whole, of a trochaic and iambic character with regard to its usual accentuation, and that accent and quantity coincide in Latin to a far greater extent than in Greek. We may, therefore, be prepared to find a general coincidence between the prosaic accent and the metrical *ictus* in the metres of the dramatists, without being at once obliged to assume that this agreement was something studiously contrived and sought after by the poets themselves.

This observation is fully borne out by the facts of the case. If the earlier poets had purposely endeavoured to reconcile the metrical ictus of their verses with the prose-accentuation of the words employed in them, it would seem a fair inference to expect that in them the proportion of agreement would be greater than in the later poets, for whom such an attempt has not been assumed. But precisely the reverse proves to be the case, and there is indeed, as has been statistically proved by Corssen[1], a far greater proportion of this coincidence in the later than in the earlier poets. This fact harmonizes with the general development of Latin poetry, which ended by becoming entirely accentual (i.e. the accent determined the quantity, as is the case in most modern languages), while it had originally been quantitative.

---

[1] See II 957 sqq. We cannot therefore agree with those critics who continue to correct all those passages in which the metrical ictus appears to be at variance with the usual accentuation. Corssen II 990—1000.

It may readily be granted that in the prosody of the comic poets many syllables had not yet received a fixed and settled quantity, and that this fact was due to the influence of the prose-accent or to the musical (rhythmical) pronunciation of that early time. Ennius, who was the first to employ dactylic hexameters in Latin poetry, was obliged to settle the prosodiacal value of most of these syllables; the reason of this was the very nature of his metre, in which the *arsis* must invariably consist in *one long* syllable, while the *arsis* of iambic and trochaic verses may just as well consist of two short syllables—there being moreover considerable liberty permitted as to the treatment of the *thesis*.

The Latin differs from the Greek only in so far as the p. lv. prosaic accent had already commenced to exercise an important influence upon the quantitative value of many syllables, when the language was first employed for literary purposes ; many traces of this we have endeavoured to point out in the metres of Plautus and Terence. The vacillating and fluctuating system of Latin prosody was p. lvi. afterwards entirely reformed by Ennius. He could not violently alter what had already become the acknowledged usage of the language, but in all those cases which were not yet finally settled, the quantity preferred by him was adopted by the subsequent poets. A full discussion of this point would, however, lead us beyond the limits of this Introduction : at present we think it sufficient to refer to L. Müller, de re metr. p. 69 and 70.

F. SYNIZESIS.

The notion of *synizesis* rests on the ambiguous nature of the two letters *u* and *i*, which may be used both as vowels and consonants, and are in the latter quality frequently expressed by *v* and *j*[1]. To these two we have to add the letter *e*, which sometimes assumes the consonantal sound of *i* (*y*). This is the case in the word *deus*,

---

[1] On the genuine pronunciation of this *j* see Key, L. G. § 9.

where we have *dei = di* even in common Latin[1], but in
the comic writers we find *deo* (Plaut. Cist. I 3, 2. Liv.
Andr. trag. Ribb. v. 9) and *deos* (Naev. com. Ribb. 95. Plaut.
Amph. I 1, 128. II 2, 86. v 1, 38. 41. Aul. IV 10, 12. 13.
Capt. III 5, 69. Curc. I 1, 70. II 2, 13. v 2, 58. Cas.
II 5, 28. 38. II 6, 37. 44. Cist. II 3, 52. IV 1, 12.
Epid. II 2, 117. v 1, 4 and in many other passages) as
monosyllables[2]. The genitive *dei* occurs with a monosyllabic pronunciation only once, Ribb. Trag. p. 202; *deae*
follows this analogy (Aul. 778. Cas. II 4, 1. Cist. II 1,
35. Epid. III 3, 15. Most. I 3, 35. Pseud. I 1, 35. I 3, 36.
Poen. III 3, 54. IV 2, 37. v 4, 102. Persa II 4, 21. 25.
27. v 2, 50). In the same way *deorum* is disyllabic in
many instances (Amph. prol. 45. Epid. v 2, 10. Bacch.
124. Men. 217. Rud. II 2, 13). This fact may be com-

p. lvii.

pared with the similar contracted pronunciation of θεός
and θεά, which is not unfrequently met with in the tragic
poets.

The word *meus* was treated much in the same way as
deus: we have therefore *mei meae meo meos meas meis*
sometimes as monosyllables, and *meorum mearum meapte*
(Truc. II 5, 18) as disyllables[3]. The real pronunciation
of these forms in such cases may be ascertained from the
spelling *mieis* (= *meis*) which occurs in the dactylic inscription on the sepulchre of one of the Scipios: this
enables us to guess that it was probably very much like
the modern Greek pronunciation of θιός (= θεός), i.e. *myîs
dyô*, etc.

Many forms of the pronouns *is* and *idem* fall under
the same head; thus we have *eo ei eodem eidem eas
easdem eapse* (Curc. I 3, 4) *eos eosdem eae eaedem ea
eadem* (abl.) *eorum*. The subjunctives *eamus eatis* appear
as disyllables according to the same rule, and in *exeundum*
(Aul. 40) we notice the same pronunciation. We may
add *eunt* Cist. I 1, 39. Poen. I 2, 117, and perhaps also
queo Aul. 190.

---

[1] *dii* is not a genuine form.
[2] See, on the whole question,
Spengel, 'Plautus,' p. 25.
[3] For the forms *dius* and

mius see Ritschl, de decl. quadam lat. recond. I p. 22. Schuchardt I 433.

The forms *eius ei huius* (*huic*) *quoius quoi* deserve particular notice. Of these *quoi* and *huic* are always monosyllables, while the others admit of a threefold triple pronunciation :

trochee,	pyrrhich,	monosyllable,
$\bar{e}\widecheck{\imath}us$[1]	$\widecheck{e}\widecheck{\imath}us$[2]	$e\overline{\imath}us = eis$
$h\bar{u}\widecheck{\imath}us$[1]	$h\widecheck{u}\widecheck{\imath}us$[2]	$h\overline{u\imath}us = huis$[3]
$qu\bar{o}\widecheck{\imath}us$	$c\widecheck{u}\widecheck{\imath}us$	$qu\overline{o\imath}us = quois$[4]
$c\bar{u}\widecheck{\imath}us$[1]		$c\overline{u\imath}us = cuis$
$\bar{e}i$	$\widecheck{e}i$	$\bar{e}i$[5]

All these forms occur in the metres of the comic p. lviii. writers: we must, however, leave it to the industry of our readers to collect as many examples of each separate measure as they find sufficient for their own conviction. Many instances of the varied metrical character of *ei* are collected by Ritschl, Opusc. ii 418 sq.

We shall now briefly enumerate some of the most frequent cases in which *i* and *u* display their variable nature. Thus we have

$$dies = dyes, \quad die = dye,$$

---

[1] I purposely do not mention the oldest forms *e-i-us ho-i-us quo-i-us* (tit. Scip. Barb. Ritschl. pr. l. m. ep. t. 37), since they are not found in Plautus and Terence.

[2] To this head we may refer the examples quoted above p. 52. See Lachmann, comm. Lucr. p. 27, and especially p. 160 s. See also Corssen ii 672.

[3] The spelling *huis* occurs in an inscription in Gruter's collection 44, 3: see Corssen, *krit. beitr. zur lat. formenl.* p. 545, and Schuchardt ii 503. In Guyet's edition of Plautus the forms *eis huis* and *quois* are several times found in the text.

[4] This pronunciation must be assumed for a line of Lucilius: *quoius voltu ac facie, ludo ac sermonibus nostris.* (Lachmann, l. l.) Lachmann shows that this form left its traces in *cuicuimodi*, i. e. *quoisquoismodi*, the dropping of the final *s* taking place as explained above p. 30 s. The *u* disappeared much in the same way as *magis* presupposes an original *magius*. The oldest ms. gives *cuicuiusmodi* in Cic. Verr. v 41, 107 which Halm is inclined to believe genuine.

[5] The same theory applies to such forms as *rĕi, rēi, rē* (=$r\overline{e}i$); *spĕi spĕi *spē* (=$sp\overline{e}i$) &c. See note on Aul. 607.

$diu = dyu,$
$scio = scyo,$
ais ain ait as monosyllables,
aibam etc. as disyllables,
$trium = tryum,$
otio filio gaudiis omnia tertiust as disyllables
(in the so-called 'free metres,' but *nescⁱⁱo*
is common throughout).

On the other hand it should be observed that in Plautus and Terence *gratiis* and *ingratiis* are always fully pronounced[1]; in later times we find *gratis* and *ingratis* as the predominant forms.

In *tuos* and *suos*[2] and their various forms the *u* assumes in many instances the consonantal sound of a *v*. The same is the case with many words where a *u* follows an initial consonant, e. g. *duo (duorum duarum duobus duabus) duellum*[3] *duellica puer puella*, or in such an instance as *quattor* for *quattuor*[4].

The verbal forms *fui fuisti fuistis fuisse*, etc. undergo very often a synizesis of the two letters *ui. fui* and *fuit* may, however, be pronounced in three different ways, viz. *fūi fŭi fûi* (monosyll.). If we add the variable quantity of the perfect termination *it* (see p. 16), we arrive at the following possible pronunciations of *fuit :*

$$f\bar{u}it \; f\breve{u}it \; f\bar{u}\breve{i}t \; f\breve{u}\bar{i}t \; f\widehat{uit} \text{ (monos.)}.$$

lix.   This instance may serve as another palpable illustration of the truth of the observation made p. 50 with regard to the elasticity of Plautine prosody.

---

[1] See Bentley on Ter. Ad. IV 7, 26.

[2] *tuus* and *suus* are not only not Plautine, but not even good Latin forms. Even Cicero knows no *uu*. (In *fluuius* the first *u* is the root vowel, the second a modification of the guttural *g*). See however, Munro's Introduction to Lucretius.

[3] The pronunciation *dvellum* was the next step to the secondary form *bellum*. In the same way we have *duonum (dvonum) bonum*.

[4] For this instance see Ritschl, Rhein. Mus. VIII 309. Lachm. Lucr. p. 192. Enn. ann. (ed. Vahlen) 96. 580, and the somewhat different statement of Corssen II 751.

We may finally draw the reader's attention to the general fact that compounds in which two vowels come together are always pronounced *per synizesin* in Plautus and Terence, e.g. *dein deinde*[1] *proin proinde*[2] *dehinc deorsum* (written *dorsum* in an inscription C. I. L. I 199, 20) *seorsum praeoptare praeesse deosculari.* See also Corssen II 712 sqq. 759 sq.

G. HIATUS.

In order to complete our sketch of the pronunciation of Latin as seen in the comic writers, we must also touch upon a subject which is, however, one of the most difficult points in Plautine criticism, viz. *the hiatus.* After the uncritical labours of Linge, Ritschl was the first to give some distinct and positive rules with regard to the admission of hiatus in the metres of the comic writers, in the XIVth chapter of his Prolegomena, though his views as given there were afterwards in many respects corrected and enlarged by himself.

There is, at least, one point on which no doubt can possibly exist, and this discriminates Ritschl's views from those of former scholars. We shall quote his own words[3]: '*impeditior est de hiatu quaestio. non dicam autem contra eos qui quovis et loco et modo admissum hiatum concocunt concoctisque bonos versus concacant: quis enim lavare laterem animum inducat? verum qui in ipsa caesura senariorum admissum tutantur atque defensitant, eos certe aliqua ratione agere concedendum est. Nec ego hoc numquam factum contendam: sed tamen ut vel id genus longe artioribus, quam vulgo creditur, finibus esse circumscriptum putem. Et tantum quidem non potest non haberi*

---

[1] The contradictory passage in Ter. Andr. 483 has been happily corrected by Fleckeisen. See L. Müller, de re metr. p. 265.

[2] Geppert (Ausspr. p. 21) says that in Amph. III 3, 27 Plautus uses *proinde* as trisyllabic; but it is easy to remove this exception by correcting *fac sis proinde adeo uti me velle intéllegis,* instead of *ut* given by the mss.

[3] Opusc II 414.

certissimum, non elegantiam quandam interpretandum
omnem hiatum esse, quam sint sectati poëtae, sed licentiam
potius quam sibi indulserint.' The truth of this assertion
p. lx. appears from Cicero's words (Or. § 150) '*nemo tam rus-*
ticus est qui vocales nolit coniungere.' The only question
which is still *sub iudice* is therefore, how far the comic
poets indulged in a license which we must admit they
used in their metres.

Parry, in his Introduction to Terence, p. LVII, sets
down three rules which would serve to explain the admis-
sibility of hiatus, viz.: hiatus, he says, is justified,

(1) by the sense of the passage,

(2) by the punctuation,

(3) in exclamations, such as *heia hercle eho heus.*

Setting aside the third rule, which has indeed a general
value for all Latin poets, we confine ourselves to a more
detailed discussion of the first two rules. We may define
the matter more accurately in the following manner :—
Hiatus is justified :

(*a*) where the line is divided among two or more
speakers,

(*b*) by *caesura* and *diaeresis.*

The latter point in its full extent was long disputed
by Ritschl, but at last he began to allow a greater free-
dom and to relax the severity of his original views, as
will be seen in the instance of the hiatus in the caesura
of the trochaic septenarius (praef. Men. p. x ss.) This
occurs in the Aulularia v. 174. 250. 638. But he does
not allow a hiatus in the caesura of an iambic senarius
' *ut quae in medium ordinem rhythmicum incidat* ' (Proll.
p. CXCVI). Still he deviates from this law in such an instance as Trin. 342,

tempúst adeundi :: éstne hic Philto qui ádvenit?

because in this case the line is divided among two
speakers. In the Aulularia we have two instances of
the same kind of hiatus, viz. 305 and 530:

immo équidem credo :: át scin etiam quómodo?
ain aúdivisti? :: úsque a principio ómnia.

In both instances it would not be very difficult to avoid the hiatus by writing *set* instead of *at* in the first, and inserting *aio* before *usque* in the second line. But as a hiatus of this kind is by no means very rare, we shall adhere to the authority of our mss.

To proceed, Ritschl allows no such hiatus as we have p. lxi. Trin. 185,

em meá malefacta, ém meam avaritiám tibi,

according to the reading of all our mss. He writes therefore

on meá malefacta, meam én avaritiám tibi,

to which Fleckeisen justly prefers Hermann's reading

en meá *tibi* malefacta, én meam avaritiám tibi[1].

Or, to give another instance, Trin. 776, the reading of all our mss. is as follows :

det álteram ílli, álteram dicát tibi,

which Ritschl changes into

illí det álteram, álteram dicát tibi.

In both cases Brix has kept the reading of the mss., and we think him the more entitled to do so, as it requires a great deal of arbitrary criticism to correct all other instances of the same kind. It is therefore possible to maintain the reading of the mss. in the following lines in the Aulularia :

695. memoráre nolo, hóminum[2] mendicábula.

561. potáre ego hodie, Eúclio[3], tecúm uolo.

704. atát, eccum ipsum. íbo, ut hoc condám, domum.

---

[1] See also the critical note on this passage in my edition.

[2] Bergk would in all such cases avoid the hiatus by writing *homōnum*. See his arguments in the Philol. xvii p.

54 sqq. jahrb. 1861 p. 633. Brix on Men. 82.

[3] It would be possible to read *hodié potare ego, Euclio, tecúm volo*. (See, however, below, where I have adopted another

5—2

Nor would I correct the ms. reading *in* v. 671

ïndeque óbservabo, aúrum ubi abstrudát senex.

We have the same hiatus v. 69 :

queo cónminisci : ita me miseram ad hûnc modum,

p. lxii. as the line stands not only in *J*γ and the recent mss.,
but in *B* itself.

Another instance which may be alleged, is somewhat
doubtful. It is v. 504,

stat fúllo phrugio aúrifex linárius.

In this case we may notice that *B* gives *phyrgio*, a
reading which might be supported by a great many analogous examples of other words[1], though it is true that this
form of the word seems to occur nowhere else. If therefore we could confidently say that a hiatus was in this
line an impossibility, we should have to give *phurgio* in
our text.

But there is a general law which protects a great
many passages in Plautus, in which a hiatus occurs, from
the corrections of modern scholars. We owe its discovery
to Fleckeisen. It is as follows :

Monosyllables terminating in a long vowel or m *need
not coalesce with a following short vowel.*

Illustrations of this law may be found in such passages as Stich. 321. Aul. 707. 708. Mil. gl. 1330[2].

reading.) A hiatus of the same kind (i.e. before a proper name) occurs Poen. v 3, 8 :

o mí ere salve, Hánno insperatíssume.

This is the reading in *BC*, and though *A* gives the scene in which this line stands, I cannot say what the reading in it is. But to show how easy it is to get rid of such a hiatus as this, if we are only determined to do so, we will remove it for the benefit of the hiatus-haters among our readers :

o mi ére, salvē : *salve* Hánno insperatíssume.

And this reading would be recommended by the '*variatio accentus*' in *salve* (see my note on v. 258).

[1] Compare *corcodilus tarpesita bardus* θáρσος Cortona *corcota* (see my dissertation *de Aulularia* p. 14).

[2] See Corssen II 783 sq.

This kind of hiatus occurs most frequently when the p. lxiii. long vowel (or a vowel together with *m*) forms the first syllable of an arsis resolved into two shorts. This may be exemplified by comparing the following passages in the Aulularia : arg. I 2. *mé ut id* 8. *quoî ego* 187. *quó abis* 201. *iám ego* 272. *rém habere* 458. *sí ita* 488. *dém hodie* 654. *mé erus* 673.

A few words in conclusion. Throughout this chapter, we have endeavoured to keep free from merely hypothetical theories which have been brought forward for the explanation of Plautine prosody. '*Difficile est et lubri- cum*,' says Ritschl, Proll. Trin. p. CLXVII, '*quid vitae consuetudo veterum probare vel potuerit vel non potuerit, assequi ratiocinando et comminiscendo velle.*' Unless we greatly mistake, Ritschl's own investigations—to follow which in their gradual development is one of the most instructive and interesting studies—prove the truth of this observation. Yet the history of his investigations appears to teach a lesson which will most likely be the basis for the labours of the coming time, viz. that we gain and learn more and arrive at more stable results by means of a critical and conservative observation of single facts than by specious but unsound emendations of seeming irregularities[1].

[1] See also Brix, *jahrb. für class. phil.* 1865 p. 58. I may also be allowed to refer to the preface of my edition of the Trinummus.

T. MACCI PLAVTI
AVLVLARIA.

ARGVMENTVM I

Senéx avarusvíx sibi credens Eúclio
domí suae defóssam multis cúm opibus
aulam ínvenit rursúmque penitus cónditam
exsánguis amens sérvat. eius fíliam
5 Lycónides vitiárat. intereá senex
Megadórus a soróre suasus dúcere
uxórem, avari gnátam deposcít sibi:
durús senex vix promíttit atque aulaé timens
domó sublatam váriis abstrudít locis.
10 insídias servos fácit huius Lycónidis
qui vírginem vitiárat: atque ipse óbsecrat
avónculum Megadórum sibimet cédere
uxórem amanti. pér dolum mox Eúclio
quom pérdidisset aúlam, insperato ínvenit
15 laetúsque natam cónlocat Lycónidi.

ARGVMENTVM II

Aulám repertam *avárus* plenam auri Eúclio
vi súmma servat, míseris adfectús modis.
Lycónides istíus vitiat fíliam.
volt hánc Megadorus índotatam dúcere,
lubénsque ut faciat dát coquos cum obsónio.
auró formidat Eúclio, abstrudít foris,
re*que* ómni inspecta cómpressoris sérvolus
id súrpit, illic Eúclioni rém refert,
ab eó donatur aúro, uxore, et fílio.

PERSONAE

LAR FAMILIARIS PROLOGVS
EVCLIO SENEX
STAPHYLA ANVS
EVNOMIA MVLIER
MEGADORVS SENEX
STROBILVS MEGARONIDIS SERVOS
STROBILVS (?) LYCONIDIS SERVOS
ANTHRAX COCVS
CONGRIO COCVS
PHRVGIA TIBICINA
ELEVSIVM TIBICINA
PYTHODICVS SERVOS
LYCONIDES ADVLESCENS.

PROLOGVS.

LAR FAMILIARIS.

Nequís miretur quí sim, paucis éloquar.
ego Lár sum familiáris, ex hac fámilia

The greater part of the prologues to the Plautine plays being spurious and prefixed to the comedies of the poet long after his death, it is very doubtful whether the prologue to the Aulularia can be held to have been written by the poet himself. It is true, none of the arguments alleged against the rest of the prologues by Ritschl (Par. I 209—226) can be applied to this: on the contrary, this prologue is remarkably distinguished for its simple grace and unaffected language. As regards the question of its being required or not, we agree entirely with Thornton, who justly observes : 'There seems to be no reason, why any account at all need be given for how many generations the treasure had remained undiscovered in the old miser's family,' though at the same time it is obvious that for the purpose of giving such information no fitter person could be selected than the Lar familiaris. Moreover, the introduction of this deity is quite conformable to the habit of the writers of the so-called New Comedy (see Meineke, Men. et

Philem. rell. 1823 p. 284) which Plautus seems to have followed here as well as in the prologues to the Rudens and the Trinummus. On these grounds, I was originally inclined to attribute this prologue to Plautus himself (de Aulul. p. 29), but without taking into consideration a metrical reason subsequently suggested by Brix, viz. that the writer uses the word *avónculus* v. 34 as quadrisyllabic, while Plautus himself has it as trisyllabic *aúnculus* (v. 677. 772. 792), in accordance with a popular pronunciation which we find confirmed by several inscriptions. It seems therefore safer to return to Bernhardy's opinion (Römische Litteraturgeschichte, 1865, p. 442) who ascribes this prologue to an older hand than the others, though we may allow the universal character and even the whole idea of it to be taken from Plautus' original prologue.

v. 2. *Lar familiaris*, the tutelar deity of the house and family. "The Roman *Lases*, at a later time called *Lares*, are subordinate deities of a kind and helpful disposition ; their

unde éxeuntem me áspexistis. hánc domum
iam múltos annos ést quom possideo ét colo
5 patríque avoque iam huíus qui nunc híc habet.
sed míhi avos huius óbsecrans concrédidit
thensaúrum auri *olim* clam ómnis : in medió foco
defódit, venerans mé, ut id servarém sibi.
is quóniam moritur, íta avido ingenió fuit,

activity is displayed in field and
garden, on roads and in path-
ways, in town and hamlet, on
the vault of heaven and in the
deep of the sea, as is proved by
the epithets given to them; but
above all they are held to be
the benevolent and helpful
spirits of the dear homestead
and house, the genial blessing
of whom pervades the whole
family, and makes it thrive
(Preller, Röm. Mythol. p. 71 sq.
486 sq. 2nd ed.). The name is
in Etruscan *Las-a*, in Latin
Las-es, *Lar-es*, (*Lar-a*, *Lar-
unda* 'the mother of the Lares')
and has been justly derived
from the root *las* 'to desire or
wish,' whence we have in Latin
las-c-iru-s, in Gothic *lus-tu-s*,
Old High Germ. *lus-ti*, 'lust.'
Las-a, *Las-es*, *Lar-es* would
thus mean 'well-wishing, benevolent' spirits like the *Holden*
in German mythology." Corssen,
Etrusker, I p. 246. See also
our note on Trin. 39.

4. The construction of this
line is somewhat negligent,
though used by Plautus himself
in another passage : Persa 137,
*sicut istic leno haudum sex
mensis Megaribus huc est quom
commigravit.* Hence may have
arisen the French way of expressing the same thought; *il y a
beaucoup d'années que—.* For
quom 'since' see also Public

School Latin Grammar, § 182,
9, and for the explanation of the
present tenses *possideo* and *colo*
see Key, L. G. § 1455 e, note†,
and § 458.—*colo = incolo*, as v.
693. Here the notion of *guard-
ing* the house is involved, in the
same way as in Virgil's expression *nemorum cultrix Latonia
virgo* (Aen. XI 557) not only 'in-
habitant,' but protectress too is
meant.

5. *patrique avoque* 'for the
advantage of—:' see Key, L. G.
§ 977.—*habet = habitat* (cf. v. 21)
according to an idiom which
is pretty frequent in Plautus.

7. *thensaurus* is the genuine
Plautine form which, in consequence of the thin pronunciation of the letter *n*, afterwards
became *thesaurus*. In the same
way we have *Megalensia = Me-
galesia*, comp. Corssen I 251
sqq.—*omnis* is acc. plur. 'unknown to all:' see Dräger,
Histor. Syntax I § 304 (p. 621).
It is very natural that *clam*
should govern the accusative
in early Latin, as it is an adverb formed from the root *cal*
seen in Greek καλ-ύπτω and
Καλ-υψώ, and was originally
calam (comp. *palam*).

8. The syllables *ans mĕ ut*
form a dactyl, according to a
metrical law explained Introd.
p. 69.

9. Donatus (on Ter. Ad.

10 nunquam índicare id fílio voluít suo,
inopémque optavit pótius eum relínquere
quam eúm thensaurum cómmonstraret. fílio
agrí reliquit éi non magnúm modum,
quo cúm labore mágno et misere víveret.
15 ubi is óbiit mortem quí mi id aurum crédidit,
coepi óbseryare, ecquí maiorem fílius
mihi honórem haberet quam éius habuissét pater.
atque ílle vero mínus minusque impéndio
curáre minusque me ímpertire honóribus.
20 item á me contra fáctumst : nam item obiít die*m*.
is húnc reliquit qui híc nunc habitat fílium
paritćr moratum, ut páter avosque eiús fuit.
huic fília unast : éa mihi cotídie

prol. 1) observes that *quoniam*
is here used in its original sense
of a temporal conjunction, being
but a compound of *quom* and
iam. Plautus has it so not unfrequently, e.g. Trin. 112 *quoniam hinc iturust ipsus in Seleu-
ciam.* ibid. 149 *quoniam hinc
profectust ire peregre Charmi-
des.* We may observe the same
change of the two notions of
temporality and causality in
the German conj. *weil*, which
has now almost entirely lost
its temporal sense, though this
was the original one. Nevertheless, Schiller uses it as an
equivalent to the English *while*,
Wilhelm Tell, act i sc. 2 '*weil*
ich ferne bin, führe du mit
klugem sinne das regiment des
hauses.' See also my note on
Trin. 14.—The words *ita avido
ingenio fuit* might stand in
brackets, at least they do not
influence the construction of
the sentence : 'when he was
about to die, he did not—such
was his avaricious disposition—
reveal the secret to his son.'
10. *id* here and v. 8 denotes

the secret in general, and should
not be referred to *thensaurus*,
though a gloss in a Vienna
ms. suggests '*nota thesaurum
neutro genere dici.*' But in the
present prologue it is doubtless
masculine, see v. 12, and such
it is indeed wherever it occurs
in Plautus. For the indefinite
and somewhat loose employment of the neuter pronoun
the student may consult my
note on Trin. 405.
13. Comp. Hor. Serm. ii
6, 1 *hoc erat in votis : modus
agri non ita magnus.*
18. *impendio* is here used
as an adverb. Cicero has it
so in his epistles, ad Att. x 4, 9
*at ille impendio nunc magis odit
senatum.* See Afranius 351 *in-
dies impéndio | ex désiderio má-
gis magisque máceror,* and Ter.
Eun. 587 *impendio magis animus gaudebat mihi.* In later
latinity, e.g. in Appuleius and
Ammianus Marcellinus, we meet
with the same adverbial use of
impendio.
23. For *mihi* see Introd.
p. 23.—*cotidie*, instead of *quo-*

aut túre aut vino aut áliqui semper súpplicat,
25 dat míhi coronas. eíus honoris grátia
fecí, thensaurum ut híc reperiret Eúclio.
nam eám compressit dé summo adulescéns loco :
is scít adulescens quaé sit quam comprésserit,
illa íllum nescit, néque compressam autém pater.
30 eam ego hódie faciam ut híc senex de próxumo
sibi uxórem poscat : íd ea faciam grátia
quo ille eám facilius dúcat qui comprésserat.
et híc qui poscet eám sibi uxorém senex,
is ádulescentis ílliust avónculus,
35 qui illám stupravit nóctu, Cereris vígiliis.
sed híc senex iam clámat intus, út solet.

tidie, is a form well supported by the best mss. and expressly recommended by Marius Victorinus I p. 2460 (Putsch).

24. *tus vinum coronae* were the usual honours offered to the household-gods : see v. 383 and the commentators upon Hor. Od. III 23, 3. Iuv. IX 137 ss.

25. Comp. *huius honoris gratia* Amph. I 2, 24.

27. After having given the *general* reason of his action, the Lar is now going to inform his hearers of the *detailed* circumstances. This is the true explanation of *nam*, a particle which never gives up its character entirely, though it may seem simply connective in some passages. The Greek γάρ is often used in exactly the same way. See note on v. 595.

29. *neque autem* ('nor on the other hand') is used by Cicero Fam. v 12 and Lucretius I 857, and VI 779.

30. *hic senex de proxumo* (*ex prox*. 169. 288) 'the old man,

our neighbour.' He means Megadorus.

31. For *sibi* ἀπό—see Introd. p. 49. In 33 the word *uxor* has its original quantity.

35. *Cereris vigiliis*] Lyconides himself confesses this fact to Euclio v. 787 s. 'The nocturnal festival of Ceres, θεσμοφόρια, *vigiliae Cereris*, used to be celebrated by married and unmarried women strolling about in the dark without lights, whence this opportunity could easily be misused by young men desirous to encounter romantic adventures. The comic poets are therefore quite true to reality in founding the plots of some of their plays upon these festivals, as e. g. Plautus does here and in his Cistellaria (where see the prol. 8).' Köpke. Cicero has several chapters against such licentious festivals as these in his second book de legibus, where he especially mentions their frequent occurrence in the comic poets, II 14: *quid autem mihi displi-*

anúm foras extrúdit, ne sit cónscia.
credo, aúrum inspicere vólt, ne subruptúm siet.

ceat in sacris nocturnis, poëtae indicant comici. See Davies' and Turnebus' notes on de leg. II 9 and 14.
38. *conscia.* In prose the dependent genitive is rarely omitted (see, however, Cic. de Fin. II 16, 53), but in poetry the adjective is occasionally used absolutely, e.g. Cistell. II 3, 46 *fac me consciam* ('tell me'). Hor. Serm. I 2, 130 *miseram se conscia clamet.*
39. *subruptum* and v. 347 *subrupias* are the archaic forms for *subreptum* and *subripias,*

which are frequently given by the best mss. of Plautus and should no doubt be uniformly introduced into the text. The *ă* of *rapere capere quatere calcare salire* became originally *ŭ* in compounds, comp. *occupo, concutio, inculco, insulto.* These forms occur even in those later writers who affect an archaic style, and even Martial has *surrupuit* XIII 38. Comp. also *contubernium* and *taberna,* and see Schuchardt, on Vulgar Latin I 173 sq.

ACTVS I.

EVCLIO. STAPHYLA. I 1

40 Ev. Exi ínquam, age exi: exeúndum hercle tibi
hinc ést foras,
circúmspectatrix, cum óculis emissíciis.
St. nam cúr me miseram vérberas? Ev. ut mísera
sis
atque út te dignam mála malam aetatem éxigas.

40. For *exeundum* see Introd.
p. 62. The accentuation of
hercle on the final syllable is
quite unobjectionable, as appears from another line Curc.
I 3, 55 (261) *síquidem herclé
mihi regnum detur*, though
Fleckeisen transposes there *mi
hercle*, which is however against
the authority of the mss. Comp.
also Mil. glor. 473, *mágis herclé
metuo.*
41. *circumspectatrix* 'pry-
about' THORNTON.—*oculi emissicii* 'inquisitive eyes,' a phrase
imitated by Tertullian de pallio
c. 3 *circumspectu emissicii ocelli
immo luminis puncta vertigi-
nant.* Cicero would have said
emissarii; Plautus has a similar
formation Poen. v 5, 24 *tunicae demissiciae*, which Horace
calls *tunicae demissae* Serm.
I 2, 25.
42. *nam cur = curnam.* Plautus and Terence frequently
change the order of such compounds with *nam*, e.g. v. 44

we have *nam qua = quanam*, and
Curc. I 1, 12 *nam quo te dicam
ego ire = quonam.* Comp. however, such passages in Virgil as
Ecl. IX 39, Georg. IV 445.—
Euclio's answer is laconic
enough, a way of speaking very
natural with an angry man.
He means 'you ask me why I
beat you, poor wretch—well to
give you some reason to call
yourself wretched.' Much of
the strength of the passage
consists in the repetition of the
word *misera*, just as in the
next line *mala malam* are put
close together. Comp. Trin.
68, *malis te ut verbis multis
multum obiurigem.* In Greek
e.g. καλὴ καλῶς Aristoph. A-
charn. 253.
43. *aetas* (originally contracted from *aevitas*), is with
the comic poets very frequently
an equivalent to *vita.* Thus
Plautus says *sibi inimicus magis
quam aetati tuae = vitae tuae,
tibi*, Men. 675. Both words

St. nam quá me nunc causa éxtrusisti ex aédibus? 5
45 Ev. tibi egón rationem réddam, stimulorúm seges?
illúc regredere ab óstio: illuc: síṣ vide,
ut incédit. at scin, quó modo tibi rés se habet?
si hercle hódie fustem cépero aut stimulum ín manum,
testúdineum istum tíbi ego grandibó gradum.   10
50 St. utinám me divi adáxint ad suspéndium

occur together Amph. ii 2, 1 s.
in vita atque in aetate agunda.
45. *stimulorum seges* 'har-
vest of whips,' a comical expression which may be parallel-
ed with Cicero's *seges gloriae*
(in pro Milone).
46. *sis* 'if you please.' This
sis is an equivalent to *si vis*,
conf. Cic. or. 45, 154, '*lubenter
verba iungebant, ut* sodes *pro*
si audes, sis *pro* si vis.' An instance of *sodes* (=*si audes*),
occurs Trin. 244, where see our
note. It is, however, more
common to say *videsis*, in one
word.
47. For *incédit* see Introd.
p. 48; *incedit* is more than
' she walks,' it is 'she creeps.'
'*incedere* est otiose et cum
dignitate quadam ambulantium.'
Westerhov on Ter. Eun. v 3, 9,
who quotes Plaut. Pseud. 411
and Verg. Aen. i 46.
48. *hercle* logically belongs
to the following line, but in
consequence of a kind of hasty
anticipation it is put into the
protasis. We find it so very
often, e.g. v. 56. 248. Pseud.
628. Stich. 610. Trin. 457.
Epid. iii 1, 10.
49. *grandibo gradum:* alliteration together with assonance.
Epid. i 1, 11 *ut tu es gradibus
grandibus.* Truc. ii 2, 31 *abire*

hinc ni properas grandi gradu.
Fragm. Clitellariae ap. Festum
v. Vegrande *nimium es vegrandi
gradu.* Pacuvius v. 37 Ribb.
has *praegrandi gradu.* The
word itself is explained by
Nonius by *grandem facere,* and
examples are quoted from Varro,
Plautus, Lucretius, Accius and
Pacuvius. For the formation
of the future in *ibo* and the
imperfects in *ibam* instead of
iebam, see Key, L. G. §§ 461 and
468. Comp. also the extensive
collections of formations of this
kind in Neue's *Formenlehre* ii
p. 448 sq. With *testudineus
gradus* 'tortoise-pace' we may
compare *formicinus gradus* Men.
888.
50. The nominative *divi* = *di*
occurs only here in Plautus;
but the formula *divom atque
hominum fidem* is repeatedly
found, Amph. v 1, 69. Aul. 297.
Merc. 842. Rud. prol. 9 (*divos*
= deos Mil. gl. 730).—*adaxint*
is said by Nonius to stand instead of *adigant,* an explanation which renders only the
general sense of the word, without accounting for its formation. This is explained by
Festus' remark (v. *axitiosi*)
'*axit antiquos dixisse pro egerit manifestum est.' axim* is
formed in the same way as

potiús quidem, quam hoc pácto apud te sérviam.
Ev. at út scelesta sóla secum múrmurat.
oculós hercle ego istos, ímproba, ecfodiám tibi,
ne me óbservare póssis, quid rerúm geram.   15
55 abscéde etiam nunc, étiam nunc.   ST. etiámne?
     Ev. ohe,
istíc astato. si hércle tu ex istóc loco
digitúm transvorsum aut únguem latum excésseris,

jaxim, see Neue ii pp. 539.
543—546. A third formation
of the same kind is *capsim
capsis*, which was misunder-
stood for *cape sis* (*si vis*) by
Cicero Or. 45, 154 (an explanation rejected by Quintilian i 5,
66). The perfects *axi* (*ag-si*),
faxi (*fac-si*), *cap-si* follow the
analogy of *duxi* (*duc-si*) *rep-si*
etc., while *ēgi fēci cēpi* lengthen
the radical vowel. See Corssen,
Krit. Beitr. zur lat. Formenl. p.
530.

52. Such alliterations as *scelesta sola secum* are very frequently found in the ancient
Roman poets and merit our
especial attention. We shall
here point out only a few examples which occur in the next
lines: *dedam discipulam* 59.
metuo male 61. *miserum modis*
66. *miseram modum* 69. *decies
die* 70. Alliteration was, it is
true, never a necessary and
organic element in Latin poetry,
at least so far as our sources
permit us to trace back its history; still, it was frequently
employed by the earliest poets
who kept close to the spoken
language of the people, which
is always fond of alliteration;
and even in the so-called classical periods of Latin poetry it
was often employed as an ad-

ditional ornament. Horace e.g.
uses it very judiciously in such
passages as *dulce decus* Od. i 1,
2. *dulce et decorum* iii 2, 13.
dulce docta iii 9, 10. *dulci
distinet a domo* iv 5, 12 etc.
See a very good essay on this
subject in Lucian Müller's
book de re metr. poet. p. 450
ss. and Mr Munro's remarks in
his edition of Lucretius ii p.
106.

53. For examples of the
phrase *oculos ecfodere* (ὀφθαλ-
μοὺς ἐξορύσσειν) see Aul. 187.
Capt. iii 1, 4. Trin. 463. Ter.
Eun. iv 6, 2, where Donatus
observes '*femineae minae sunt.*'

54. The phrase *quid rerum
geram* is not unfrequently met
with in Plautus; thus we have
it again Aul. 117.

57. Gronovius Lect. Pl. p.
48 sq., quotes the expression
digitus transversus from Cato
de re rust. c. 45 and 48, and
the equivalent *patens digitus*
is quoted from Caes. b. c. ii 10.
unguis transversus occurs in two
passages of Cicero's, ad Att.
xiii 20 and Fam. vii 25. In
the latter passage the addition
of the words *quod aiunt* shows
the proverbial character of the
expression, which would however be perfectly evident even
without this hint.

aut sí respexis, dónicum ego te iússero,
contínuo hercle ego te dédam discipulám cruci. 20
60 sceléstiorem me hác anu certé scio
vidísse numquam, nímisque ego hanc metuó male,
ne mi éx insidiis vérba imprudentí duit
neu pérsentiscat, aúrum ubi est abscónditum :
quae in óccipitio quóque habet oculos péssuma. 25
65 nunc íbo ut visam, sítne ita aurum ut cóndidi :
quod mé sollicitat plúrimis miserúm modis.
St. noenúm mecastor, quíd ego ero dicám meo

58. *respexis = respex(es)is =
respexeris:* Key, L. G. § 566.
59. 'I'll send you for a
schooling to the gallows,' THORN-
TON. The cross shall teach you
to shut your eyes for ever, if
you cannot keep them shut for
a few moments.
60. In the ms. B we find
here the marginal note ' *hoc
secum loquitur,*' which is perfectly adapted to the situation.
61. For the prosody of *ni-
mìsque,* see Introd. p. 31.
62. *duim* (compare v. 236
perduim v. 664) is an archaic
subj. pres. See Neue II p.
441 sq. The ending *im* is the
same as seen in *edim velim
nolim malim sim.* Cicero has
this form in the formulas *di te
perduint* pro rege Deiot. 7, 21,
and *utinam tibi istam mentem
di immortales duint* Catil. I 9,
22. The expression *verba dare*
which properly means ' to give
mere words instead of deeds '
commonly assumes the more
general sense ' to deceive.'
63. *persentiscat :* ' smell the
place out, where the gold is
hidden.'
64. *occipitium* is the form
more frequently found than
occiput; comp. also *sincipitium*

Men. 506, instead of *sinciput,*
the latter being the only recog-
nised form in good writers.
67. *noenum=ne oenum (u-
num),* according to the explanation first given by Jacob Grimm.
The word corresponds therefore
entirely with the Greek οὐδ-
αμ-ῶς, and οὐδ-έν, the latter
being frequently used as a simple negation in later Greek and
constantly so in modern Greek,
where we have moreover the
shortened form δέν. As to the
Latin word, we may observe
that this passage seems the
only one in which at least one
good ms. has kept it. In Ennius we read it in three places :
ann. 161 *somnia vera aliquot,
verum omnia noenu necessest*
(*non nunc* the mss., *noenu*
H. Ilberg) ; ann. 314 *noenum
rumores ponebat ante salutem*
(*non enim* the mss., *noenum*
Lachmann) ; and ann. 411 *noenum sperando cupide rem pro-
dere summam (non in* the ms.).
When judging from these examples, it is not without probability that in many passages
in Plautus where we now read
non enim, we should reintroduce
the original reading *noenum,*
e. g. in the Aulularia itself

malaé rei evenísse quamve insániam,
queo cónminisci : íta me miseram ad húnc modum
70 deciéns die uno saépe extrudit aédibus.   31
nesció pol quae illunc hóminem intemperiaé tenent :
pervígilat noctis tótas, tum autem intérdius
quasi claúdus sutor dómi sedet totós dies.
neque iám quo pacto célem erilis fíliae   35
75 probrúm, propinqua pártitudo quoi áppetit,
queo cónminisci : néque quicquam meliúst mihi,
ut opínor, quam ex me ut únam faciam lítteram

v. 586 where *non enim* seems to have no clear meaning. See Bücheler, jahrb. für class. phil. 1863 p. 774.

69. For the hiatus in the caesura, see Introd. p. 68.

71. For the disyllabic pronunciation *nescĩo* see Introd. 64.—*intemperiae* 'whimwhams' (THORNTON), see v. 634. Epid. III 4, 39. Mil. gl. 434.

72. *Interdius* (δν' ἡμέραν) is read here and Most. 444 ; the simple *dius* occurs in opposition to *noctu* Merc. 862, and Charisius expressly states that Titinius used *noctu diusque:* see Ribb. Com. p. 116 ; from this an old acc. neutr. *diu* (as seen in the usual form *interdiu*) arose after the final *s* had been dropt (Introd. p. 30). From the Sanskr. *divas* we have in Latin both *dies* and *dius* (comp. *di-ur-nus,* where the original *s* is changed into an *r*). See Corssen, Krit. Beitr. zur Formenl. p. 499 s. 504. Lachmann on Lucr. p. 226 s.

73. *claudus sutor:* 'of course, lame people would be the most likely to take to such a sedentary employment as that of a cobbler.' RILEY. Comp. v. 508.

—For *dómĭ* (not *d'mi*) see Introd. p. 23 s.

74. *erus* and its derivatives are better spelt without an initial *h;* see Ritschl, Proll. Trin. p. 98, praef. Stichi p. 23, and Opusc. II 409.

76. The repetition of the words *queo conminisci* may perhaps appear strange, but such repetitions are not inconsistent with the character of a garrulous old woman, and afford no ground for entertaining any suspicion of the genuineness of the reading. Such seeming negligence must be granted to a comic poet.

77 s. Famianus Strada has written a special paper on this *littera longa,* but the right explanation has been found out by Lipsius who compares an epigram of Ausonius (128, 10): *Quid, imperite, P putas ibi scriptum, ubi locari iota convenit longum?* This epigram is directed against Ennius, a man of very bad repute, who, as the poet insinuates, ought to be sent to the gallows. The figure of a long I is indeed somewhat like the appearance of a hanging body, especially

longám, meum laqueo cóllum quando obstrínxero.
Ev. nunc défaecato démum animo egrediór domo,
80 postquám perspexi, sálva esse intus ómnia.   [I 2
redi núnciam intro atque íntus serva.   St. quíp-
    pini?
ego íntus servem? an né quis aedis aúferat?
nam hic ápud nos nihil est áliud quaesti fúribus :
ita inániis sunt óppletae atque aráneis.   6

if that body should happen to be very thin and slender. *longae litterae* are also mentioned Rud. v 2, 7 and Poen. iv 2, 15, but without any special reference to the letter I: comp. *littera pensilis* Pseud. 17.—*unam* is not pleonastic, as Weise says (see note on v. 563); Staphyla intends making of herself *one* long letter; i.e. a letter exhibiting one long stroke.

79. *animo defaecato* is explained by Camerarius 'liquido minimeque turbido, i.e. hilari;' see Pseud. 760 *nunc liquet, nunc defaecatumst cor mihi.* The same meaning is expressed by *animo liquido et tranquillo es* Epid. v 1, 36 and *liquido es animo* Pseud. 232. In one passage (Most. 158) the word *defaecatus* is metaphorically used of a person cleaned by a bath.

81. For *nunciam* (which is always trisyllabic in Plautus and Terence) we may refer to our note on Trin. 3.—*quippini*, instead of *quippeni*, is very frequently given by the best mss. e.g. Most. 948. 1109. Pseud. 361. The final *ĕ* in *quippe* was changed into *i* before an *n*, in the same way as we have *tutin* =*tutene.* The right punctuation of this passage is first seen in Pareus' edition, and is here

of much importance for the construction of the sentence. The sense is 'why should I not? Shall I really take care of all within? Perhaps you are afraid, somebody might run away with our house?'

83. *quaesti:* for this genitive see Key, L. G. § 141 and a valuable paper by Ritschl in the Rhein. Mus. viii p. 494 [now Opusc. ii]. Fleckeisen, Krit. Miscellen p. 42 ss. The following is an extract from Ritschl's prooemium de titulo Aletrinatium (1853) p. viii 'longe longeque latius per sextum septimumque saeculum altera terminatio (*i*) patuit. qua et Plautus usus est constanter in *quaesti tumulti victi senati sumpti gemiti,* et Ennius *strepiti tumulti* declinans, Pacuvius *flucti aesti parti soniti,* Caecilius *quaesti sumpti soniti,* Terentius *quaesti tumulti fructi ornati adventi,* Turpilius *quaesti tumulti fructi sumpti piscati parti,* Titinius *quaesti,* Attius *flucti tumulti exerciti aspecti lucti salti,* Lucilius *sumpti,* Afranius *tumulti,* Pomponius *quaesti tumulti piscati,* bis Lucretius *geli,* Calpurnius Piso *senati,* Cato *fructi,* Sisenna *senati soniti,* Sallustius *tumulti soniti.'*

85 Ev. mirúm quin tua me caúsa faciat Iúppiter
    Philíppum regem aut Dárium, trivenéfica.
    aráneas mihi ego íllas servarí volo.
    paupér sum, fateor, pátior : quod di dánt, fero.   10
    abi íntro, occlude iánuam : iam ego híc ero.
90 cave, quémquam alienum in aédis intro míseris.
    quod quíspiam ignem quaérat, extinguí volo,
    ne caúsae quid sit quód te quisquam quaéritet.
    nam si ígnis vivet, tu éxtinguere extémpulo.   15

84. The word *inania*, instead of *inanitas*, probably owes its origin to nothing more than the assonance of *aranea*. The ὀξύμωρον 'full of emptiness' can hardly be imitated in any modern language, so as to preserve its entire strength of expression. Plautus ventures on a similar phrase Capt. iii 1, 6 where the parasite calls a fast-day *dies ecfertus fame*. Catullus uses a similar expression (8, 48) *plenus sacculus est aranearum*, and the same is found in a line of Afranius (Ribb. Com. p. 184) *anne arcula tua plenast aranearum?* Hence we may safely conclude that this simile was proverbially used in popular speech.

85. *mirum quin:* ' I wonder, Jove does not make me a wealthy king.' Comp. Persa 339 s. *mirum quin regis Philippi causa aut Attali | te potius vendam quam mea, quae sis mea*. See also our note on Trin. 495.

86. King Philippus and Darius are here mentioned as the most obvious and best-known instances of wealthy kings, the one as a European, the other as an Asiatic monarch. Comp. 696 *ego sum ille rex Philippus*.

For the usual quantity of *Philippus* in Plautus see Introd. p. 46 s., but in both passages of the Aulularia the common quantity is well supported by the best mss.—The form *trivenefica* occurs only here; Bacch. 813, we read *tervenefica*, which is likewise unexampled in any other passage.

90. For *cavĕ* see Introd. p. 25.

91. *quod* 'if,' properly 'as regards the case that,' is always connected with the subjunctive, see the instances from Plautus given by Brix on Mil. gl. 162, and for the occurrence of this construction in Cicero and later writers C. F. W. Müller, Rhein. Mus. xx 480.

92. 'qui *petit*, vult obtinere : qui *quaerit*, vult scire aut invenire.' LAMBINUS.

93. *ignis vivet*, comp. πυρὸς φλὸξ ἔτι ζῶσα Eur. Bacch. 8. Lipsius compares Arist. Lys. 306 τουτὶ τὸ πῦρ ἐγρήγορεν θεῶν ἕκατι καὶ ζῇ. Hildyard appropriately quotes Shakespeare, Othello v 2, 7 '*put out the light, and then put out the light*,' i.e. of life. Comp. also Dickens, *Old Curiosity Shop*, chapt. 44 '*The fire has been alive as long as I have.*' In German we

tum aquam aúfugisse dícito, si quís petet.
95 cultrúm securim písttillum mortárium,
quae uténda vasa sémper vicíní rogant,
furés venisse atque ábstulisse dícito.
profécto in aedis meás me absente néminem   20
volo íntro mitti. atque étiam hoc praedicó tibi:
100 si Bóna Fortuna véniat, ne intro míseris.
ST. pol ea ípsa, credo, ne íntro mittatúr, cavet.
nam ad aédis nostras númquam adit quaquám prope.
Ev. st, táce atque abi intro.   ST. táceo atque abeo.
    Ev. occlúde sis   25
forís ambobus péssulis: iam ego híc ero.

have the phrase 'einem das lebenslicht ausblasen.'

95. As regards the accentuation *pistillúm* I may here repeat Ritschl's expression on *árgentúm* (Men. 930): 'accentus non insolentia at insuavitas,' Men. praef. XIII. See also my note on Trin. 410.

96 s. *utendum rogare* 'to borrow;' *utendum dare* 'to lend.' See v. 309 and Ov. ars am. I 433 *multa rogant utenda dari, data reddere nolunt.—utendum petere* occurs Aul. 397.

100. On *Bona Fortuna* see Preller Röm. Myth. p. 559. It appears from a passage of Diomedes, that the words *Bona Fortuna te quaesivit* were commonly used in the sense of *nemo te quaesivit*. In a fragment of Afranius first pointed out by L. Müller (Rhein. Mus. xx 374) we have an instance of this expression; it runs as follows: '*Adulescens*. num quis me quaesiit? *Servos*. Bona Fortuna.' There is, however, no reason to suppose that Euclio alludes to this, as is the opinion of some commentators; it is,

perhaps, more natural to understand the words simply such as they are 'Let nobody enter my house, not even Good Luck itself.'

102. We need not suppose that a temple of *Bona Fortuna* was close to Euclio's house. There is a temple of *Fides* in the vicinity, into which Euclio afterwards carries his treasure (v. 575), and as there is also Megadorus' house on the stage, we can hardly accommodate another temple. There occur, besides, no other allusions to such a temple of Fortuna, which would doubtless be the case, had it been a necessary part of the scenery. The adverb *quaquam* is commonly used in *nequaquam* and in *haud quaquam* (Sall. Catil. 3). *numquam quaquam* is a very strong negation 'never by any means.' Comp. *numquam quicquam* Amph. II 2, 40. *numquam quisquam* Ter. Eun. IV 4, 11. See moreover Ter. Andr. I 2, 3. Ad. I 2, 18. IV 1, 12. v 4, 1.

104. *ambobus pessulis* 'supero et infero.' See Guhl u.

105 discrúcior animi, quía ab domo abeundúmst mihi.
nimis hércle invitus ábeo. sed quid agám scio.
nam nóbis nostrae qui ést magister cúriae,
divídere argenti díxit nummos ín viros.   30

Koner, Leben der Griechen u.
Römer 1, 146. 2, 206 s.
105. For *animi* we may compare such expressions as *discrucior animi* Ter. Ad. iv 4, 1
(= 640 Fl.) *Antipho me excruciat
animi* Phorm. i 4, 10 (=187).
excrucias animi Plaut. Mil. gl.
1068 and 1280. *angas te animi*
Epid. iii 1, 6. *in spe pendebit
animi* Ter. Haut. tim. iv 4, 5
(=727), where the genitive
should not be joined with *spe*,
see Plaut. Merc. i 2, 18 (=127
R.) *animi pendeo* and my note
on the passage. Cicero uses
the same expression Tusc. disp.
i 40, 96 *pendemus animi, excru-
ciamur, angimur :* but there
animi is due to an emendation
by Ursinus, the mss. giving
animis. In another passage,
Tusc. iv 16, 35 the reading
of the mss. is as follows *is qui
adpropinquans aliquod malum
metuit, exanimatusque pendet
animi.* We have to range
under the same head such instances as *falsus animi est* Ter.
Eun. ii 2, 43, where the reading *animi* is expressly mentioned by Donatus, though the
mss. give *animo :* comp. *me
animi fallit* Lucr. i 922. In the
same way we have *vagus animi*
Cat. 63, 4, and *dubius animi*
Verg. Georg. iii 289. See also
Dræger i p. 443 sq., and my
note on Trin. 454 *satin tu's
sanus mentis aut animi tui* which
passage seems to show that
animi is in these constructions
a real genitive (used of relation),

and not a locative, as has been
asserted by some scholars.
Comp. also Epid. i 2, 35 *desi-
piebam mentis* and ibid. ii 2, 55
sermonis fallebar.
106. *sed* is necessary on account of *nam* in the following
line. Euclio says that, although
he does not like to go out, he
has nevertheless his reason for
doing so. This reason is given
by *nam.*
107. *Vtrum legitimos habent
omnes tribus divisores suos, quos
Plautus magistros curiarum in
Aulularia vocat?* is the question
raised by Asconius on Cic. Verr.
i 8, 23, although there is no
serious foundation for it, the
divisores being no legally autho-
rised persons, but distributors
of bribery money. See Long's
note and Cic. pro Plancio 19,
48. We may however remark
that the expression *magister
curiae* is a ἅπαξ λεγόμενον, and
was doubtless meant as a translation of the τριττυάρχης of the
Greek original (see de Aul. p.
15). The whole passage treats
of Athenian life: distributions
of money among the citizens
were very frequent at Athens,
but almost unknown at Rome
before the time of the emperors.
—Observe the fulsomeness of
expression in *nobis nostrae,* instead of which O. Seyffert has
ingeniously conjectured *Nestor
nostrae.*
108. *dividere* instead of *se
divisurum esse,* in accordance
with the loose construction so

id sí relinquo ac nón peto, omnes ílico
110 me súspicentur (crédo) habere aurúm domi.
nam véri simile nón est, hominem paúperem
pauxíllum parvi fácere quin nummúm petat.
nam núnc quom celo sédulo omnis, né sciant,   35
omnés videntur scíre et me benígnius
115 omnés salutant quám salutabánt prius.
adeúnt consistunt, cópulantur déxteras,
rogitánt me, ut valeam, quíd agam, quid rérum
geram.
nunc quó profectus sum íbo : postideá domum   40
me rúrsum quantum pótero tantum récipiam.

common in Plautus and Terence.
For instances see the Index to
my edition of Terence, s. v.
infinitive, and note on Trin. 5.
—*nummus* 'has a different sense
in Plautus according as it means
Greek or Roman money. As a
Roman coin, it is equivalent to
a sestertius (Epid. i 1, 52. Most.
ii 1, 10): in the other case to a
drachma (Trin. 844) or didrach-
ma (Truc. ii 7, 10. Pseud. iii
2, 20. Pers. i 1, 38. iii 3, 33. v
2, 70). It is impossible to decide whether drachma or di-
drachma be meant in such passages as Aul. 445. Men. i 4, 1.
ii 2, 16. Epid. iii 2, 36; nor
is it clear whether drachma or
sestertius should be understood
Epid. v 2, 36. As drachma the
word is taken by Bentley in Ter.
Haut. tim. iii 3, 45. Where
aureus is added, the *nummus
Philippeus* is meant.' Brix on
Trin. 844.—*in viros, κατ' ἄνδρας*,
viritim ; see Public School
Latin Gramm. § 93, C, i, 5.
109. For *id* see my note on
Trin. 405. *ilico* is the legiti-

mate spelling, not *illico*: see
Ritschl, proll. Trin. cii.
114. *benignius salutant* ' they
are more *profuse* in their compliments.' Comp. Hor. Ep. i
5, 11 *sermone benigno* 'copious,
plentiful talk.' See also Od. i
17, 15. ii 18, 10. In most cases,
where we are generally inclined
to translate *benignus* by 'kind,'
the original sense of the word
'generous, profuse' will give a
more distinct and impressive
idea of the meaning of the passage.
116. *copulantur* 'shake hands
together:' this verb occurs as
deponent only in this passage.
See also Brix on Mil. gl. 172.
118. *profectus sum* 'where
I've set out to go.' Ter. Eun.
ii 2, 49 *fortasse tu profectus alio
fueras*, on which passage Westerhov rightly observes 'profectus dicitur etiam de eo qui inci-
pit proficisci.' This explains
such a phrase as *profectu's ire
Rud. iii 6, 9.
119. *quantum potero tantum
recipiam* 'I shall come back

as quick as possible.' Ter. Ad.
III 2, 52 *tu quantum potes abi,*
where Fleckeisen adopts Guyet's
emendation *potest.* It is true
that in this phrase either the
best or at least good mss. give
potest as an impersonal in Ter.
Ad. v 7, 11. Phorm. v 8, 3. IV
3, 69. Ad. IV 5, 66; but Andr.
v 2, 20 and Ad. III 2, 52 *potes*
alone is recorded as the reading of the mss. It should therefore not have been changed into
potest; moreover, this line of
the Aulularia proves that in this
phrase the verb could be personal as well as impersonal: a
fact which appears also from
Capt. II 3, 88 *ut quam primum
possis redeas,* where Brix compares Ter. Andr. III 3, 45 *quantum queam* and Eun. v 2, 5 *quantum queo.* See also Brix on
Men. 432, and both Lorenz and
Brix on Mil. gl. 115.

ACTVS II.

EVNOMIA. MEGADORVS. II 1

120 EVN. Velím te arbitrári, me*d* haéc verba, fráter,
meáï fidéï tuáïque réi
causá facere, ut aéquomst germánam sorórem.
quamquam haúd falsa súm, nos odiósas habéri:
nam múltum loquáces merito ómnes habémur,   5
125 nec mútam profécto repértam ullam esse hódie
dicúnt ullo in saéclo.
verum hóc, frater, únum tamén cogitáto,
tibí proxumám me mihíque esse itém te.
ita aéquomst, quod ín rem esse utríque arbitrémur, 10
130 et míhi te et tibí me consúlere et monére,

120. The forms *med* and *ted* are used by Plautus both in the accus. and abl. sing.
122. *ut aequomst* sc. *facere.* The infinitive in such constructions is sometimes omitted and *aequomst* seemingly assumes the same construction as *decet.* Comp. Rud. 47 *is leno, ut se aequomst, flocci non fecit fidem.* See below v. 721.
124. *multum* has here an adverbial sense, comp. Stich. 206 *multum miseri.* Examples of this use from Horace are generally known: Ep. i 10, 3 *multum dissimiles.* Serm. ii 5, 92 *multum similis*, and others. *multiloquaces*, the word proposed for this line by Passerat, has for itself the authority of an old glossary, but cannot be admitted on account of the metre. Plautus employs the word *multilocus*

Cistell. i 3, 1 and Pseud. 794.
125. Lambinus' note on this line is well worth preserving. 'Ego tamen,' he says, 'qui cum haec scriberem, annum aetatis agebam LVI, duas mutas mulieres vidi.' This provokes old Taubmann's fun, who for his part assures Lambinus, that at the age of 29 he knew already more than two dumb women.— Ben Jonson (Silent Woman i 5) calls a woman's silence 'a wealthy dowry.'
126. Adelphasium uses almost the same words Poen. i 2, 28 *itást: verum hoc únum tamén cogitáto.*
130. A construction *monere alicui* does not exist. It is therefore clear that in this line the datives depend on *consulere*, and *monere* follows its analogy by way of zeugma.

neque óccultum habéri id neque pér metum mussári,
quin párticipem páriter ego te ét tu me ut fácias.
eo núnc ego secréto forás te huc sedúxi,
utí tuam rem ego técum hic loquerér familiárem.   15
135 MEG. da mi, óptuma feminá, manum.   EVN. ubi
eást? *et* quis east nam óptuma?
MEG. tu.   EVN. túne ais?   MEG. si negás, nego.
EVN. decet te équidem vera próloqui.
nam optúma nulla eligí potest: alia ália peior,
fráter, est.   20

131. *mussare* is explained by
Nonius 427, 15 '*hominum occulte
quid et pressa voce loquentium.*'
The frequentative *mussitare* (e.g.
metu mussitant Cas. III 5, 33)
is explained by Donatus on Ter.
Ad. II 1, 53 '*proprie est dis-
simulandi causa tacere, dictum
vel a muto vel ab M, quae littera
est nimium pressae vocis ac
paene nullius, adeo ut sola omnium, cum inter vocales incide-
rit, atteratur atque subsidat.*'
Comp. the English *to mutter*
and see Munro on Lucr. VI 1179.
133. Though it appears to
us strange that a confidential
conversation should purposely
take place in a public street,
we should not forget that the
constant habit of the Roman
comedy compelled the poets
to let all such things pass in
the streets as would otherwise
require a more appropriate
scenery. Comp. Pompon. 142 ss.
Ribb. *ego dedita opera te, pater
solum foras Seduxi, ut ne quis
esset testis tertius Praeter nos.*
135. *feminā*] For the long
quantity of the voc.-*a* see Introd.
p. 12.—*quis east*] *quis* is more
frequently found in Plautus as
the feminine than *quae*, see the
copious collection of passages

in Brix's note on Mil. gl. 361.
See v. 168. Instances of this
usage are collected by Nonius
197, 30 ss.—For the separation
of *nam* from *quis*, see note on v.
42.
136. *ais* and *ait* are generally monosyllables in Plautus,
aio and *aiunt* never. See
Ritschl, proll. Trin. CLXII.—For
the pronunciation of *decet = dece*
see Introd. p. 34.—We should not
write *quidem* instead of *equidem*,
which is the reading of the mss.,
as it has been shown that *equidem* is merely a strengthened,
and as it were emphatic, form
instead of *quidem*, comp. *hem
ehem, heu eheu, nam enim.* The
common opinion, according to
which *equidem* is a contraction
of *ego quidem*, should be given
up now. See Ribbeck's valuable
treatise, on Latin particles
(Leipzig, 1869), p. 36—42, and
my note on Trin. 352.
137. The accentuation *optúma* would be startling to those
who believe in a general tendency of Plautine prosody to
preserve the common accentuation of daily life. There are,
however, many instances of such
metrical paroxytona as *optúma*
to be found in Plautus and the

MEG. ídem ego arbitror,
néc tibi advorsári certumst *me* de istác re umquám,
soror.
140 EVN. da mi óperam, amabo.
MEG. tuást: utere átque imperá si quid *mé* vis.
EVN. íd quod in rém tuam óptumum esse árbitror,
te id mónitum advento.
MEG. soror, móre tuo facis.   EVN. fácta volo.   25
145 MEG. quid ést id, sorór ?   EVN. quod tibí sempi-
térnum
salútare sít, liberís procreándis—
MEG. (ita dí faxint) EVN. volo te úxorem
domum dúcere. MEG. heia, occidís. EVN. quid ita ?
MEG. quia mí misero cerebrum éxcutiunt
150 tua dícta, soror : lapidés loqueris.   30
EVN. heia, hóc face, quod te iúbet soror.   MEG. si
lúbeat, faciam.
EVN. in rem hóc tuamst.   MEG. ut quidem *ego*
émoriar,
priúsquam ducam.

---

other comic poets. Comp. *de-
sine* (Naev. 60. Caec. 60. Ribb.).
piscibus Rud. ii 6, 29. *omnibus*
Trin. 54. *consúlit* Pseud. 1092.
moribus Aul. 500. *unícus* Poen.
prol. 65. *altéra* ibid. 85. *filius*
Cas. prol. p. 55. See Ritschl,
proll. Trin. p. ccxxiv.
140. *amabo* 'pray ;' see my
note on Ter. Eun. 130. It is
ordinarily used parenthetically
without influencing the construction of the sentence.
141. Comp. Capt. v 3, 1
*Hegio, adsum : si quid me vis,
impera.*
144. *facta volo* 'est non
comica magis formula quam
translaticiae humanitatis. quod
est : cupio tibi fieri quod vis,
et quantum in me est, ut fiat,

operam dabo. Bacch. 495. Asin.
685.' J. F. Gronovius ad Gell.
vii 3. Compare Ter. Ad. v 7,
21. Phorm. v 3, 4.
148. *occidis*] The present
stands in this phrase Pseud.
931 and Men. 922, the perfect
occidisti Aul. 712 and Ter.
Phorm. iv 3, 67.
150. *lapides loqueris* 'you
speak stones.' (Aristoph. Eq.
628, κρημνοὺς ἐρείδων.) Compare
Shakespeare, Hamlet iii 7 'I
will speak daggers to her, but
use none.' Much Ado about
Nothing ii 4 '*She speaks poniards,
and every word stabs.*' The
contrary is expressed by Aristophanes Nub. 910 ῥόδα μ' εἴρη-
κας.

[sed his legibus, quam dare vis, ducam :]
quae crás veniat, peréndie foras écferatur.
soror, hís legibus si quám dare vis,
155 cedo, núptias adorna.   35
EVN. cum máxuma possúm tibi, fratér, dare dote:
sed grándior es : múlieris est aétas media.
eam sí iubes, fratér, tibi me póscere, poscam.
MEG. núm nevis me intérrogare te ? EVN. ímmo
si quid vís, roga.
160 MEG. póst mediam aetatém qui media dúcit uxorém domum,   40
si éam senex anúm praegnantem fórtuitu fécerit,

154. *perendie* ' the day after:'
this is the original meaning of
this word which will thus be
constantly met with in Plautus.
Comp. the phrase used in the
legis actiones '*in diem tertium
sive perendinum*' (see Bergk,
Rhein. Mus. xix 606) and Merc.
378 *cras agito, perendie agito.*
Megadorus seems to have the
same opinion of married life
which Hipponax expresses in
the following lines δύ' ἡμέραι
γυναικός εἰσιν ἥδισται, 'Οταν
γαμῇ τις κἀκφέρῃ τεθνηκυῖαν.
Another sentence of the same
kind is reported of Chaeremon
γυναῖκα θάπτειν κρεῖσσόν ἐστιν ἢ
γαμεῖν.
157. The reading of this
line is very uncertain. In the
reading adopted in our text we
have the final syllable in *gran-
dior* long (see Introd. p. 14),
and the last syllable in *mulieris*
as anceps, which in the caesura
may be excused.—*aetas media,*
i. e. *inter senem iuvenemque, sed
propior seni,* as Seneca expresses
it Oed. 776. *aetatis mediae mu-
lier* Phaedr. ii 2, 3, the same

person being subsequently styled
anus (10). Cicero has *media
aetas* de sen. 17, 60 and 20,
76.
159. *nevis* is a reading not
absolutely certain in this place,
and it is possible that Plautus
wrote the common *non vis.*
See Ritschl, Opusc. ii 249.
But in support of our reading
we may quote the analogous
passage, Poen. v 2, 119, *at te
moneri num nevis?* See, however, also Most. 336.
161. Megadorus contemptu-
ously calls a wife of somewhat
maturer years *anus,* to express
that she is nearly old enough
to deserve this title. The epithets *senex* and *anus* are, however, not to be taken as expressive of a very old age, as
they are sometimes applied to
persons of about 45 to 50 years.
E. g. Amphitruo is styled *senex* in the comedy bearing his
name v 1, 20, and iv 2, 12,
though he seems a newly-
married man in the prime of his
years.

quíd dubitas, quin sít paratum nómen puero Pós-
　tumus?
núnc ego istum, sorór, laborem démam et demi-
　nuám tibi.
égo virtute déum et maiorum nóstrum dives súm
　satis:
165 ístas magnas fáctiones ánimos dotis dápsilis　　45
clámores impéria eburna véhicla pallas púrpuram
níl moror, quae in sérvitutem súmptibus redigúnt
　viros.
Evn. díc mihi quaeso, quís east quam vis dúcere
　uxorem? Meg. éloquar.
nóstin hunc senem Eúclionem ex próxumo paupér-
　culum?
170 Evn. nóvi hominem haud malúm mecastor. Meg.
　eíus cupio fíliam　　50

162. *postumus* is a formation
of the same kind as *infumus*
intumus extumus. It generally
means a son born after his
father's death, but sometimes
even sons born when their fa-
thers were very old were called
so. See Virgil, Aen. VI 763
Silvius, Albanum nomen, tua
postuma proles, Quem tibi long-
aevo serum Lavinia coniunx
Educet silvis. Gellius gives us
the note of an ancient grammarian, Caesellius, on this passage '*postuma proles non eum*
significat qui patre mortuo, sed
qui postremo loco natus est. si-
cuti Silvius qui Aenea iam sene
tardo seroque partu est editus.'
Noct. att. II 16 with Gronovius'
note.—For the nominative, see
note on Trin. 8, and E. Becker
in Studemund's 'Studien' I p.
170.
164. The same expressions
are used Trin. 346 and the

whole line appears again Capt.
321, where it is however considered spurious by Fleckeisen
and Brix. See also Ritschl's
conclusive remarks Opusc. II
284.
165. For *factio* we may compare such passages as Trin.
452. 464. 497. Cistell. II 1, 17.
The adjective *factiosus* (v. 225)
means therefore ' multis innix-
us et florens clientelis.'—*dotis:*
the gen. plur. *dotium* occurs
Digest XXIII 3 '*de iure dotium.*'
dapsilis = δαψιλής. *dapsilus* is
no Latin form : the passage
generally quoted, Pseud. 396, is
too corrupt to prove anything.
The adverb *dapsile* is read in a
fragment of Pomponius (v. 161.
Com. Ribb. p. 210).
168. For *quis east* see note
on v. 135.
169. *pauperculum* 'rather
poor.' The diminutive ex-
presses commiseration.

W. P.　　7

vírginem mihi désponderi.   vérba ne faciás, soror :
scío quid dicturá's, hanc esse paúperem. haec pau-
pér placet.
Evn. dí bene vortant.   Meg. ídem ego spero.
    Evn. quíd? me numquid vís?   Meg. vale.
Evn. ét tu, frater.   Meg. égo conveniam Eúclionem,
    sí domist.
175 séd eccum *video.*   néscio unde sése homo recipít
    domum.   55

Evclio.   Megadorvs.

Ev. praésagibat mi ánimus, frustra me íre, quom
    exibám domo :   II 2
ítaque abibam invítus.   nam neque quísquam cu-
    riálium
vénit neque magíster, quem divídere argentum
    opórtuit.
núnc domum properáre propero : nam égomet sum
    hic, animús domist.

---

172. *quid dictura's,* i.e. dictura es, though we should expect either *sis* or *quod es dictura.*
But in Plautine language the
difference between the subjunctive and indicative in constructions like the present is not yet
accurately developed. We may
compare Bacch. 78 *scio ego quid
ago* : : *at ego pol scio quid metuo*
with Aul. 106 *sed quid agam scio.*
173. Seeing her brother determined on his choice, Eu-
nomia gives her assent with the
words generally used on such
occasions *di bene vortant:* see
Trin. 573.—'Abituri, ne id dure
facerent, *numquid vis* dicebant
iis quibuscum constitissent.'
Dónatus on Ter. Eun. II 3, 49.
Comp. Hor. Serm. I 9, 6.

174. For the hiatus *convéni-
am | Eúclionem* see Introd. p.
66.
175. *nescio unde* should be
joined : 'from some place or
other.'
179. *properare propero* is a
comical exaggeration frequently
met with in Plautus : see v.
242. Comp. Curc. 637 *propere
propero.*—*animus domist :* comp.
Persa 709 *animus iam in navist
mihi.* Merc. 589 *si domi sum,
foris est animus : sin foris sum,
animus domist.* Similar expressions are found Pseud. 32. Men.
584 ; Ter. Eun. IV 7, 46 and
Cic. ad Att. XII 12. Hence we
should explain Cas. III 3, 9 s.
Thus also Aristoph. Acharn.
398 sq., ὁ νοῦς μὲν ἔξω ξυλλέγων

180 MEG. sálvos atque fórtunatus, Eúclio, sempér sies. 5
Ev. dí te ament, Megadóre.   MEG. quid tu? récten
   atque ut vís vales ?
Ev. nón temerariúmst, ubi dives blánde adpellat
   paúperem.
iam íllic homo aurum mé scit habere : eo mé salutat
   blándius.
MEG. aín tu te valére ?   Ev. pol ego haud pérbene
   a pecúnia.
185 MEG. pól si est animus aéquos tibi, sat hábes qui
   bene vitám colas.   10
Ev. ánus hercle huic indícium fecit de aúro : per-
   spicué palamst :
quoí ego iam linguám praecidam atque óculos ecfodiám domi.
MEG. quíd tu solus técum loquere ? Ev. meám
   pauperiem cónqueror.
vírginem habeo grándem, dote cássam atque in-
   locábilem :

ἐπύλλια, οὐκ ἔνδον. We may compare even such a passage as in
Shakspere's Henry V. I 2 : *sub-
jects, whose hearts have left
their bodies here in England,
And lie pavilion'd in the fields
of France.*
182. *non temerariumst* ' it's
not for nothing ' (Thorn.), comp.
v. 616.
183. *eo* has here a monosyllabic pronunciation: see Introd.
p. 62.—*blandius* 'very kindly,'
i.e. more kindly than he usually
does. In this way the comparative is sometimes equal to a
strengthened positive, comp.
Amph. prol. 56 *sed ego stultior,*
i.e. ' I'm very stupid.' The same
expression occurs Merc. 919.
184. *a pecunia* ' as to my
pecuniary circumstances,' comp.

ab ingenio improbust Truc. IV 3,
59.
185. For *habẽ(s)* see Introd.
p. 40.
186. Euclio misunderstands
the philosophic sentence with
which Megadorus tries to com-
fort him, viz. that a contented
mind is the best foundation of
happiness, and at once jumps to
the conclusion that Megadorus'
expression *sat habes* alludes
to his treasure.—*perspicue palamst:* the two synonyms express together only one idea
' it is *quite* clear.' Here, as in
properare propero (v. 179), alliteration helps to strengthen the
expression.
187. For the hiatus *quoi
ego* see Introd. p. 68.
189. *virgo grandis* ' a full

7—2

190 néque eam queo locáre quoiquam. MEG. táce, bonum habe animum, Eúclio.   15
dábitur: adiuvábere a me: díc si quid opust: ímpera.
Ev. núnc petit, quom póllicetur: ínhiat aurum, ut
   dévoret.
áltera manú fert lapidem, pánem ostentat áltera.
némini credó qui large blándust dives paúperi.
195 úbi manum inicít benigne, ibi ónerat aliquam zá-
   miam.   20
égo istos novi pólypos qui ubi quídquid tetigerúnt
   tenent.

grown girl.' *grandis* is idio-
matically used of growth, see
note on Trin. 374. *cassus* is,
as Priscian justly observes, of
the same root as *carere*, and
therefore governs the same case
as the verb.

190. The words *neque eam
queo locare quoiquam* are no
superfluous addition after *inlo-
cabilis* in the preceding line,
as some commentators say.
The sense is 'I've an unmar-
riageable daughter, and indeed
I can't dispose of her.' These
two expressions together ex-
haust, so to say, the whole of
the idea, such fulness as this
being one of the characteristic
features of popular speech.
Comp. Mil. gl. 452 *neque vos
qui homines sitis novi neque
scio*. Amph.' v 1, 8 *nec me
miserior feminast nec ulla vide-
atur magis*. Trin. 130 *quid
secus est aut quid interest?*—
See v. 211.

191. *dabitur*, sc. auxilium,
pecunia.

192. *inhiare* c. acc. 'to gape
for something,' ἐγχαίνειν τι in
Alciphron, a phrase very frequent with Plautus: e.g. Aul.

265. Trin. 169. Mil. gl. 715.
1199. Truc. II 3, 18. Stich.
605: later writers use the dative after this verb. See Ritschl
in Reifferscheid's Suetonius p.
490.

193. Erasmus suggests that
the allusion is taken from en-
ticing a dog by holding bread in
one hand and a stone in the
other, ready to throw as soon as
the dog comes nearer. Comp.
also St Matth. vii 9 ἢ τίς ἐστιν
ἐξ ὑμῶν ἄνθρωπος ὃν αἰτήσει ὁ
υἱὸς αὐτοῦ ἄρτον, μὴ λίθον ἐπιδώ-
σει αὐτῷ;

195. *manum inicere=copu-
lari manus* v. 116.—*onerare* is
sometimes synonymous with *imponere, inferre*, e.g. in Virgil's
expressions *vina onerare cadis*
(Aen. I 195) and *dona Cereris
canistris onerare* (Aen. VIII 180).
zamia, ζαμία (ζημία), i.e. damnum, detrimentum. The word
seems a ἅπαξ λεγ.—Brutus (in
Cicero's Ep. ad fam. II 13) expresses the same meaning by
iniungere detrimentum.

196. According to the usual
idiom, we ought to have *quidque*
instead of *quidquid*. But it is
unnecessary to correct the pre-

MEG. dá mi operam parúmper: paucis, Eúcliost, quod
té volo
dé communi re ádpellare méa et tua.　　Ev. ei
miseró mihi.
aúrum mihi intus hárpagatumst: núnc hic eam rem
vólt, scio,
200 mécum adire ad páctionem.　　vérum intervisám
domum.　　　　　　　　　　　　　　　　　25
MEG. quó abis?　　Ev. iam *huc* ad té revortar:
nam ést quod visam *ad mé* domum.
MEG. crédo edepol, ubi méntionem ego fécero de
fília
míhi ut despondeát, sese a me dérideri rébitur.

*　　　　*　　　　*　　　　*　　　　*　　　　*

néque illo quisquamst álter hodie ex paúpertate
párcior.

sent passage, as there are numerous other passages of the
same kind to support it. Comp.
Most. 831 *ut quidquid magis
contemplor, tanto magis placet,*
with Lorenz's note.

199. *harpagare,* a hybrid verb
formed from the Greek ἁρπαγή,
repeatedly occurs in Plautus:
Bacch. 657. Pseud. 139. 957.
Trin. 289.

200. *adire ad pactionem* =
pacisci, and thus the construction should be explained. See a
similar case v. 281.—*intervisam:*
as *vis*-means 'go and see,' so *in-
tervis*- means 'go and hunt up,'
'go and see thoroughly into.'
Key, Transactions of the Phil.
Soc. 1854 p. 67. This explanation accounts for the acc. *domum* here and in the next line,
which some editors change into
domi, but compare Merc. 555
*interea tamen huc ad me inter-
visam domum.*

202. The construction is

most peculiar and, we suppose,
unexampled by any other passage. Even *mentionem facis ut
filiam mihi despondeat* would
be strange, as *mentionem facio*
would still be used in the sense
of *postulare,* whence also the
dependent sentence with *ut.*

203. After this line I have
marked a gap, as there is no
connexion between 203 and 204.
I have formerly observed 'ea
quae interciderunt ad hanc fere
sententiam composita fuisse cre-
diderim: etenim se meis opibus
parem esse suasque fortunas ad
meos sumptus aequandos suffi-
cere negabit; cf. Trin. 467 ss.,
ubi similia leguntur.'

204. *quisquam alter* is read
here and Asin. 492. Camerarius
explains *ex paupertate* 'ex ordine seu numero pauperum ut
ex nobilitate.' This use of *pau-
pertas* is not, however, supported
by other examples.

205 Ev. dí me servant, sálva res est. sálvomst, si quid
    cómperit.   30
nímis male timuí : priusquam intro rédii, exani-
    matús fui.
rédeo ad te, Megadóre, si quid mé vis. MEG. habeo
    grátiam.
quaéso, quod te.pércontabor, ne íd te pigeat próloqui.
Ev. dúm quidem ne quid pérconteris quód mi haud
    lubeat próloqui.
210 MEG. díc mihi : quali me árbitrare génere pro-
    gnatúm ? Ev. bono.   35
MEG. quíd fide ? Ev. boná. MEG. quid factis ?
Ev. néque malis neque ímprobis.
MEG. aétatem meam scís ? Ev. scio esse grándem
    item ut pecúniam.
MEG. cérte edepol equidém te civem síne mala omni
    málitia
sémper sum arbitrátus et nunc árbitror. Ev. aurum
    huíc olet.

205. The mss. read *non perit*,
which is unintelligible, unless
we assume *perit* to be a contracted form of the perfect—an
assumption entirely unwarrant-
ed in Plautus, and especially
at the close of a line. I
have, therefore, admitted Vahlen's emendation, *comperit*. The
sense is now ' The money is
safe, if indeed Megadorus has
heard anything of its existence. '
    206. *intro redii*, ' went back
into the house.'—*exanimatus :*
see v. 179.
    211. *neque mala neque im-
probis :* see note on v. 190.
    213. For *mala malitia* see
on v. 42. *malitia* is often used
by the comic writers in the
sense of *cunning* or *shrewdness,*

e. g. Ter. Phorm. IV 3, 54. Plaut.
Epid. in fine : *hic is homost qui
libertatem malitia invenit sua.*
Cicero too has the word in this
sense, ad Att. xv 26.—Instead
of *omni*, Cicero would have preferred *ulla :* see my note on Ter.
Andr. 723 and on Trin. 338,
sine omni malitiast.
    214. For *arbitrōr* comp. Cas.
II 4, 5 *bónae frugi hominem té
iam pridem esse arbitrōr : : in-
té.ligo,* and see Introd. p. 17.—
aurum huic olet : " A faint suspicion about anything language
is apt to represent under a
figure borrowed from the sense
of smell. Thus *subolet mihi* is
the favourite mode of expressing
this idea with Plautus and Terence [*oboluit huic marsuppium*

215 quíd nunc me vis? MEG. quóniam tu me et égo te
    qualis sís, scio: 40
quaé res recte vórtat mihique tíbique tuaeque
    fíliae,
fíliam tuám mi uxorem pósco. promitte hóc fore.
Ev. heía, Megadore, haú decorum fácinus tuis factís
    facis,
út inopem atque innóxium abs te atque ábs tuis me
    inrídeas.
220 nám de te neque ré neque verbis mérui, ut faceres
    quód facis.   45
MEG. néque edepol ego té derisum vénio neque
    derídeo,
néque dignum arbitrór. Ev. cur igitur póscis meam
    gnatám tibi?
MEG. út propter me tíbi sit melius míhique propter
    te ét tuos.
Ev. vénit hoc mi, Megadóre, in mentem, téd esse
    hominem dívitem,

Men. 384]. The medium by which the scent is conveyed is of course the air, and thus we have the phrase 'to wind,' meaning 'to catch a scent of anything,' so also 'to get wind of,' or as the Germans say *wind davon haben."* KEY.

215. For the prolepsis see note on v. 440.

216. Formulas of this kind were usual on such occasions as this: see v. 780.

218. *decorum tuis factis* should be joined: 'a deed becoming your general behaviour.' We may, moreover, draw attention to the assillabation perceptible in *dor* and *decorum. facinus facere* is an instance of the so-called *figura etymologica*, of which Plautus makes fre-

quent use, e.g. this very phrase occurs again Curc. I 1, 24. Cicero too has it, de fin. II 29, 95, most probably in consequence of a remembrance from some poet. Comp. Trin. 446. 599.

219. 'A poor man, who never gave offence to you or yours,' (Thornton). For *abs* see Draeger I § 285, 4 (p. 579 sq.).

220. For the construction *mereri ut* Brix on Capt. 419 quotes the following passages: Capt. 419. 740. Epid. v 2, 47. Ter. Andr. I 5, 46. Cic. de or. I 54, 232. Liv. XL 11.

221. Comp. Trin. 448 *neque te derisum advenio neque dignum arbitror*, where *advenio* is the reading of the Ambrosian palimpsest, and *veni* that of the other mss.

225 fáctiosum: me *aú*tem esse hominem paúperum pau-
pérrumum: 50
núnc si filiám locassim meám tibi, in mentém venit,
té bovem esse et me *ésse* asellum: ubi técum con-
iunctús siem,
úbi onus nequeam férre pariter, iáceam ego asinus ín
luto,
tú me bos magis haú respicias, gnátus quasi numquám siem;
230 ét te utar iníquiore et méus me*d* ordo inrídeat: 55
neútrubi habeam stábile stabulum, sí quid devortí
fuat.
ásini mordicús me scindant, bóves incursent córni-
bus:
hóc magnumst períclum ab asinis me ád boves tran-
scéndere.

225. *item* never has the sense attributed to it by Hildyard 'on the other hand,' and the passage quoted by him (Aul. prol. 20) very well admits of the common sense of the word. I have therefore adopted Brix's emendation of this passage.— For *factiosum* see note on v. 165.

226. *locassim* arises from an original form *locavesim* (from which the common form *locaverim* is derived with the change of an *s* into an *r*); by a compression of the middle syllables we get *locasim* or *locassim* (comp. *causa caussa* and Introd. p. 44). —*locare* is frequently used by the comic poets where later writers would have said *conlocare*: see the examples given by Bentley in his note on Ter. Phorm. v 1, 32.

229. With the collocation of the words *magis hau* compare Trin. 233 *de hac re mihi satis hau liquet.*—*quasi* stands here in its 'original sense as the equivalent of its decomposition *quam si* (see Bentley on Ter. Ad. IV 1, 12). Comp. Trin. 265 *peius perit quasi saxo saliat.* Mil. gl. 481 s. *neque erile hic negotium Plus curat quasi non servitutem serviat* (*quam si* Bb and late mss). Curc. 51 *tam a me pudicast quasi soror mea sit* (*quam si* Jγ). See also Bücheler, On Latin declension p. 30.

230. For *utār* see Introd. p. 17.—*iniquiore* 'quite unequal.' See note on v. 183.

231. *stabile stabulum*: see note on v. 42.—For *fuat* see Key, L. G. § 725, and my note on Trin. 594.

232. For the adv. *mordicus* see Ritschl Opusc. II 248, who has collected all the Plautine examples of it.—For *bovĕs* (or *bous*) see Introd. p. 39.

MEG. quam ád probos propínquitate próxume te
    adiúnxeris,
235 tam óptumumst. tu cóndicionem hanc áccipe. aus-
    cultá mihi   60
    átque eam mihi despónde. EV. at nihil est dótis
    quod dem. MEG. né duas.
    dúm modo moráta recte véniat, dotatást satis.
EV. eó dico, ne mé thensauros répperisse cénseas.
MEG. nóvi: ne doceás. desponde. EV. fíat. sed pro
    Iúppiter,
240 num égo disperii? MEG. quíd tibist? EV. quid
    crépuit quasi ferrúm modo?   65
    ní mirum occidór, nisi ego intro huc própere propero
    cúrrere.   II 8, 23
MEG. híc apud me hortúm confodere iússi. sed ubi
    hinc ést homo?

234 s. *quam proxume, tam
optumumst* = quo propius, eo melius, a construction not unfrequently met with in the comic
writers : e.g. Ter. Haut. tim. v
2, 44 *quam minima in spe situs
erit, tam facillime...pacem...
conficiet.* Ad. III 4, 56 s. *quam
vos facillume agitis, quam estis
maxume, tam maxume vos aequo
animo aequa noscere oportet.* The
same construction is found in
Sallust, Iug. 31 *ita quam quis-
que pessume fecit, tam maxime
tutus est.* See also Ruddimann,
Inst. gramm. lat. II p. 306 ed.
Lips.

235. The right spelling of
condicio is with a *c*; see Bram-
bach, on Orthography p. 21.
The word is often used in the
sense of 'marriage-offer,' e.g. v.
472. See my note on Ter. Andr.
79.—Plautus often uses *auscul-
tare* instead of *auscultari*.

236. For *duas* see note on
v. 62. In another passage, Men.
267, it is doubtful whether *duas*
or *duis* is the true reading.

237. The adjective *mōratus*
is by no means confined to
Plautine language; just as we
have here *recte mōratu*, Cicero
says *vir bene moratus* Or. I 43 :
see the lexica.

240. *num disperii*, 'let me
hope I am not *totally* undone?'
Comp. Most. v 1, 36.   Trin.
1089.   Ter. Ad. III 3, 1.
Haut. tim. v 2, 17.   Similar
compounds are : *discrucior* Aul.
105. *discupio, dispudet* Bacch.
481. Most. 1166. Ter. Eun. v
2, 16. *distaedet* Amph. I 3, 5.
Ter. Phorm. v 9, 22. All these
expressions belong to every day
life, which is always fond of ex-
aggerations.

242. The infin. act. *confodere* should be explained by sup-

ábiit neque me cértiorem fécit: fastidít mei,
quía videt me súam amicitiam vélle. more hominúm
    facit.
245 nám si opulentus ít petitum paúperioris grátiam,
    paúper metuit cóngredi*ri:* pér metum male rém
    gerit.   70
    ídem quando occásio illaec périit, post seró cupit.
Ev. si hércle ego te non élinguandam dédero usque
    ab radícibus,
    ímpero, auctor sum, út me quoivis *hómini* castrandúm
    loces.
250 Meg. vídeo ego hercle, me árbitraris, Eúclio, homi-
    nem idóneum,
    quém senecta aetáte ludos fácias, haud meritó meo. 75

posing the ellipsis of an accus.
like *servos.* Hildyard justly compares the following passages
from Virgil: Aen. ii 185—6.
iii 472. v 385. 773. This negligent construction is very frequent after *iubeo:* see the examples given by Zumpt § 617.
—We should explain *ubi hinc
est* by assuming a σύγχυσις of
two constructions: *quo hinc ivit
et ubi est.* It is, however, possible that we should write *hic,*
comp. Ter. Andr. 965.
    243. *fastidit mei* ' he scorns
me :' see Key, L. G. § 939.
    246. *congrediri,* from the
crude form *con-gredi*—, see
Key, L. G. § 555. Comp. also
242.
    247. *post* is redundant, but
a similar instance of *post* at the
beginning of the apodosis occurs Trin. 417.
    248. For *hercle* see note on
v. 48.—The verb *elinguare* occurs only in this passage and in
the treatise *de differentiis verborum* by Cornelius Fronto (p.

2200 Putsch) '*elinguis* habet
linguam, sed usu eius caret :
elinguatus amisit.' Comp. also
elinguatio γλωσσοτομία and *elin-
guo,* as ἀπογλωττίζω gloss. Lab.
p. 64.—*usque ab* is not so frequently met with as *usque ad.*
Terence has it only once, Phorm.
ii 3, 48.
    249. Comp. Poen. i 18 *auc-
tor sum, sino.* For the omission
of the copula *que* see Key, L. G.
§ 1436.
    250. For the constr. *idoneus
qui* (like *dignus qui*) comp. Ter.
And. 492 s.
    251. In *senecta aetas* the
first word should be considered
as an adjective, see on Trin.
43. *aetate iuenta* (i. e. *iuu*) occurs at the end of a hexameter in an ancient inscription :
Ritschl, P. L. M. E. tab. 80, c.
Terence has *senecta* alone Ad.
v 8, 31 ; in all other passages he
uses *senectus.*—*ludos facere* =
ludere, ludificari, and hence we
should explain the construction
c. acc. (see an analogous case

Ev. néque edepol, Megadóre, facio, néque si cupiam,
      cópiast.
Meg. quíd nunc ? etiam míhi despondes fíliam?
      Ev. illis légibus,
cúm illa dote quám tibi dixi.   Meg. spónden ergo?
      Ev. spóndeo.
255 dí bene vórtant.   Meg. íta di faxint.   Ev. íllud
      facito ut mémineris
cónvenisse, ut né quid dotis méa ad te adferret
      fília.   80
Meg. mémini.   Ev. at scio vos quó soleatis pácto
      perplexárier.

v. 194 s.). Plautus joins this
phrase also with a dative (Merc.
ii 1, 1. Rud. iii 1, 1. Truc.
iv 2, 46. Most. ii 1, 80. Cas.
iv 1, 3), but the accusative appears to be more frequent. See
Ritschl, Par. i 428, where a special essay on this phrase will
be found showing that *ludo
facere aliquem, ludum facere
aliquem, ludos dare aliquem* are
not Plautine expressions.

252. In *cupiam copiast* observe the alliteration together
with assonance. Thornton remarks ' There is a poor conceit
here. Megadorus had said *ludos facias*, which m ay signify
you make sport of me, or *you
give a public show, play or spec-
tacle;* in which latter sense
Euclio takes it and replies *I
could not, if I would*, by reason
of his poverty.' This play on
the expression used by Megadorus is really so very poor
that we cannot believe it to be
intended by Plautus himself,
but it seems rather due to the
refinement of the commentators.
Euclio very strongly expresses
the idea ' how could so poor a

man as I make sport of so rich
a gentleman as you ?' *copia* is
not rarely equivalent to ' possibility, chance.'

254. It is of course equally
correct whether we accent *cúm
illa* or *cum illa*, but the first
pronunciation seems to har-
monize more with the habit of
Plautus : see Introd. p. 68.—
Comp. Trin. 571 *nunc tuam so-
rorem filio posco meo, Quae res
bene vortat.*—Le. *di bene vortant : spondeo.* Other instances
of the same phrase are Pseud.
646. Trin. 302. Ter. Ad. 725.
Eun. 390. Hec. 196. (O. Seyffert, Studia Plautina, p. 2.)

255. *facito ut memineris* is a
phrase recurring in other passages : Bacch. 328. Curc. i 3,
54. Pseud. 515. Stich. 47. *facito in memoria habeas* occurs
Poen. v 4, 108. Cas. iii 1, 9.
(O. Seyffert, l. c.)

257. The verb *perplexari*
occurs only here in Plautus ;
Terence expresses the same by
perplexe loqui Eun. v 1,1. Comp.
verbum perplexabile As. iv 1,
47.

páctum non pactúmst, non pactum páctumst, quod
vobís lubet.
MEG. núlla controvórsia mihi técum erit.   sed núptias
260 hódie quin faciámus, numquae caúsast?   Ev. immo
hercle óptuma.
MEG. íbo igitur, parábo.   numquid mé vis?   Ev.
istuc.   MEG. síc: vale.   85
heús, Strobile, séquere propere me ád macellum
strénue.
Ev. íllic hinc abiit.   di ínmortales, óbsecro, aurum
quíd valet.
crédo ego illum iam inaúdivisse, míhi esse thensau-
rúm domi:
265 íd inhiat, ea affínitatem hanc óbstinavit grátia.

---

258.   *páctum non pactúmst*
'hac (accentus) variatione boni
poëtae saepissime utuntur in
repetitione, ne idem vocabulum
eodem accentu recurrat. .Italis
quoque haec perquam familiaria
sunt nec nostris poëtis (i.e. *Ger-
manis*) Anglisve aliena.' Lachmann on Propert. II 3, 43.—*quod
vobis lubet* 'just as it pleases
you.' *quod*=*quoad :* comp. Mil.
gl. 1160 *impetrabis, imperator,
quód ego potero, quód voles* 'thou
shalt have anything, as far as
it is in my power' (*quot* or
quod the mss., *quoad* Ritschl's
edition). In a tetrameter bac-
chiacus Men. 769 we have the
same *verúmst modus tamén, quod
pati úxorem opórtet,* ' still there
is a measure whereto a wife
must be patient' (*quod* CD, *quo
adpati* B, *quoad* Ritschl after
Lambinus). In Terence we find
two instances of this meaning
of *quod :* Eun. II 1, 7 s. *munus
nostrum ornato verbis quod poteris, et illum aemúlum, Quod*

poteris ab eo pellito, and Haut.
tim. III 1, 7, *quod potero, adiu-
tabo senem.*   In the construction *quod eius* it is generally
known in this sense, see Key,
L. G. § 922.
260.   Translate: 'I hope there
is no reason why we should not
have the wedding even to-day.'
For the construction compare
Capt. II 2, 103 s. Amph. II
2, 222. Amph. fr. ap. Non.
327, 2. Cas. v 4, 24. Ter.
Phorm. II 1, 42. Most. 434.
Capt. III 4, 92 s. Hor. Serm.
I 1, 20. Euclio answers *immo
edepol optima (causa est ut fa-
ciamus).*
261.   For the phrase *numquid
me vis* see note on v. 173.—
Euclio is going to say *istuc de
dote facito ut memineris* (see v.
255), but Megadorus cuts him
short by saying *sic* 'yes ' (comp.
Ter. Phorm. 813).
262. *propere strenue* express together only one notion 'directly.'
264.   *inaudire* always means

*   *   *   *   *   *

úbi tu es quae debláteravisti iám vicinis ómnibus II 3
meaé me filiaé daturum dótem ? heus, Staphyla, té
voco.
écquid audis? váscula intus púre propera atque élue.
fíliam despóndi ego, hodie núptum huic Megadoró
dabo.

270 St. dí bene vortant. vérum ecastor nón potest, subi-
túmst nimis.   5
Ev. táce atque abi. curáta fac sint, quom á foro re-
deám domum,
átque aedis occlúde. iam ego hic ádero. St. quid
ego núnc agam ?
núnc nobis prope adést exitium, míhi atque erili
fíliae.
núnc probrum atque pártitudo própe adest ut fiát
palam.

'to hear by chance,' see Brix on Mil. gl. 212.

265. *id* represents the general notion of the thing—'that's what he is after.' So we have *eo* in reference to *quadraginta minae* Trin. 405. Comp. As. i 1, 76 *viginti iam usust filio argenti minis: Face* id *ut paratum iam sit.* — *obstinare* is explained by Festus to be 'affirmato et perseveranti animo expetere.' It occurs thus only here in Plautus.

266. *deblāterare* is an intension of the simple verb *blāterare* used by Horace (Serm. ii 7, 35) and some earlier poets, e. g. Afranius and Caecilius (Nonius p. 78, 30). Plautus has *blātire* Amph. ii 1, 71. Epid. iii 1, 13. Curc. iii 82. See Gellius i 15, where a whole chapter is devoted to loquacity. The Ger-

man *plappern* and the English *to blab* are derived from the medieval form *blaberare*.

267. The Future Infinitive is one of the cases in which the auxiliary may be omitted even in Plautus.—Comp. Curc. v 3, 8 *heus tu, leno, te volo.* It is not impossible that *volo* is likewise the true reading in this passage, although *voco* gives a good sense and is, moreover, the reading of the mss.

268. We should observe the hyperbaton in the words *pure propera atque elue,* instead of *propera atque intus pure elue vascula;* comp. Ter. Ad. 917 *tu illas abi et traduce.*

270. *potest=pote est* or in later latinity *possibile est.* So again v. 275. This usage is confined to the language of the earlier poets.

275 quód celatum atque óccultatumst úsque adhuc, nunc
     nón potest.   10
     íbo intro, ut erus quae ímperavit, fácta quom veniét
     sient.
     nam écastor malúm maerorem métuo ne inmixtím
     bibam.

277. We may comp. Most.
352 *mali maeroris montem max-*
umum. In the present passage, however, we may doubt the
phrase, and perhaps we should
correct *malum et maerorem.*
There' are *two* things necessary
for a mixture. For the formation of the adverb *inmixtim* see

Key, L. G. § 780. Munro on
Lucr. ɪ 20. Bücheler, on Lat.
declension p. 23. It is however
a ἄπ. λεγ.—Comp. Cas. v 2, 52
ut senex hoc eodem poculo quo
ego bibi biberet. In English we
may say with the same simile
to empty the cup of misfortune.

ACTVS III.

STROBILVS.   ANTHRAX.   CONGRIO.   (PHRYGIA.
ELEVSIVM.)

STR.   Posquam óbsonavit érus et conduxít coquos II 4
tibícinasque hasce ápud forum, edixít mihi,
280 ut díspertirem obsónium hic bifáriam.
CON.   me quídem hercle *hic hodie tá*m palam non
dívides :

STROBILUS returns from the
market with two cooks and two
music-girls whom Megadorus has
hired for the celebration of his
nuptials with Euclio's daughter.
In the following dialogue between Strobilus and the cooks
we have a lively, though comi-
cally exaggerated, picture of
Euclio's meanness and avarice.
Comp. Athen. XIV p. 659 b
μάλιστα δὲ εἰσάγονται (sc. ἐν τῇ
νέᾳ κωμῳδίᾳ) μάγειροι σκωπτικοί
τινες, and Meineke, Men. et Philem. rell. 1823 p. 64, and see
also my note on Ter. Eun. 776.
278. *posquam* instead of *postquam* is repeatedly attested by
the best authorities (here the
ms. *B*); see Ritschl, Opusc. II
548 sqq.—*obsonare* 'to get vic-
tuals,' 'to market,' e.g. Bacch.
97. 143. *obsonari* as deponent
stands v. 293. Comp. Stich.
681 *Stichus obsonatust* ' has
bought provisions.'
279. *apud* here drops its
final *d:* see Introd. p. 34.—*apud
forum* is the usual expression,
not *in foro.—forum :* comp.

Pseud. 790 s. *forum coquinum
qui vocant, stulte vocant: Nam
non coquinumst, verum furinum
forum.*
281. Congrio plays upon his
own name and the expression
dispertire obsonium used by
Strobilus.   By *obsonium* and
ὄψον especially *fish* was understood, whence ὀψάριον in the
language of the New Testament
simply means 'fish' (comp. the
modern Greek ψάρι).   Strobilus
having signified his intention to
divide the *obsonium* into two
parts, Congrio replies that he
shall certainly not divide him,
just as if he was afraid of being
comprehended under the category of *fish*, the *conger* being a
kind of eel, which was cut into
pieces before it was cooked
(comp. v. 396).   For *dispertire*
he substitutes *dividere*, a word
which is sometimes used in a
dishonest sense: see Petron. 11
p. 13 Bücheler.   Comp. also
Cic. ad fam. IX 22, 4 *non hones-
tum verbum est divisio? at inest
obscenum.*

112   AVLVLARIA.   [II. 4. 5—16.

si quó tu totum me íre vis, operám dabo.   5
A.   bellum ét pudicum véro prostibulúm popli.
po*l*, sí quis vellet, té*d* haud nolles dívidi ?
285 Con. atque égo istuc, Anthrax, áliovorsum díxeram,
non ístuc quo tu insímulas.   Str. sed erus núptias
meus hódie faciet.   Con. quoíus ducit fíliam ?   10
Str. vicíni huius Eucliónis *hinc* e próxumo.
ei ádeo obsoni hinc dímidium iussít dari,
cocum álterum itidemque álteram tibícinam.
290 Con. nempe húc dimidium dícis, dimidiúm dom*um?*
Str. nempe sícut dicis.   Con. quíd hic non poterat
dé suo   15
senex óbsonari fília*i* núptiis ?

282. *operam dabo* 'I will hold myself ready for your service.'
283. *popli* instead of *populi :* comp. Lorenz on Most. 15, who shows that Plautus employs the shorter form only at the end of a line or before the principal caesura.
284. Anthrax, the other cook who seems more honest but less witty than Congrio, catches at Congrio's expression *hic tam palam*, and calls him therefore *pudicum prostibulum*, adding as his suspicion that Congrio would perhaps not refuse to yield to such a proposal, if made at a fitter time and place.—*haud nolles*, an intensifying λιτότης for *velles* 'you would be quite ready.' (See Ritschl Opusc. II 250.)
285. Congrio replies that he meant *operam dare* v. 282 in a different sense, not obscenely as Anthrax would insinuate.—*aliovorsum dicere :* comp. Ter. Eun. I 2, 2 *aliorsum accipere.*

286. *istuc* is here adverb= *istoc*, see Key, L. G. § 366.— Strobilus intends to avoid all further quarrel and says therefore *sed erus* &c. 'but to come to the point, my master is going to marry.' For this usage of *sed* see Zumpt § 739.
288. *huius* is here monosyllabic = *huis*, see Introd. p. 63, note 3.
291. 'Do you mean to say that you are going to send one half here, the other to your own house?'
292. *nempe* has its first syllable short: see Introd. p. 51.
293. The same expression *filiai nuptiis* occurs v. 370. 532. 790. In these three passages the mss. rightly omit *in*, which must be omitted, since the final *i* in *filiai* cannot be elided : comp. Lachmann, Lucr. p. 161. In this passage we are at liberty to take *nuptiis* either as a dative or an ablative (see Key, L. G. § 992. Zumpt § 475), but in others it must be ablative.

Str. vah. Con. quíd negotist? Str. quíd negoti
sít, rogas?
295 puméx non aequest áridus atque hic ést senex.
Con. ain tándem? Str. ita esse ut díxi, tute exís-
tima.
quin dívom atque hominum clámat continuó fidem,20
suam rém perisse séque eradicárier,
de suó tigillo fúmus si qua exít foras.

295. This was a proverbial
expression, comp. Persa i 1, 41
*aquam e pumice postulas qui
ipsus sitiat* and Pseud. 73 *pumi-
cei oculi.*—For *aridus* see the
commentators on Ter. Haut.
tim. iii 2, 15 *sed habet patrem
quendam avidum miserum atque
aridum.* It is frequently used
to denote the nature of the pu-
mice-stone, e. g. Catull. 1, 2.
Martial viii 72. *pumex* is generally a masculine, but sometimes we have it also as a feminine, see Priscian vi 712 (P.).
Servius on Aen. xii 587 '*pumi-
cem autem iste* (Vergilius) *masculino genere posuit, et hunc
sequimur; nam et Plautus ita
dixit*' seems to allude to this
passage in the Aulularia. We
should probably pronounce *ardus* in the present passage, in
order to avoid an incorrect anapaest in the fourth foot of the
trimeter. *ardus* occurs in an
inscription, C. I. L. i 577, 2, 21,
and was used by Lucilius. See
O. Seyffert Stud. Plaut. p. 6.
296. *tandem* expresses Congrio's unwillingness to believe
what Strobilus tells him. See
Zumpt § 237. The same in-
dignant question *ain tandem*
occurs Ter. Andr. 875. Phorm.
373.
297. *quin* here and v. 300

means 'even:' see Zumpt § 542.
If found with an indicative, this
particle is quite different in origin from *quin* c. coni. In the
latter case, it is a compound of
the relative pronoun *qui* and
the original negation *ne;* in the
first, it is the interrogative *qui*
and *ne*. In translating it by
'why,' we may preserve its original meaning.
298. *eradicari*=*usque ab ra-
dicibus* (v. 248) *perire:* see the
commentators on Ter. Andr. iv
4, 22. Haut. tim. iii 3, 28.
299. *tigillum* is a diminutive
of *tignum*, formed in the same
way as *sigillum* from *signum*.
Isidore's derivation from *tegulae*
(Orig. xix 10) is quite groundless.
Most of the commentators take
de suo tigillo in the sense of
'from his house,' or, as Hildyard
says, 'through the rafters of his
house.' As there is no other
passage in any author, where
tigillum would have the sense
of *domicilium breve*, I prefer
the explanation given by Pareus
according to which we need not
invent a new sense for this
passage. Euclio thinks that he
is undone, when the smallest
piece of wood is burned in his
house, and he therefore keeps
no wood in the house: see
v. 355.

W. P.   8

300 quin quom ít dormitum, fóllem obstringit ób gulam.
Con. cur?   Str. né quid animae fórte amittat
dórmiens.
Con. etiámne opturat ínferiorem gútturem?   25
Str. cur?   Con. né quid animae fórte amittat dórmiens.
Str. haec míhi te ut tibi me aequom ésse credo
crédere.
305 Con. immo équidem credo.   Str. át scin etiam quó
modo?
aquam hércle plorat, quóm lavat, profúndere.
Con. censén talentum mágnum exorarí pote   30
ab istóc sene ut det quí fiamus líberi?
Str. famem hércle utendam, sí roges, numquám
dabit.

---

300. 'Some commentators suppose, by *follem* is meant a *purse*, but the plain and obvious sense of this word appears to be a kind of *bag*, which Strobilus supposes Euclio to fasten to his mouth and throat to catch his breath in, while he is asleep. The thought is extravagant, but humorous.' Thornton.

302. *guttur* is masculine in two other Plautine passages, Mil. gl. 835, and Trin. 1014. Novius too has *usque ad imum gutturem* v. 118, Ribb.

304. 'Innuit neutri ab altero esse credendum.' Acidalius. Comp. Poen. 494 *an mi haec non credis?—Credo ut mi ae-quomst credier.*

305. The words *at scin etiam quomodo* simply form a connexion between the preceding jokes and those that follow. This same phrase is generally used to express threats, and thus we have it v. 47: see

Weise's note on Poen. i 2, 165; but it occurs in the same way as here in another passage, Poen. i 3, 29.—For the hiatus in this line see Introd. p. 67.

306. *plorat* 'he cries his eyes out;' for the infin. comp. Hor. Od. iii 10, 4. Aristophanes has a similar joke about a mean Athenian, Patrocles, Plut. 84 ἐκ Πατροκλέους ἔρχομαι, ὃς οὐκ ἐλούσατ' ἐξ ὅτουπερ ἐγένετο. This however means that Patrocles never took a bath since his birth, because he was too mean to pay for it.

307. *pote* alone stands not only for *potes* (e.g. Trin. 353) and *potest*, but even for *posse*. See Ritschl, Proll. cxi.—For the so-called 'great' talent, see Smith's Dictionary of Antiquities s. v. *Talentum.*

308. For *ab* ĭstóc see Introd. p. 46.—*qui* = ut inde, see Key, L. G. § 312, 2.

309. See note on v. 96.

310 quin ípsi pridem tónsor unguis démpserat,
    conlégit, omnia ábstulit praeségmina.
    Con. edepól mortalem párce parcum praédicas.   35
    censén vero adeo párce et misere vívere?
    Str. pulméntum pridem erípuit ei míluos :
315 homo ád praetorem plórabundus dévenit,
    infit ibi postuláre plorans éiulans,
    ut síbi liceret míluom vadárier.   40
    sescénta sunt, quae mémorem, si sit ótium.
    sed utér vostrorumst célerior ? memorá mihi.
320 Con. ego et múlto melior.   Str. cócum ego, non
        furém rogo.

311.   *praesegmina, ἀπονυχί-
σματα,* 'parings.'
    312.   *parce parcus* 'a most
stingy wretch' (Thornton). For
the expression comp. Pseud. 11
misere miser or Cas. iii 1, 8
scite scitus and similar passages: see also note on v. 42.
    313.   *censen vero* etc. 'do
you indeed believe that he lives
so economically and miserly?'
Perhaps this line should be attributed to Strobilus. It would
then form a kind of prelude to
the example related in v. 314—
317.
    314.   *miluos* and *larua* are
always trisyllabic in Plautine
prosody.
    317.   The subj. *liceret* is
conceived dependent upon the
historical present *infit.* But
liceat would not have been incorrect.—*vadarier* 'aliquem est
accipere ab eo vades, h. e. fide-
iussores locupletes qui certa
sponsione pecuniae illum, unde
petebatur, vadimonium obitu-
rum seu in ius venturum reci-
piant et promittant. dabantur
autem vades, ne in carcere atti-
nerentur usque in diem iudicii.'

Gronovius, Lect. Plant. p. 51.
See Plaut. Curc. v 2, 23—27
and the commentators on Hor.
Serm. i 9, 74—78. (Walter,
röm. Rechtsgesch. § 728 ss.)
    318.   On *sescenta* see Dona-
tus' note on Ter. Phorm. iv 3,
63 'perspicere hinc licet con-
suetudinem utriusque sermonis.
nam Apollodorus μυρίας dixit
pro multis, et ut apud Graecos
μυρία, ita apud nos *sescenta*
dicere pro *multis* usitatum est.'
Hildyard observes that *sescenta
tanta,* Pseud. ii 2, 37, might be
translated *five hundred times.*
    319.   '*vostrorum* multifariam
scriptum est pro *vostrum*' according to Gellius xx 6, 12.
Plautus has also *nostrorum* instead of *nostrum.* See Lorenz
on Most. 270, and Brix on Mil.
gl. 174.
    320.   Cooks enjoyed a bad
repute at Rome, as the whole
scene in the Pseudolus iii 2
between Ballio and the cook
shows. *Celeres manus* are an
attribute of thieves, e.g. in a
line quoted from Plautus' Cornicularia (p. 1470 Taubm.)
mihi, Laverna, in furtis cele-

8—2

Con. cocum érgo dico. Str. quíd tu ais? A. sic
sum út vides.

Con. cocus ílle nundinálist : in nonúm diem   45
solet íre coctum. A. tún trium litterárum homo
me vítuperas? Con. fur? étiam fur trifúrcifer.

325 Str. tace núnciam tu atque ágnum hinc uter est
pínguior...   II 5
A. licét... Str. tu, Congrio, eúm sume *actutúm tibi*

rassis manus. Congrio himself prays to Laverna, v. 442.

321. With *sic sum ut vides* comp. Theocr. Id. xxii 59 τοιόσδ' οἶον ὁρᾷς. The same phrase occurs Pl. Amph. ii 1, 57.

322. The explanation of the expression *cocus nundinalis* is not quite settled, and we learn from Festus (p. 173 M.) that the ancient grammarians themselves were not quite agreed with regard to the explanation of this passage. *nundinalis* would come from *nundinae* (=*novendinae*) and would of course mean a very bad and worthless cook hired only on fair-days. I should however prefer the other reading, which is clearly indicated by Festus, but generally confounded with *nundinalis*, and this is *nundialis*. *novendialia* are explained in an old glossary ἔνατα ἐπὶ νεκροῦ ἀγόμενα (see e.g. Petron. 65): *cocus nundialis* would thus signify a cook hired for the so-called 'silicernium,' and for festivals of that nature not the best cooks seem to have been generally hired. The *leno* Ballio says of a very bad cook in this sense *quin ob eam rem Orcus recipere ad se hunc noluit, Vt esset hic qui mortuis cenam coquat:* Pseud. 795 s. It may be added that in the ms. *B* the

third *n* in the word *nundinalis* is by the hand of a corrector; see Lorenz's progr. p. 9.

323. I have not adopted the spelling *littrarum*, though there is little doubt that we should actually pronounce so. It is not very probable that *trium* is capable of a monosyllabic pronunciation.

324. Congrio is not slow to understand Anthrax's meaning, and retort upon him. (Comp. Cas. ii 2, 49 where *fures* are called *littrati.*) Anthrax gives him the title of thief (Fvr), and he calls him *fur trifurcifer.* On *furcifer* I add the explanation given by Donatus on Andr. iii 5, 12 '*furciferi* dicebantur qui ob leve delictum cogebantur a dominis ignominiae magis quam supplicii causa circa vicinos *furcam*ʹin collo ferre, subligatis ad eam manibus, et praedicare peccatum suum simulque conmonere ceteros ne quid simile admittant.' *tri-* adds to the strength of the expression, comp. *trivenefica* v. 86. The same word *trifurcifer* occurs twice Rud. iii 2, 29 s. It is by no means the same with *trifur* v. 625.

325. For *tacĕ* see Introd. p. 26.

326. *licet* 'it shall be done:' for instances see Men. 158. 213.

atque íntro abi illuc, ét vos illum séquimini.
vos céteri illuc ád nos. A. hercle iniúria
dispértivisti : pínguiorem agnum ísti habent.   5
330 STR. at núnc tibi dabitur pínguior tibícina.
i sáne cum illo, Phrúgia. tu autem, Eleúsium,
huc íntro abi ad nos. CON. ó Strobile súbdole,
hucíne detrusti me ád senem parcíssumum ?
ubi sí quid poscam, usque ád ravim poscám prius 10
335 quam quícquam detur. STR. stúltus et sine grátia's.
tibi récte facere ? quándo quod faciás, perit.
CON. qui véro ? STR. rogitas ? iám principio in
aédibus
turba ístic nulla tíbi erit. si qui utí voles,
domo ábs te adferto, ne óperam perdas póscero. 15
340 hic ápud nos magna túrba ac *magna* fámiliast,
supéllex aurum véstis vasa argéntea :
ibi sí perierit quíppiam (quod té scio

Most. 401. 930. 1153. Capt. v
1, 28. Bacch. 35.
330. Such proceleusmatics
as -*tibi dábi*- are not rarely
found in the second foot of iambics, though they are more common in the first. See Ritschl,
Proll. CCLXXXIX.
331. *Phrygia*, i. e. Φρυγία,
was a very appropriate name for
a music-girl, a peculiar kind of
flutes being called *tibiae Phry-
giae*. See the commentators
on Tib. II 1, 86. Cat. 63, 23 and
J. F. Gronovius' Obs. lat. I 17.
336. *tibi recte facere* 'how
could I please you?' The use
of the infinitive of indignation
is very common in the third
person, but very rare in the
second and first. Of the first,
Lachmann in his note on Lucr.
II 16 gives only two instances :
the present passage in the Aulularia and Ter. Andr. v 2, 29
tantum laborem capere ob talem

filium? 'that I should have so
much trouble for such a son.'
337. *qui vero* (*mihi recte
facis*)? 'but how are you favour-
ing me?' Congrio does not understand the *gratia* which Strobilus
pretends to confer upon him.
338. *qui* is the old ablative
instead of *quo* (= *qua re*).
339. The infinitive *poscere*
is here negligently used instead
of the regular construction *pos-
cendo*. See Key, L. G. § 1255
and Lorenz on Most. 1159.
Hildyard quotes Epid. II 2, 13
*omnem per urbem sum defessus
quaerere* (= *quaerendo*): see also
v 2, 54 s. Catullus expresses
the same, *defessus . . essem te
mihi, amice, quaeritando:* c. 55
in Haupt's edition.
340. For the pronunciation
of *apud* see Introd. p. 34.
342. For *quod abstinere* ('to
abstain from which') see Key,
L. G. § 909. The Plautine

facile ábstinere pósse, si nihil óbviamst)
dicánt 'coqui abstulérunt, comprehéndite,   20
345 vincíte verberáte, in puteum cóndite.'
horúm tibi istic níhil eveniet, quíppe qui
ubi quód su*br*upia*s* níhil est. sequere hac mé.   Con.
sequor.

STROBILVS.   STAPHYLA.   CONGRIO.   II 6

STR. heus, Stáphyla, prodi atque óstium aperi.   St.
quí vocat ?
STR. Strobílus.   ST. quid vis?   STR. hósc*e* ut ac-
cipiás coquos
350 tibícinamque obsóniumque in núptias.
Megadórus iussit Eúclioni haec míttere.
ST. Cererín, Strobile, hi súnt facturi núptias?   5

passages, in which this construction occurs, have been collected by Brix in his note on
Men. 985.
345. For *puteus* comp. v.
363. I do not find any other
passages where this kind of
punishment for slaves is mentioned. In Greek the corresponding word λάκκος means
also a kind of cellar.
346. The construction of the
words is *quippe qui ubi nihil
est quod subrupias.* For *quippe
qui* with a following indicative
see Key, L. G. § 1194 note.
qui in this connexion is an
archaic asseverative particle,
which in later language is only
known in the compound *atqui.*
For instances see Rud. 384.
Truc. I 1, 49. Bacch. 368.
Pseud. 1274. Ter. Haut. tim.
538. In the same way we have
ut qui in several instances which

have perversely been corrected
by the editors: As. 505. Trin.
637. Capt. 553. Bacch. 283.
See Fleckeisen, Krit. Miscellen.
p. 32 s.
347. For *subrupias* see note
on v. 39.
348. For *qui* as a direct interrogative see Madvig, § 88, 1.
351. The active infinitive
mittere is defended in note on
v. 242.
352. In the festivals called
Cereris nuptiae the use of wine
was not permitted: see Servius
on Verg. Georg. I 344 and Ma-
crobius, Saturn. III 11. The
original significance of these
festivals is not quite evident;
Preller (röm. Myth. p. 439)
thinks that they commemorated
the wedding of Pluto and Pro-
serpina, at which Ceres was
conceived in the character of
hostess.

STR. qui? ST. quía temeti níhil adlatum intéllego.
STR. at iam ádferetur, si á foro ipsus rédierit.
355 ST. ligna híc apud nos núlla sunt. CON. sunt ásseres?
ST. sunt pól. CON. sunt igitur lígna: ne quaerás
    foris.
ST. quid, ímpurate, quámquam Volcanó studes,   10
    cenaéne causa aut tuaé mercedis grátia
    nos nóstras aedis póstulas combúrere?
360 CON. hau póstulo. STR. duc ístos intro. ST. séqui-
    mini.

PYTHODICVS.   II 7

curáte: ego intervísam quid faciánt coqui,
quos pól ut ego hodie sérvem cura máxumast:
nisi únum hoc faciam ut ín puteo cenám coquant:
inde cóctam sursum súbducemus córbulis.
365 si *illi* aútem deorsum cómedent, si quid cóxerint,   5

353. '*vinum temetum prisca
lingua adpellatur*' Gellius, x 23:
the word is very rare in the
language of prose-writers (only
Plin. xiv 90 and Cic. de. rep.
iv ap. Non. p. 5): see Riese,
Rhein. Mus. xxi 119.

354. *ipsus*, i.e. erus, Megadorus, 'the governor.' This
use of *ipsus* is probably an imitation of the Greek αὐτός, for
thus disciples and slaves called
their masters: e.g. αὐτὸς ἔφα
ipse dixit, where αὐτός means
the all-revered master Pythag-
oras. See also Aristoph. Nubes
219. Comp. Aul. 806 and Cas.
iv 2, 11 *ego eo quo me ipsa
misit*, i.e. era. Verg. Ecl. ix
66.

359. *postulare* is in the language of the comic poets frequently an equivalent for *velle*

or *cupere;* thus we may translate here 'would you have us
burn our house?' Hence we
should explain the infinitive
which follows. For instances see
v. 581. Capt. iii 5, 59. 81. Cas.
i 53. Truc. i 2, 39; with the
whole sentence comp. Capt. iv
2, 64 s. *quid me, volturi, Tuan
causa aedis incensurum censes?*

361. *intervisam* 'I'll go and
see;' see on v. 200.

364. For *inde* see Introd.
p. 45.

365. According to the in-
variable practice of Plautus,
deorsum is disyllabic: see Introd.
p. 59.—The word does here apparently not mean 'downwards,'
but 'down.' Forcellini gives
one instance for this sense,
Varro de re rust. iii 5 *deorsum
in terram est aqua quam bibere*

superi íncenati súnt et cenati ínferi.
sed vérba hic facio, quási negoti níl siet,
rapácidarum ubi tántum sit in aédibus.

EVCLIO.   II 8

volui ánimum tandem cónfirmare hodié meum,
370 ut béne *me* haberem fíliaí núptiis.
venio ád macellum, rógito piscis: índicant
carós—agninam cáram—caram búbulam—
vitulínam cetum pórcinam, cara ómnia.   5
atque eó fuerunt cáriora—aes nón erat.
375 abeo íllim iratus, quóniam *mihi* nil ést qui emam.
ita illís impuris ómnibus adií manum.

possint. Another example is
given by Douza: Varro de re
rust. I 8 *qui colunt deorsum,
magis aestate laborant; qui
sursum, magis hieme.* Cicero
too has *sursum* in the sense
'higher up:' de nat. deor. II
56, 141, *nares…recte sursum
sunt.*
368. *rapācida* is a comical
formation after the analogy of
Pelopida Aeacida and other
patronymics. Plautus has the
similar words *Saturides* Most.
III 1, 44, *plagipatidae* Capt. II
1, 12 and *collicrepidae cruricre-
pidae* Trin. 1022. *sit* appears
here long; see Introd. p. 15.
369. Euclio had been to the
market to make some trifling
purchases for his daughter's
nuptials, but found everything
too expensive.—With *animum
confirmare* comp. *affirmare animum* Merc. 81.
373. With *pórcinám* comp.
pistillám v. 95.
374. Thornton rightly trans-

lates 'what made them dearer
still, I had no money.' In
prose we should add *quod* before *aes.*
375. *illim* is an archaic form
equivalent to *illinc,* see Ritschl
Opusc. II 453 sqq. The mss.
read *iratus illinc* and do not
give *mihi.* It is, perhaps, possible that the line is due to an
interpolator, though I have now
ventured to make some alterations in order to reduce it into
a metrical shape.
376. For *ita íllís* see Introd.
p. 42.—In *ómnibús* the final
syllable is probably long: see
Introd. p. 17. It is, however,
also possible to read *-mnibús
ad-* as a tribrach.—*adire manum*
is not unfrequently found in
Plautus (e.g. Poen II 11. Persa
v 2, 18. Cas. v 2, 55) in the
sense 'to deceive,' to impose
upon.' Acidalius justly observes that the phrase seems
to have arisen from some arti-
fice practised in wrestling.

deinde égomet mecum cógitare intér vias
occépi 'festo dié si quid prodégeris,   10
profésto egere líceat, nisi pepérceris.'
380 postquam hánc rationem véntri cordique édidi,
accéssit animus úd meam senténtiam,
quam mínumo sumptu fíliam ut nuptúm darem.
nunc túsculum emi hoc ét coronas flóreas :   15
haec ímponentur ín foco nostró Lari,
385 ut fórtunatas fáciat gnatae núptias.
sed quíd ego apertas aédis nostras cónspicor ?
et strépitust intus. númnam ego compilór miser ?
CON. aulám maiorem, sí pote, *ex* vicínia   20
pete : haéc est parva, cápere non quit. EV. eí mihi.
390 perii hércle. aurum rápitur, aula quaéritur.

---

377. *inter vias* 'while I was walking home.' Comp. the German *unterwegs*.

378. Thornton translates 'feast to-day makes fast to-morrow.'—*die* is here a monosyllable : Introd. p. 58.

379. Comp. Hor. Serm. II 3, 143 s. *qui Veientanum festis potare diebus, Campana solitus trulla vappamque profestis.* Afranius 262 Ribb. *aeque profesto ac festo concelebrat focum.* Festus p. 229 with a doubtful etymology explains *profesti dicti, quod sunt procul a religione numinis divini.—parcere* in the sense ' to live sparingly,' comp. *parcus.*

380. *ventri* in the first place, as being mainly concerned in this deliberation: *cor*, because his common sense would advise him to venture on a small expense : *animus* (381) the domineering principle, 'will and inclination.' The whole sounds like the description of a transaction in the senate or some

other powerful body.

383. See note on v. 24.

384. *haec*, sc. *coronae*. In Plautus the nom. plur. of the feminine is commonly *haec*, not *hae*.

387. The particle *numnam* occurs several times in Plautus and Terence ; of *numne* Ritschl (Proll. LXXV) gives only one instance Poen. v 2, 119 : see also Sueton. rell., ed. Reifferscheid, p. 524. Euclio hopes that his fear is groundless. Zumpt, § 351 note.

388. Congrio does not appear on the stage, but is merely heard to say these words within the house.—*si pote, εἰ δυνατόν.*—*aula* is the ancient form instead of *olla*. *au* was pronounced like *o*, and Plautus and his contemporaries did not employ double consonants. The name of the present play is derived from the dimin. *aulula.*

390. We should probably assume a hiatus after *hercle*, i.e. a pause should be made after

Apóllo, quaeso súbveni mi, atque ádiuva,
quia ín re tali iám subvenisti ántidhac: 26
confíge sagitis fúres thensaurários.   25
sed césso prius quam prórsus perii cúrrere?

ANTHRAX.   II. 9

395 Dromó, desquama píscis : tu, Machaério,
congrúm muraenam exdórsua, quantúm potest.
ego hínc artoptam ex próxumo utendám peto
a Cóngrione. tú istum gallum, sí sapis,   5
glabriórem reddes míhi quam volsus lúdiust.
400 sed quíd hoc clamoris óritur hinc ex próxumo?

the exclamation. Various attempts have been made to fill
up the hiatus by the addition
of some syllable or other, but
none appears to be satisfactory.
  392.   Euclio implores Apollo
in his quality as ἀλεξίκακος.
The line may possibly be an
allusion to some event in which
Apollo protected by his personal
interference the treasures of
some temple against thieves or
hordes of barbarous invaders.
This may possibly have been
the aggression of the Gauls under Brennus who threatened
Delphi: see Justin's account
XXIV 6 sqq. It should, however,
be confessed that this allusion
(no doubt intelligible to a Greek
audience at the time of the first
performance of the Greek original of the Aulularia) reads somewhat obscurely in the Latin ad-
aptation.—antidhac is archaic
instead of antehac. The full
form of the preposition ante was
antid or anted (comp. postid
prod red).
  393.   For ságitis see Introd.

p. 47. This pronunciation had
already been suggested by Hare
in his ms. notes where he
compares Trin. 725.—What is
meant by fures thensaurarii, is
clear enough ; but thesaurarius
appears to be a ἅπαξ λεγ.
  396.   With this line a passage
from Ter. Ad. III 3, 23 ss. is
generally compared. The word
exdorsuare occurs only here and
in Appuleius.
  399.   ludius is in Labbaeus'
Glossaries p. 109 rightly explained ὑποκριτής. Thornton remarks 'The ludii were young
lads employed in the public
spectacles ; our author adds
volsus (plucked), because they
used at the time of puberty to
have the down or hairs plucked
from their chins to keep their
faces smooth.' The word is no
doubt connected with ludere
'to play,' and the common
spelling lydius due to the erroneous derivation from the Ly-
dii, i. e. Etruscans : see Dionys.
Halic. II 97. Comp. ludio.

coqui hércle, credo, fáciunt officiúm suom.
fugiam íntro, ne quid túrba*rum* hic itidém *fuat.*

CONGRIO.   III. 1

óptati civés, populares, íncolae, accolae, ádvenae omnes,
dáte viam qua fúgere liceat, fácite totae pláteae pateant.
405 tótus doleo atque óppido perii: íta me iste habuit sénex gymnasium.   5

101. *faciunt officium suum* is of course ironically meant: 'you could not expect cooks to do otherwise, they only do their duty, at least according to their own notions.' Hildyard compares Asin. II 2, 113 *quin tu officium facis ergo ac fugis?* and Pseud. 913 *fuit meum officium (ut abirem).*

402. *ne* should be conceived as dependent upon an omitted *metuens* or *veritus*, which appears to be implied in the general character of the sentence. Translate 'I will hasten into our house, lest any disturbance should take place there as well as here.'

403 ss. Congrio comes running out of Euclio's house and implores the assistance of the citizens against the old man's fury.

403. *optati cives* 'beloved, dear citizens:' comp. Cic. ad Quintum fr. II 8 *vale, mi optime et optatissime frater.* This sense is very familiar in the compound *exoptatus.* Similar scenes to this are frequent in the comic poets: see e. g. Rud. III 2 and Ter. Ad. II 1.

404. 'The Greek words which Plautus employs, are first naturalized and assume something of a Roman dress. πλατεῖα, for example, with its long penult becomes in Plautus, and indeed in Terence also, *platĕa,* and so easily passes through the Italian *piazza* into the French and Norman-English *place.* Similarly γυναικεῖον takes in Latin comedy the shape of *gynaecĕum.*' KEY, Trans. of the Phil. Soc. 1861 p. 177 s. See also Corssen, II 679, who enumerates *platĕa, chorĕa, balinĕum, gynaecĕum, Seleucĭa* alongside of πλατεῖα, χορεία, βαλανεῖον, γυναικεῖον, Σελεύκεια.

405. The same expression *oppido perii* recurs v. 793, comp. the similar *oppido interii* v. 721 and Amph. I 1, 43.—For the expression *habuit me gymnasium* comp. Asin. II 2, 31 where Leonidas greets his fellow-slave Libanus with the words *gymnasium flagri, salveto.*—In pronouncing the word *senex* the final *x* should be dropped: see Introd. p. 36.

néque ego umquam nisi hódie ad bacchas véni in
    bacchanál coquinatum :   3
íta me miserum et meós discipulos fústibus male
    cóntuderunt.   4
neque lígna ego usquam géntium praebéri vidi
    púlcrius :   8
itaque ómnis exegít foras, me atque hósce onustos
    fústibus.   9
410 atát ut perii hercle égo miser: a, périi, bacchanál
    adest :   6
sequitúr : scio quam rém geram : hoc ipsús magister
    mé docet.   7

406. I have spelt the words *baccha* and *bacchanal* with a small *b*, because they should rather be considered as general terms than as proper nouns. Plautus frequently mentions *bacchae :* see Cas. v 4, 9 ss. Merc. 469. (Vidular. fragm. p. 483 Ern.) Bacch. 371. 53. Amphitr. ii 2, 70 ss. Mil. gl. 1016. Men. 834 ss. Pseud. 109 s. In Greek, βάκχαι in general means 'furious women,' and the word has the same sense in Plautus, where we should not always think of an allusion to the *bacchanalia* so severely punished by the Roman senate. It is not therefore admissible to use this passage to fix the time when Plautus wrote the Aulularia.—The verb *coquinatum* is attested by Nonius and given by our mss.: it is therefore quite preposterous to write *coquitatum*, as G. Hermann and Goeller do. The same verb occurs Pseud. 853 *an tú coquínátum te ire quoquam postulas* and ibid. 875 *quanti istuc unum mé coquináre perdoces ?* In the dictionaries we generally find it

marked with the wrong quantity *coquino;* but *coqu-ina-* is derived from *coqu-* in the same way as *car-ina-* from *cär-* (Sanskr. *skar* laedere): *carinare* is used with this quantity by Ennius, Ann. 181 and 229; although Forcellini here again gives *carino*, while Freund rightly has *carino*. See also Sauppe's remarks on this point in the Ind. schol. Gott. 1858-59 p. 10, where he likewise defends the short quantity of the *i* in *coquino*.

407. Congrio calls the inferior cooks (*quingentos coquos* v. 545) his ' disciples,' because he has to direct them what to do. In using the plural *contuderunt*, Congrio continues the simile of the *bacchae*, just as if in Euclio all the Furies were represented together.

408. Instead of wood, which was of course a necessary article for cooks, Euclio most liberally provides them with *fustes : onustus fustibus* meaning ' thoroughly thrashed.'—*ligna praebere* is known from Hor. Serm. i 5, 46.

Evclio. Congrio.   III 2

Ev. redi: quó fugis nunc? téne tene. Con. quid,
   stólide, clamas ?
Ev. quia ad trís viros iam ego déferam nomén tuom.
   Con. quam obrem ?
Ev. quia cúltrum habes. Con. cocúm decet. Ev.
   quid cómminatu's
415 mihi? Con. ístuc male factum árbitror, quia nón
   latus fodi.
Ev. homo núllust te sceléstior qui vívat hodie,   5
   neque quoi égo de industria ámplius male plús
   lubens faxim.
Con. pol etsí taceas, palam íd quidem est: res ípsa
   testist.

411. The *magister* is of
course Euclio: see v. 405.

412. On seeing Euclio issu-
ing from the house, Congrio had
taken to his heels, and therefore Euclio shouts *tene tene*
'stop him, stop him:' cf. v. 705.
For the quantity *tĕnĕ tenē* see
Introd. p. 26.

413. The *tresviri* are the
tresviri capitales who had charge
of the prisons and awarded
punishment to those whom they
found trespassing against the
security of the public; Amph.
i 1, 3 Sosia is afraid of being
taken up by the tresviri : *quid
faciam nunc, si tresviri me in
carcerem compegerint?* and Asin.
i 2, 5 Argyrippus threatens the
cruel mother of his mistress to
lodge a charge against her with
the tresviri : *ibo ego ad trisvi-
ros, vóstraque ibi nómina Fáxo
erunt: cápitis te pérdam ego et
filiam.* Comp. also Persa 72 *ut
aequa parti prodeant ad trisvi-*

ros. See Walter, röm. Rechtsgesch. § 141.—*quam obrem* is
the spelling adopted by Fleckeisen throughout his edition of
Terence, on the very practical
purpose to show at once that
in the comic poets *quam* should
always be elided before *ob*.

416. *vivere* is frequently an
equivalent of the simple *esse:*
e. g. Amph. prol. 75 *victores
vivere.* Trin. 390 *lepidus vivis*
'you are a jolly man.' Men.
202 *vivis meis morigera moribus.*
ibid. 908 *ego homo vivo miser.*
Catullus has the same use of
vivere : 10, 34 *sed tu insulsa
male ac molesta vivis,* and 111,
1 *vivere contentas viro solo.*

417. We should join *plus
male faxim* 'I would ill-treat
more.' But not improbably we
should write *plus mali,* as has
been done by Guyet and Weise.
—In *lubens* the final letters *ns*
should be entirely dropped: see
Introd. p. 35.

ita fústibus sum móllior magis quam úllus cinaedus.
420 sed quíd tibi nos táctiost, mendíce homo, quae res?
Ev. etiám rogitas? an quía minus quam *me* aéquom
erat feci?   10
Con. sine: at hércle cum magnó malo tuo, si hóc
caput sentit.

419. *mollior magis:* to strengthen a comparative by adding *magis* or *mage* seems to have been quite familiar to the conventional language of the Romans: comp. Men. prol. 55 *magis maiores nugas egerit.* Stich. 698 *hoc magis est dulcius.* Capt. iii 4, 111 *nihil invenies magis hoc certo certius.* Poen. ii 15 *contentiores mage erunt atque avidi minus.* Among prose-writers, constructions of this kind occur only in Valerius Maximus, Justinus, Arnobius and Boëthius. In Greek μᾶλλον is frequently added to comparatives, even by the best writers: see Krüger, *griechische Sprachlehre* § 49, 7, 5. But it would be quite misleading to say that the Latin constructions were imitations of the Greek; the very fact that we find them only in the comics or in later and negligent writers, would speak against such a theory. The vulgar dialects of the English language are not free from the same pleonastic comparative, e.g. Dickens lets a carter say that his beer *'is more flatterer than it might be:'* Old Curiosity Shop, chap. xxvi (p. 121 people's edition). In *magis* the final *s* should be dropped.—*cinaedus* (κίναιδος) means a public dancer of a rather loose character: see Mil. gl. 668 *tum ad saltandum non cinaedus malacus aequest atque*

ego. For the expression *mollis fustibus* Hare justly compares Mil. gl. 1424 *mitis sum equidem fustibus.*
420. The construction *tibi nos tactiost* is explained by Key, L. G. §§ 907 and 1302. We have the same v. 737. Curc. v 2, 27 (=626 Fl.). Cas. ii 6, 54. Poen. v. 5, 29. Men. 1016, and in the same way we read *quid tibi huc receptio ad test meum virum?* Asin. v 2, 70 (=920), and *quid tibi huc véntiost? quíd tibi hanc áditiost? quíd tibi hanc nótiost, inquam, amicám meam?* Truc. ii 7, 62 ss. (=611 s. Geppert).—*quae res* is a phrase expressing indignation and surprise=*quae ista tandem res est.* Thus we have Asin. ii 4, 71 (= 477) *quae res? tun libero homini male servos loquere?* For other instances see Poen. v 4, 29. Cas. ii 8, 18. iii 6, 8.
421. With *rogitas* comp. v. 337.—For the construction of the words *quam me aequom erat* see note on v. 122.—In *erat* the final *t* should be dropped: in the same way we should pronounce *capu* in the following line.
422. *sine* appears almost as a threatening interjection in several passages in Plautus and Terence: e. g. Hec. iv 4, 85 where Donatus observes '*sine* separatim accipe, quia vim habet conminantis.' See also Eun. i 1, 20. Plaut. As. v 2,

Ev. pol ego haúscio quid póst fuat: tuom núnc caput
    sentit.
    sed in aédibus quid tíbi meis nam erát negoti
425 me absénte, nisi ego iússeram? volo scíre. CON. tace
    ergo.
    quia vénimus coctum ad núptias... Ev. quid tú
    malum curas,   15
    utrúm crudum*ne* an cóctum edim, nisi tú mihi es
    tutor?
CON. volo scíre, sinis an nón sinis nos cóquere hic
    cenam?
Ev. volo scíre ego item meaé domi mea sálva futura.
430 CON. utinám mea mihi modo aúferam quae *ad te*
    ádtuli salva.

48.—Ussing on Pl. Asin. 893
aptly renders it by the Greek
εἶεν.—The commentators observe that the ancients used to
direct their blows against the
head: see Hor. Serm. I 5, 22.
Amph. I 1, 162 Mercurius says
of his fist that it *exossat os
hominibus*. Comp. also v. 437
non fissile hoc haberes caput and
451. Congrio means *si hoc*
(i. e. meum) *caput sentit* in the
sense of 'si quid ego sapio, si
quid in me sensus est,' as
Lambinus justly explains it;
for *caput* frequently signifies
the entire person, e. g. Ter.
Andr. II 2, 35. Ad. II 3, 8.
Verg. Aen. IV 435, and instances
of *sentio* in the sense of 'sapere'
are given by the dictionaries.
Euclio ironically replies ' *tuom
nunc caput sentit*' by which he
alludes to the blows inflicted
upon Congrio's head.
423. *hauscio* is in Plautus
one word formed in the same
way as the common *nescio*: see
Key, L. G. § 1401, 1.

424. *nam* should be joined with *quid*: see note on v.
42.
426. In *venimus* and *malum*
the final consonants should be
dropped.—*malum* is here an interjection apparently belonging
to conversational language and
frequently met with in the
comic writers. Even Cicero uses
it occasionally, e. g. Off. II 15,
13 *quae te malum ratio in istam
spem induxit?* 'what the deuce
could lead you to such a hope?'
Verr. I 20, 54 *quae malum est
ista tanta audacia atque amen-
tia?* It always expresses a
strong degree of indignation
and anger.
427. The disjunctive question *utrum—ne—an* is explained
by Key, L. G. § 1425 (with note),
Zumpt, § 554, Madvig, § 452, 1:
examples will be found Trin.
306. Capt. II 2, 18. Bacch. 75.
500. Poen. supp. 32. Pseud.
709. Enn. frag. 38, ed. Vahlen:
see also my note on Ter. Eun.
IV 4, 54.

me hau paénitet, tua ne éxpetam.   Ev. scio, né
    doce, novi.   20
Con. quid est quá nunc prohibes grátia nos cóquere
    hic cenam ?
quid fécimus, quid díximus tibi sécus quam velles ?
Ev. etiám rogitas, sceléste homo ? qui*ne* ánglos
    omnis
435 mearum aédium et conclávium mihi pér*turb*atis ?
id úbi tibi erat negótium, ad focúm si adesses,   25
non físsile *hoc* haberés caput: merito íd tibi factumst.
a*t* út tu meam senténtiam iam nóscere possis,   27
si ad iánuam huc accésseris, nisi iússo, propius,
440 ego té faciam, misérrumus mortális ut sis.
scis iám meam senténtiam? quo abís? redi rursum. 30
Con. ita mé bene amet Lavérna, te iam*iám* nisi
    reddi

431. *me hau paenitet* 'I am
very well satisfied :' see my
note on Ter. Eun. v 6, 12.
Zumpt, § 441. Translate 'I am
content enough, so do not suppose that I should steal your
property.' *ne expetam tua* is
a brief expression instead of
ne existumes me tua expetere :
see Key, L. G. § 1228. Zumpt,
§ 573. For *doce͂* see Introd. p.
26.
    434. For the syncopated form
anglos comp. Probus, p. 197, 22
'*baculus* non *baclus*, *angulus*
non *anglus*,' whence *anglus* appears to have been a vulgar or
popular contraction.
    435. For the pronunciation
of *mearum* see Introd. p. 62.—
The mss. read *pervium* or *perviam facitis*, but *perviam* is no
Latin word, though one might
support it with the analogous
obviam. I have, therefore,
written *perturbatis* 'you upset,'

though I do not think this conjecture absolutely certain.
    437. *fissile caput* 'a broken
head.' The adjective *fissilis* is
of rare occurrence, and is in no
other passage added to *caput* or
any other part of the human
body.
    438. Comp. Ter. Phorm. v
8, 54 *immo ut tu iam scias
meam sententiam.*
    439. *iusso* = *iussero*, which is
here given by the mss., though
inadmissible on prosodiacal
grounds. *nisi iusso* 'contrary
to my orders.'
    440. The prolepsis *te faciam
ut sis miserrumus* needs no further explanation: comp. v. 790.
Examples of this kind of construction are given by Gronovius in his note on Gellius II 1.
    442. For *ita* comp. v. 754.
Key, L. G. § 1451 e.—*Laverna*
was originally a goddess of
darkness and hence naturally

mihi vasa iubes, pipulo hic differam ante aedis.
quíd ego nunc agám ? ne ego edepol véni huc auspi-
ció malo :
445 númmo sum condúctus : plus iam médico mercedíst
opus.
Ev. hóc quidem hercle quóquo *ego* ibo, mécum erit,
mecúm feram,   III. 3
néque ist*ic* in tantís periclis úmquam committam
út siet.
íte sane intro ómnes nunciam ét coqui et tibícinae :
étiam *huc* intro dúce, si vis, vél gregem venálium.
450 cóquite facite féstinate núnciam, quantúm lubet.   5
Con. témperi, postquam ímplevisti fústi fissorúm
caput.

became the patroness and protectress of thieves. In a fragment of Plautus' Cornicularia a
thief prays to Laverna: comp.
Hor. Ep. i 16, 60 *pulcra La-*
verna, Da mihi fallere, da iusto
sanctoque videri : Noctem pec-
catis et fraudibus obice nubem,
on which passage Porphyrio observes 'larvearum dea, quae
furibus praeest.' See Preller,
röm. Myth. p. 218. 459. Comp.
also Webster ed. Dyce (1866)
p. 294 a : *Success then, sweet*
Laverna! I have heard That
thieves adore thee for a deity.
From Paulus we learn '*laver-*
niones fures antiqui dicebant,
quod sub tutela deae Lavernae
essent, in cuius luco obscuro
abditoque solitos furta prae-
damque inter se luere:' another
derivation of the name ἀπὸ τοῦ
λαβεῖν is of course only a *mau-*
vais jeu d'esprit. By praying to
Laverna, Congrio himself proves
that Strobilus (v. 320) was not
mistaken in his character.
443. The reading and the

scansion of this line are anything but certain. *pipulus* is
said to mean *convicium.* Comp.
Mil. gl. 584 *nam nunc satis pi-*
pulo impio merui mali, where
the reading is, however, not
quite settled. To a scene similar to the present may have
belonged the lines quoted from
Matius' Mimiambi by Gellius
xx 9 : *dein coquenti vása cuncta*
deiéctat, Nequámve scitaménta
pipuló póscit. Except these
passages, the word is quoted
from no other author but Ap-
puleïus.
445. For *nummus* see note
on v. 108.
449. *grex venalium* 'a gang
of slaves:' comp. Cist. iv 2, 6*l*
mirum quin grex venalium in
cistella infuerit una. The same
expression occurs in the Pseudo-
Ciceronian speech *cum senatui*
gratias egit 6, 14 *Cappadocem*
modo abreptum de grege venali-
um diceres.
451. *temperi* occurs nineteen
times in Plautus, but never in

Ev. íntro abi*te*: opera húc conductast vóstra, non
    orátio.
Con. heús, senex, pro vápulando hercle égo abs te
    mercedém petam.
cóctum ego, non vápulatum, dúdum conductús fui.
4.55 Ev. lége agito mecúm: molestus né sis: i, cenám
    coque,   10
aút abi in malúm cruciatum ab aédibus. Con. abi
    tú modo.
Ev. íllic hinc abiit. di ímmortales, fácinus audax
    íncipit   III. 4
quí cum opulento paúper coepit rém habere aut
    negótium.
véluti me Megadórus temptat ómnibus miserúm
    modis :
460 quí simulavit meí *se* honoris míttere huc causá coquos,
ís ea causa mísit hoc qui súbru*p*erent miseró mihi. 5
cóndigne etiam méus me*d* intus gállus gallinácius

Terence. In all the Plautine
passages, *temperi* is the reading
of the best authorities, not *tempori*, except Capt. 183 where
the best ms. reads *tempori*.
The comparative *temperius* is
used by Cicero, Ovid, Columella,
Appuleius and Palladius : *tem-
porius* is found only in inferior
mss. See Ritschl in Reifferscheid's Suetonius p. 507 ss.—
With the whole sentence comp.
Cas. ii 7, 60 *temperi, postquam
oppugnatumst os. — fissum* as
subst. is reported from only one
other passage, in Celsus. Weise
compares *fissa volnera* Val.
Flacc. i 479. For the genitive
see Key, L. G. § 941. In Cas.
i 1, 35 *ego te implebo flagris* we
have the same way of speaking
with a different construction.
    453. For the shortened
quantity of *abs* see Introd. p. 57.

454. The long final *o* in *ego*
may be defended, nor do we
deem it necessary to write *cóctum ego [huc]* after the example
of v. 452.
    455. *lege agito* 'go to law,
if you want any further expos-
tulation,' i. e. you won't get
anything out of me by talking
on ever so much. The same
phrase occurs with this sense
Ter. Phorm. v 7, 91.
    456. *in malam rem abire, in
malam crucem* or *in malum cruciatum abire* are all expressions
of the same kind 'to go to the
d—.'
    458. For the hiatus *rém ha-
bere* see Introd. p. 68.
    462. In all the passages
where *condigne* occurs, it gives
the expression a sarcastic or
ironical colouring: e.g. Poen.
ii 17 *condigne haruspex, non*

qui ánui erat pecúliaris pérdidit paeníssume.
úbi erat haec defóssa, occepit íbi scalpurrire úngulis
465 círcumcirca. quíd opust verbis ? íta mi pectus pér-
acuit :
cápio fustem, optrúnco gallum, fúrem manufestá-
rium.   10
crédo edepol ego illí mercedem gállo pollicitós coquos,
si íd palam fecísset. exemi éx manu *istis* mánubrium.

---

homo trioboli—aiebat portendi mihi i.e. what else could I have expected? Cas. I 1, 43 *noctu ut condigne te cubes* (i.e. very badly) *curabitur.* See also Bacch. 392. Men. 906 ; only Capt. I 2, 22 the adverb has not an ironical sense.—*gallinācĕus* is the quantity of this word in Plautus, Lucilius, Titinius (126 Ribb.) and Phaedrus : see Lachmann on Lucr. p. 36.—Bücheler (rhein. Mus. xx 441) quotes the spelling *gallinacius* (instead of the common *gallinaceus*) from the best authorities in Varro Ονος λ. II, Cicero Mur. § 61, Phaedrus III 12, 1, Petron. 86 and an inscription Orelli 4330. In the same way we have the otherwise unexampled formation *viracius* in a fragment of Varro's Meleager (see Riese, rhein. Mus. xxI 121).

463. The adverb *paenissume* recurs v. 660. That the first syllable should be spelt with a diphthong, appears from Priscian who in two passages declares *paenissime* to be the superlative of *paene :* see Ritschl's note on Most. 656. This derivation is also borne out by the meaning 'very nearly.'

464. *scalpurrire* appears to be a ἅπ. λεγ.: it is by no means a desiderative, in which case

the *u* would be short and we ought to have *scalpturire* (as indeed most editors perversely read : conf. also *scalpturio* κατακνάω Gloss. Labb. p. 165), but it is of the same formation as *ligurrire* and *scaturrire* (Zumpt § 232): for *ligurrire* (not *ligurire*) see Bentley's note on Ter. Eun. v 4, 14.

465. *peracuit* ' became exasperated,' comp. Bacch. 1099 *hoc hoc est quo pectus peracescit.* The word does not occur elsewhere.

466. The adjective *manufestarius* recurs Trin. 895. Mil. gl. 444. Bacch. 918 : in allusion to the last passage the word is used by Gellius I 7. All other writers say *manifestus.* — ' *manifestus fur est qui in faciendo* [ἐπ' αὐτοφώρῳ] *deprehensus est* ' Paullus, Sent. II 31, 2.

468. The *u* in *manŭbrium* cannot be lengthened by the following letters *br*, since muta cum liquida never has that effect in Plautus. *manubrium* properly means a hilt or a handle, but here it assumes a figurative sense ' occasion, opportunity.' Plautus has the word in only one other passage, Epid. 516 (Bothe) *málleum sapiéntiorem vídi excusso mánŭbrio,* a line which is omitted in all our

séd Megadorus, méus adfinis, éccum.incedit á foro.
470 iam húnc non ausim praéterire, quín consistam et
cónloquar.

MEGADORVS.   EVCLIO.   III. 5

MEG. narrávi amicis múltis consilíúm meum
de cóndicione hac: Eúclionis fíliam
laudánt : sapienter fáctum et consilió bono.
nam meó quidem animo, si ídem faciant céteri
475 opuléntiores, paúperiorum fílias   5
ut índotatas dúcant uxorés domum :
et múlto fiat cívitas concórdior
et invídia nos minóre·utamur quam útimur,

mss. except the Ambrosian palimpsest.
469. *incedit:* see note on
v. 47.
470. For *ausim* see Key,
L. G. § 482.
471 ss. Megadorus, who as
a worthy old man is naturally
inclined and entitled to criticise social nuisances and com-
plaints, supports in the following scene the reforming views
entertained by Cato and his
political friends. There are
besides the present passage so
many allusions in the comedies
of Plautus to the great luxu-
ry of the Roman ladies, that
it would be preposterous to rely
on them for the chronology of
the plays themselves : but only
two scenes are found in the
nineteen plays extant, where a
considerable number of lines
is exclusively devoted to this
subject, and surely such long
passages cannot be treated like
occasional allusions, as their

tendency and purpose are open-
ly avowed (comp. here v.
474 ss.). The one of these
passages, Epid. ii 2, 38—51,
cannot originally have formed
part of the scene in which it
stands now, as I have shown
elsewhere, and should therefore
be left out of the question ; but
the other, i. e. the present scene
in the Aulularia, we are entitled
to use for placing the Aulularia after the year 560, nay we
may even go further and range
it among the later plays of the
poet.
472. *condicio* 'match:' see
on v. 235.
473. *laudant* or rather a
more general notion which we
may infer from this verb, e.g.
dicunt, governs the construction of the words *sapienter factum*.
478. For the short quantity
of the first syllable in *invidia*
see Introd. p. 48.—In this
line, v. 479, 480 and 489 we

et illaé malam rem métuant quam metuónt magis,
480 et nós minore súmptu simus quám sumus.   10
in máxumam illuc pópuli partemst óptumum :
in paúciores ávidos altercátiost,
quorum ánimis avidis átque insatietátibus
neque léx neque tutor cápere est qui possít modum.
485 namque hóc qui dicat : quó illae nubent dívites   15
dotátae, si istuc iús pauperibus pónitur ?
quo lúbeat nubant, dúm dos ne fiát comes.
hoc sí ita fiat, móres meliorés sibi
parént pro dote quós ferant quam núnc ferunt.

may briefly draw the attention
of the student to a peculiarity of Latin : in comparisons
the same verb is repeated,
while in modern languages, e.g.
English and French, the most
general verb in the language
' to do ' ' faire' is substituted.

479. *mala res* frequently denotes ' punishment ' in the language of the comic writers.

481 ss. This line seems the
sole instance of the construction *bonum est in aliquem* ' it is
good for.' *in* would however
admit of the same explanation
as in such phrases as *pessume
in te atque in illum consulis*
Ter. Haut. tim. III 1, 28. The
next line contains another difficulty first pointed out by
Linge de hiatu p. 8: 'alterca-
tionem facimus *cum aliquo*,
non *in aliquem;*' but *in* seems
here to denote the object a-
gainst which the *altercatio* (i.e.
political contention) is directed :
see Zumpt § 314. This very
meaning of *altercatio* is, however, only assumed for this
passage.

483. *insatietas* ' a greedy disposition,' ἅπ. λεγ. Ammianus

Marcellinus has *insatiabilitas*.

484. Very probably we should
suppose that Plautus found in
the Greek original of his play a
passage treating of the un-
protected position of wealthy
ἐπίκληροι, orphan heiresses.
Though they have a *tutor*
(guardian), they are nevertheless exposed to the aggressions
of those who are on the look
out for rich matches. The expression is, however, somewhat
peculiar, as the common phrase
appears to be *capere modum
legis alicuius* (in legal phrase-
ology), but not *lex capit modum alicuius rei.* Possibly, we
should have to write *facere* instead of *capere*, or we should
take *capere modum* in the sense
of *ponere (imponere), statuere
(constituere) modum alicui rei.*
We may also say that *capere
modum* = *moderari.*

488. For the hiatus *si ita*
see Introd. p. 68.

489. *pro* ' instead of :' see
Key, L. G. § 1361 c. The phrase
mores ferre is to be explained
on the analogy of the usual expression *dotem ferre.*

490 ego fáxim muli, prétio qui superánt equos,   20
sint víliores Gállicis canthériis.
Ev. ita mé di amabunt, út ego hunc auscultó lubens:
nimis lépide fecit vérba ad parsimóniam.
Meg. nulla ígitur dicat 'équidem dotem ad te
ádtuli
495 maiórem multo quám tibi erat pecúnia.   25
enim míhi quidem aequomst púrpuram atque aurúm
dari,
ancíllas mulos múliones pédisequos
salútigerulos púeros, vehicla quí vehar.'
Ev. ut mátronarum hic fácta pernovít probe :

490. For *faxim* see Key,
L. G. § 566.—'It was the cus-
tom for ladies of rank to have
their carriages drawn by mules.'
Thornton. Martial says in one
of his epigrams (iii 62) that
mules were sometimes sold at
a higher price than whole
houses. Hildyard quotes Juv.
vii 181.
491. *viliores* has here its
original meaning 'cheaper.'—
'*cantherius* = κανθήλιος (with the
interchange of *l* and *r*) 'geldings.'
They were not highly valued
and generally considered to be
lazy and sleepy, comp. Men. 395
canterino astans ritu somniat.
493. The syllables *nimis lépi-*
form a proceleusmatic, the *s* in
nimis being dropped : Introd. p.
31.—*lepidus* is very difficult to
translate by one word in its
different shades, though the
schoolboy's English furnishes
us with the equally flexible term
jolly. The word is very frequent in the comic writers, we
find it afterwards in Catullus
(1, 1. 6, 17. 36, 10) and even in
Horace, ars poët.273.—*ad* 'for:'
see Key, L. G. § 1305 e.

496. *enim* frequently has the
sense of *enimvero:* see Key, L.
G. § 1449. Ruhnken on Ter.
Phorm. iv 4, 13 justly observes
'solis comicis quos Appuleius
imitatur, usitatum est hanc
particulam adversativam ab initio ponere.'
498. *salutigerulus* is a ἅπ.
λεγ. The editors quote '*salutigerulus ἐπισκέπτης*' from the
glosses collected by Labbaeus
p. 163; we may compare the
analogous formations *sandali-
gerula* Trin. 252, and *nugige-
rulus,* as our mss. read Aul. 518.
salutiger occurs in Ausonius
(*salutiger Iuppiter* and *salutigeri libelli*), Prudentius (*salutigeri ortus*) and Appuleius speaks
of demons as *salutigeri* '*qui
ultro citroque portant hinc peti-
tiones, inde suppetias.*' The
meaning is rightly explained by
a French translator 'petits la-
quais qu'on envoye de côté et
d'autre pour savoir des nou-
velles de ses amis, leur faire des
compliments de notre part'—
in short *tigers.*—For *qui* see
Key, L. G. § 312.

500 moríbus praefectum múlierum hunc factúm velim. 30
MEG. nunc quóquo venias, plús plaustrorum in
aédibus
videás quam ruri quándo ad villam véneris.
sed hoc étiam pulcrumst praéquam sumptus úbi
petunt.
stat fúllo phyrgio aúrifex linárius
505 caupónes patagiárii indusiárii   35

500. For the accentuation
moríbus see note on v. 137.
For the whole passage we may
coñpare a fragment from Cic.
de republ. iv *nec vero mulieri-
bus praefectus praeponatur qui
apud Graecos creari solet : sed
sit censor qui viros doceat moderari uxoribus.* It would be
somewhat gratuitous to conjecture that there actually was a
scheme on foot to propose the
institution of γυναικονόμοι or
γυναικοκόσμοι in Rome such as
there were in several Greek re-
publics, and that Plautus ventured to hint at this.
503. *pulcrumst* is of course
ironical.—Of the particle *prae-
quam* there are five instances
in Plautus: this line, Merc. 23.
Most. 982. 1146 and Amph. ii
2, 3; it does not occur in
Terence and the fragments of
the other comic writers, but in
later times Gellius uses it again
xvi 1. In the same way Plautus has the particle *praeut:*
Amph. i 1, 218. Men. 376.
935. Mil. gl. 20. Bacch. 929.
Merc. 470. Ritschl and Fleckeisen write *prae quam* in two
words, and should consequently
also write *prae ut* which they
do not.
504. The word *linarius* occurs only here in Plautus, but

is also quoted from an inscription, Gruter p. 649, 3.
505. *caupones* 'retail deal-
ers.' '*patagium*' *est quod ad
summam tunicam assui solet,
quae et patagiata* (Epid. ii 2,
47) *dicitur, et 'patagiarii' qui
eiusmodi opera faciunt.* Festus :
the word *indusiarii* is however a ἀπ. λεγ.—Our mss. give
here *indusiarii,* and *indusiatam*
Epid. ii 2, 47 : but Varro derives the word from *intus* de l.
l. v 131 p. 51 M. and accordingly writes *intusium,* and from
this source Nonius derives his
information p. 539, 31 '*indusi-
um est vestimentum quod cor-
pori intra plurimas vestes ad-
haeret, quasi intusium.* Plautus
in Epidico' etc. p. 542, 22 he
quotes from Varro de vita pop.
Rom. i (=p. 237 ed. Bip.)
'*posteaquam binas tunicas habere coeperunt, instituerunt vocare subuculam et indussam*
(thus the mss.). The adjective
indusiatus occurs in Appuleius
and the verb *indusiare* in Mar-
tianus Capella. On the *indu-
sium* itself, Böttiger (Sabina 2,
113 sec. ed.) has the following
remarks. 'The shirt was a
kind of under-tunic (*interula*)
made either of linen (*linea,*
Salm. ad scr. h. a. i 972) or of
cotton (*byssinae*). It was worn

flammárii violárii carárii
propólae linteónes calceolárii
sedentárii sutóres di*a*bathrárii—
soleárii astant, ástant molocinárii,   40
[strophiarii astant, astant semisonarii]
510 petúnt fullones, sárcinatorés petunt
pro illís crocotis stróphiis sumptu uxório.
iam hosce ábsolutos cénseas : cedúnt petunt
trecén*ti* : *ci*rcumstánt phylacistae in átriis,

by both sexes : for men it was
called *subucula*, for women *intusium* (Ferrar. de re vest. 3, 1
p. 175), precisely as the English
distinguish between *shirt* and
shift. The negligé or morning-
dress of ladies indoors consist-
ed, as we see from many passages in Ovid and Propertius,
in nothing but such a shirt
which when fitting very tightly,
did not even require to be fast-
ened by a belt...but as it might
easily become very troublesome
on account of its length, it was
generally kept together by a
semizona, at least until the proper tunic was thrown over it.'
506. *cararius* occurs only
here: *ceraria* stands in the
mss. Mil. gl. 694, where the
reading seems however very uncertain. Comp. Ov. ars am.
III 184 *et sua velleribus nomina
cera dedit.*
507. *linteo* 'a linen-weaver'
occurs here, in Servius on Aen.
VII 14, and an inscription Gruter p. 38, 15.—*calceolarius* 'a
shoemaker,' *ἀπ*. *λεγ*.
508. *diabathrarius* 'a maker
of slippers,' occurs only here,
diabathrum (i. e. the Greek *διά-
βαθρον*) is quoted from Naevius
by Varro.
509. *solearius* occurs only

here and Gruter 648, 13 ; *molo-
cinarius* (or *moloch.*) here and
in an inscription Muratori 939,
6. I am inclined to consider
this line as spurious : for, first
of all, why should the *solearii*
be named after the *diabath-
rarii ?* and then, how could the
poet name *solearii* and *moloci-
narii*, members of very different
professions, in one and the
same breath?
510. In this line the two
professions which mend old
garments are appropriately
mentioned together.
511. The *strophium* or *mam-
millare* and *fascia* was a kind
of belt worn to keep the female
bosom straight : see Smith's
Dictionary of Antiquities s. v.
512. *cedunt=incedunt*, comp.
colere=incolere v. 4.
513. *trecenti* denotes here
a great number or multitude,
much in the same way as *sescenta* v. 318. Hildyard quotes
the following examples of this
use : Cat. 9, 2. 11, 18. 12, 10.
Hor. od. III 4, 79. See also
Plaut. Mil. gl. 250.—*phylacistae :* the importunate credi-
tors waiting for their money
are compared with *jailers*. The
word only here. Comp., however, *phylaca* Capt. 747. The

textóres limbulárii arculárii : 45
515 aut áliqua mala crux sémper est quae aliquíd
petat.
Ev. compéllem ego illum, ní metuam ne désinat
memoráre mores múlierum : nunc síc sinam. 50
Meg. ubi núgigerulis rés solutast ómnibus,
ibi ád postremum cédit miles, aés petit.
520 itúr, putatur rátio cum argentário :
milés impransus ástat, aes censét dari.
ubi dísputatast rátio cum argentário, 55
[etiam plus ipsus ultro debet argentario]
spes prórogatur míliti in aliúm diem.
haec súnt atque aliae múltae in magnis dótibus
525 incómmoditates súmptusque intolerábiles.
nam quae índotatast, éa in potestate ést viri : 60

reading of this line and the following is however not quite
certain.
514. *arcularii* ' cabinet-
makers.' Hildyard quotes Cic.
Off. ii 7, 25 *scrutari arculas
muliebres*, and Varro de l. l.
viii 45 (?) *ut lectus et lectulus,
arca et arcula, sic alia.*
518. For *ubi—ibi* Brix on
Trin. 417 quotes Curc. i 2, 7
and Epid. ii 1, 1.
519. ' The public expenses,
of which the payment of the
army formed a considerable
part, fell of course mostly on
the shoulders of the richer
classes which possessed more
landed property : and accordingly the husband of a rich
wife had to bear all the taxes
laid on her property.' Koepke.
The military tax was called *aes
militare*, an expression also
found Poen. v 5, 7, though in
a different sense.
520. ' Disputatio *et* compu-
tatio *cum praepositione a* putan-

do *quod valet purum facere.
ideo antiqui purum* putum *ad-
pellarunt, ideo* putator *quod ar-
bores puras facit : ideo* ratio
putari *dicitur in qua summa sit
pura.*' Varro de l. l. vi 63
p. 97. M. Scaliger in his note
on the passage observes that
Plutarch uses the analogous expression ἐκκαθᾶραι λογισμόν ; we
may also compare the English
phrase *to clear one's debts* and
the German *eine rechnung in 's
reine bringen.* For examples
see Trin. 417. Most. 299. Cas.
iii 2, 25.
521. The last syllable of
miles is used long by Plautus
here and Curc. 728; in the
same manner, we read *divēs*
Asin. 330. See C. F. W. Müller,
Plaut. Pros. p. 49.
524. *haec* is frequently found
as the fem. plur. in the best
mss. of Plautus, Terence and
Cicero, nay Lucretius never
uses *hae*: see Munro on iii 601
and vi 456.

dotátae mactant ét malo et damnó viros.
sed éccum adfinem ante aédis. quid agis, Eúclio ?
Ev. nimiúm lubenter édi sermoném tuom.   III. 6
530 MEG. ain, aúdivisti? Ev. úsque a principio ómnia.
MEG. tamen meó quidem animo aliquánto facias
      réctius
si nítidior sis fíliai núptiis.
Ev. pro ré nitorem et glóriam pro cópia.   5
qui habént, meminerint sése unde oriundí sient.
535 neque pól, Megadore, míhi nec quoiquam paúperi
opínione melius rés structást domi.
MEG. immo ést et *ita* di fáciant ut *sempér* siet
plus plúsque istuc *tibi* sóspitent quod núnc habes.   10

527. On *mactare* and the use of this word in Plautus and Terence it suffices to refer to the commentators on Ter. Phorm. v 8, 39. *mac-tus* is derived with the suffix *tu* from *mag-*, the root of *mag-nus* : see Corssen, krit. Beitr. p. 423.—*malum* wretched life, *damnum* unnecessary expense.

529. *edi* 'I have devoured.' Thornton compares Shakespeare, *Othello* I 3 '*She'd come again and with a greedy ear Devour up my discourse.*' Plautus uses a similar expression, Cist. IV 2, 54 *mihi cibus est quod fabulare* and Most. 1062 *gustare ego eius sermonem volo*, and in the Asinaria we read the exact expression *devorare dicta*. In Greek we have similar phrases: φαγεῖν ῥήματα in Aristophanes, and εὐωχεῖσθαι λόγους in Plato.

530. For the hiatus in this line see Introd. p. 67.—*usque a :* note on v. 248.

531. This line might be metrically, though awkwardly, explained: tam mó | quid áni|mo aliquán|to faci|as réc|tius, but

there are important reasons to suspect the genuineness of the reading.

532. *nitidus* is here synonymous with *lautus* or *splendidus :* thus Plautus says Pseud. 774 *curari nitidiuscule* and Cist. I 1, 10 *lepide atque nitide accipere.* In Hor. Ep. I 4, 15 *me pinguem et nitidum, bene curata cute vises* the word has its original sense.

533. *pro* 'in proportion to, in accordance with:' see Key, L. G. § 1361 g. Gronovius appropriately compares Hor. Serm. I 2, 19 *pro quaestu sumptum facit* 'he lives up to his income.'—*gloria* show, pomp, parade: comp. Hor. Ep. I 18, 22 *gloria...supra vires et vestit et ungit.* The *gloire* of the French nation is very frequently *gloria* in this sense of the Latin word. Thornton uses in his translation the proverb *to cut one's coat according to the cloth.*

534. *habere* absolutely used 'to possess, to be rich:' comp. Truc. IV 2, 3.

Ev. illúd mihi verbum nón placet 'quod núnc habes.'
540 tam hic scít me habere quam égomet: anus fecít
     palam.
Meg. quid tú te solus é senatu sévocas?
Ev. pol ego út te accusem, mécum meditabár. Meg.
     quid est?
Ev. quid sít me rogitas, quí mihi omnis ángulos   15
     furum ímplevisti in aédibus, miseró mihi
545 qui intró misisti in aédis quingentós coquos
     cum sénis manibus, génere Geryonáceo.
     quos si 'Argus servet, qui óculeus totús fuit,
     (quem quóndam Ioni Iúno custodem áddidit)   20
     is númquam servet. praéterea tibícinam
550 quae mi ínterbibere sóla, si vinó scatat,
     Corínthiensem fóntem Pirenám potest.

541. *senatus* ' a consulta-
tion,' comp. Mil. gl. 592 and
594. This expression is foreign
to Terence.
    542. For the apparent vio-
lation of the usual rules of the
consecutio temporum in *medita-
bar ut accusem*, see the examples collected by Draeger I
p. 298.
    544. For the genitive *furum*
see Key, L. G. § 941. See above
v. 451. In the same way *com-
plere* has the genitive after it
Amph. I 2, 8 s. Men. 901. *re-
plere* Poen. III 3, 88.
    545. *quingentos* denotes here
a great number, in the same
way as we have *sescenta* v. 318
and *trecenti* v. 513. Mercklin
(ind. schol. Dorpat. 1862 p. xiii)
compares Mil. gl. 52 and Curc.
587.
    547. Appuleius Metam. II
p. 40 ed. Bip. manifestly imitates this passage in describing
a restless, suspicious fellow who
pries into everything: *vides*

*hominem insomnem, certe per-
spicaciorem ipso Lynceo vel
Argo, et oculeum totum.*
    548. For *custodem addere*
comp. Mil. gl. 146. 298. 305
(where the mss. read *tradidit*,
but Ritschl rightly gives *addidit*
from Douza's conjecture) and
Capt. III 5, 50. The same expression occurs Hor. Od. III 4,
78.
    550. For *interbibere* see Key,
L. G. § 1342, 1 d.—*scatat*, not
from *scatēre*, but *scatĕre*: this
infinitive occurs in a fragment
of an anonymous tragic poet
quoted by Cic. Tusc. I 28, 69
(Ribb. trag. 217) and three
times in Lucretius, who has
also *scatit*, see Munro on v 40.
    551. The earlier Roman
poets always turn Greek names
and words into the appearance
of Latin forms, and accordingly
give them Latin terminations.
The forms *Oresten Echion Sala-
mina* as found in Ennius and
Pacuvius are solitary excep-

tum obsónium autem pól vel le*gi*oní sat est.
MEG. etiam ágnum misi.　Ev. quó quidem agno
　　sát scio　　　　　　　　　　　　　　　　25
magis cúrionem núsquam esse ullam béluam.
555 MEG. volo ego éx te scire quí sit agnus cúrio.
Ev. quia óssa ac pellis tótust : ita curá macet.
quin éxta inspicere in sóle e*i* vivó licet :
ita ís pellucet quási lanterna Púnica.　　　30
MEG. caedúndum illum ego condúxi.　Ev. tum tu
　　idem óptumumst

tions. The introduction of pure
Greek forms is one of the characteristic features of the Augustan period. Hence we have
in the present passage *Pirenam*,
not *Pirenen*.

552. Hildyard appropriately
compares Massinger, City Ma-
dam 1 1 *provision enough to serve
a garrison.*

554. Appuleius imitates this
passage in calling a fat lamb
agnus incuriosus Flor. 2. p.
113 ed. Bp., whence it appears
that he found in his text the
gloss *curiosam* which has super-
seded the genuine reading *curi-
onem* in all mss. The peculiar
meaning of *curio* is of course
coined on purpose for the present passage. Euclio, too, im-
parts to *curio* the sense of *care-
worn*.

556. Comp. *ossa atque pellis
sum miser aegritudine* 'only skin
and bones' Capt. 1 2, 32. The
expression appears to be proverbial : comp. Theoc. 11 89
αὐτὰ δὲ λοιπὰ ὄστι᾽ ἔτ᾽ ἦς καὶ
δέρμα. Horace has a similar
expression *ossa pelle amicta
lurida* Epod. 17, 22.

558. I have kept the form
lanterna as given by the ms. *B* :
in the only other two passages

where this word occurs in Plautus, Amph. prol. 149 and ib. 1
1, 249, *B* has *laterna*, and in *J*
the lines in question are illegi-
ble. In the line from the prologue to the Amphitruo I should
propose to read *Illíc a portu
nunc cum laterna ádvenit.* For
lanterna see also Bücheler,
rhein. Mus. xviii 393 and W.
Schmitz ibid. xix 301. Compare the French *lanterne* and
the Italian *lanterna*. The *laterna Punica* is only here mentioned ; Weise says ' forte e
vitro facta :' and this opinion
seems not quite without foundation, when we consider that
the invention of glass is generally ascribed to the Phoeni-
cians.—Beaumont and Fletcher,
poets who like to show off their
learning, manifestly imitate this
passage in 'The Scornful Lady'
11 3 p. 301 ed. Lond. 1750 :
'*Serv.* Yonder's a cast of coach-
mares of the gentlewoman's, the
strangest cattle.　*Wel.* Why?
Serv. Why, they are trans-
parent, sir, you may see through
them.'

559. ' Qui opus aliquod, hoc
est materiam aliquam efforman-
dam effingendam elaborandam
alicui tradit, is *locare : condu-*

560 loces écferendum. nám iam credo mórtuost.
MEG. potáre ego hoc die, Eúclio, tecúm volo.
Ev. non *quód* potem ego quidem *hábeo* hercle.
MEG. at ego iússero
cadum únum vini véteris a me adférrier.　　35
Ev. nolo hércle: nam mihi bíbere decretúmst aquam.
565 MEG. ego te hódie reddam mádidum, si vivó, probe,
tibi quoí decretumst bíbere aquam. Ev. scio quám
　　rem agat.
ut mé deponat víno, eam adfectát viam :

cere vero qui illud opus susci-
piat, dicitur.' Lindemann on
Capt. ɪv 2, 39. *conducere* is
here simply *to buy, locare* in
the next line *to put out.* Euclio
plays upon the word *locare*
which would remind any one
of the phrase *funus locare* 'to
contract with an undertaker
about a funeral.' This becomes
the more pungent, as Euclio
advises Megadorus to bespeak
the lamb's funeral while it is
still alive.

562. The future perf. *ius-
sero* stands here, as it often
does in the comic writers, in
the sense of the simple future
iubebo or rather the subj. perf.
iusserim: see Key, L. G. § 476.

563. Translate *cadum unum*
'just one bottle.'– *a me = a mea
domo:* in the same way we have
a nobis 'from our house' Mil.
gl. 339, and both together *a
nobis domost* Cist. ɪv 1. 6.

565. *madidus* and the Greek
βεβρεγμένος often mean 'drunk,'
e.g. Amph. ɪɪɪ 4, 18. As. v 2, 9.
madide madere Pseud. 1297.
Hildyard compares the English
expression *to moisten one's clay.*
See also Heindorf's note on
Hor. Sat. ɪɪ 1, 9.—*si vivo* 'by
my life' ('so wahr ich lebe' in

German) is frequently found in
Plautus and Terence. Pareus
gives the following examples:
Cas. ɪ 1, 28. Most. 1067. Men.
903. Bacch. 766. Ter. Andr.
v 2, 25. Eun. v 6, 19. Haut.
tim. v 1, 45.

566. *tibi quoi* stands for *te
quoi* in consequence of a kind
of attraction or assimilation,
of which I find two other instances: Epid. ɪɪɪ 1, 8 *tibi quoi
divitiae domi maxumae Sunt is
nummum nullum habes* and Curc.
ɪɪ 2, 17 *namque incubare satius
te fuerat Iovi, Tibi quoi auxilium in iure iurando fuit.*

567. *deponere vino* is used
in precisely the same way by
Aurelius Victor, de vir. inl. 71
*Caepio cum aliter vincere non
posset, duos satellites pecunia
corrupit qui Viriathum* vino
(others *humi*) depositum *pere-
merunt.—adfectare viam* is 'to
try, to attempt,' Men. 686 *ut
me defrudes, ad eam rem adfec-
tas viam.* Terence has the
same phrase Haut. tim. ɪ 3, 60
and Phorm. v 7, 71, where
Donatus observes '*adfectant
viam, plenum, quod nos* ἐλ-
λειπτικῶς.' Cicero has *iter
adfectare* pro Roscio Am. 48,
140.

post hóc quod habeo ut cómmutet colóniam.   40
ego íd cavebo : nam álicubi abstrudám foris.
570 ego fáxo et operam et vínum perdiderít simul.
Meg. ego nísi quid me vis, éo lavatum ut sácru-
    ficem.
Ev. edepól ne tu, aula, múltos inimicós habes,
atque ístuc aurum quód tibi concréditumst.   45
nunc hóc mihi factust óptumum, ut te*d* aúferam,
575 aula, ín Fidei fánum : ibi abstrudám probe.
Fidés, novisti me ét ego te : cave sís tibi
ne tu ímmutassis nómen, si hoc concréduo.
ibo ád te, fretus tuá, Fides, fidúcia.   50

---

568. *colonia* appears here in its original sense (from *colo = incolo*), 'a dwelling-place:' see Epid. iii 2, 7 and Pseud. 1100. In the Asin. ii 2, 32 *catenarum colonus* means a familiar inmate of the prison.— For *cónmutét* see note on *pistillúm* v. 95.

571. Servius on Aen. iii 136 observes *apud veteres neque uxor duci neque ager arari sine sacrificiis peractis poterat.*—It is not at all improbable that a line has dropped out after v. 571, in which the leave-taking of the two *affines* was contained.

573. For *tibi* see Introd. p. 23.

574. With the construction *optimum factu* we may comp. Mil. gl. 101, *qui est amor cultu optumus.*

575. *Fidēi:* Introd. p. 14. Key, L. G. § 147.

577. For the form *immutassis = inmutaveris* see note on v. 226. The verb *immutare* occurs three times in Plautus.—*concreduo:* see on v. 62.—The sense is 'Do not allow yourself to be called *infida*, though your name is *Fides;*' comp. 607. 659 s.

ACTVS IV.

STROBILVS (II)   IV. 1

Hóc est servi fácinus frugi, fácere quod ego pér-
    sequor :
580 né morae moléstiaeque impérium erile habeát sibi.
nám qui ero ex senténtia servíre servos póstulat,
ín erum matura, ín se sera cóndecet capéssere.
sín dormitet, íta dormitet, sérvom sese ut cógitet :   5
[nám qui amanti ero sérvitutem sérvit, quasi ego
    sérvio,   6

One of the greatest difficulties in the Aulularia consists in the name and character of the slave *Strobilus* who makes his appearance in the first scene of this act. That the *Strobilus* of the first scene of the third act cannot be the same person with this, may be readily perceived ; nor is it easy to believe that Plautus would have designated two different characters by one and the same name. The most probable assumption is that the two characters, that of the slave of Megaronides and that of Lyconides' servant, were acted by one and the same performer, whence they were subsequently thrown together under one name. It is idle to speculate what may have been the original name of the second Strobilus, but it is certain that he is a very different person from the Strobilus of the first three acts of our play. We should ob-serve that, like his slave, Megadorus has now disappeared from the scene of action, and that Lyconides now steps forward.

579. *facinus* would in prose be generally omitted ; translate 'it behoves a good servant.'— From Cicero Tusc. III 8, 16 we learn that the Greek for *frugi* would be χρήσιμος, and the same writer informs us that *hominem frugi omnia recte facere, iam proverbi locum obtinet* ib. IV 16, 36.

581. *ex sententia* 'to his satisfaction'; for the phrase see note on Ter. Haut. tim. IV 3, 5.—*postulat=volt*, ἀξιοῖ, see on 359.

582. Comp. Verg. Aen. I 80 *iussa capessere fas est*. Plaut. Trin. 299 *capesses mea imperia*.

584—590. After I had first observed (de Aul. p. 29) that the reading of these lines could not be genuine, and had thought of transposing 591—594 after

585 si érum videt superáre amorem, hoc sérvi esse offi-
     ciúm reor,
  rétinere ad salútem, non enim quo íncumbat eo
     impéllere.
  quási pueris qui náre discunt scírpea induitúr ratis,
  quí laborent mínus, facilius út nent et moveánt
     manus :   10
  eódem modo servóm ratem esse amánti ero aequom
     cénseo,
590 út *eum* toleret né pessum abeat támquam * * *]
  éri *ille* imperium edíscat ut quod fróns velit oculí
     sciant,   13
  quód iubeat citís quadrigis cítius properet pérsequi.

583, Brix (jahrb. 1865 p. 56) pointed out that the lines which I have now included in brackets, were but a parallel passage originally added in the margin of the archetype of our mss. and did not therefore belong to the Aulularia. For, as he judiciously says, we can only understand them of an *amor meretricius*, in which case it would indeed be the duty of a faithful servant to restrain his master: but in the present case Lyconides is bent on lawful marriage without being very deeply in love, and as he does not doubt of Euclio's consent (which appears from IV 10), it would be a superfluous presumption of his slave to attempt to keep him back (*retinere ad salutem*). Such parallel passages have sometimes been added in the mss. of the Plautine comedies, e.g. Men. 984 a passage from the commencement of the fourth act of the Mostellaria.

584. For *erŏ* see Introd. p. 27.-- *servitutem servire* occurs several times in Plautus, once even in Cicero Mur. 29, 61. Comp. note on *facinus facere* 218.

586. For *non enim* we should probably write *noenum;* see note on 67.—For *incumbāt* see Introd. p. 15.

589. For *modŏ* see Introd p. 21.

590. *tolerare* has here the sense of *sublevare*, as Trin. 338. 358. 371.—*pessum abire* 'go to the bottom ;' comp. Cist. II 1, 11 sq.

591. *frons* eri, *oculi* servi : an attentive slave should understand how to read his master's looks. The expression was no doubt proverbial like the German '*er sieht dir deine wünsche am gesichte ab.*'

592. *citis quadrigis citius :* comp. Poen. I 2, 156 *quadrigis cursim ad carnuficem rapi*, and Asin. II 2, 13 *numquam edepol quadrigis albis indipisces postea.*—Plautus has *persequor* here and 579 : Ter. Haut. tim. IV 1, 22 says *imperium exequi.*

qui éa curabit, ábstinebit cénsione búbula   15
néc sua opera rédiget umquam ín splendorem cóm-
pedes.
595 nam érus meus amat fíliam huius Eúclionis paúperis:
éam ero nunc renúntiatumst nuptum huic Megadoró
dari.
ís speculatum huc mísit me ut quae fíerent fieret
párticeps.
núnc sine omni suspítione in ára hic adsidám
sacra: 20
hínc ego et huc et ílluc potero quíd agant arbitrárier.

593. What *censio bubula*
means, should be clear without
further explanation: comp. however Trin. 1011 where the slave
Stasimus exhorts himself *cave
sis tibi ne bubuli in te cottabi
crebri crepent*, and Stich. 63
Antipho threatens his servants
*vos monimentis conmonefaciam
bubulis*. Slaves are therefore
called *bucaedae* Most. 884 : ibid.
882 we read (*erus*) *male casti-
gabit eos exuviis bubulis*.
594. The hiatus *únquam ín*
is legitimate in the caesura;
see Introd. p. 66.
595. *nam* indicates here no
internal, but only an external
connexion of the following sentence with the preceding speech:
or, to speak more clearly, we
should supply such a sentence
as 'I make all these observations not in vain, for my master
etc.' *nam* is in this way very
frequently used by the comic
writers. See also on v. 27.—

huius, i.e. who lives here, in this
house. In the same way we
have *huic Megadoro* in the next
line. He points towards the
house.
598. *sine omni* = *sine ulla*,
see note on v. 213.—*suspitio* is
the spelling frequently found
in the best mss. of Plautus,
Terence, Caesar, Cicero, Curtius
and Tacitus: the word is a contraction from *suspicitio*, an etymology which at the same time
accounts for the different quantity of *suspītio* (noun) and *sus-
pĭcio* (verb) *suspĭcor*. Another
theory is propounded by Corssen, Beitr. p. 15 s.
599. *arbitrarier* is here = *inspicere*, comp. *arbiter* = *specta-
tor* Capt. 208 and Poen. III 3,
50. Milton has ventured to
introduce this sense of the word
into the English language, Par.
Lost I 785 '*while over-head the
moon sits arbitress.*'

EVCLIO.   STROBILVS.   IV 2

600 Ev. tú modo cave quo*i*quam índicassis, aúrum meum
    esse istíc, Fides.
nón metuo ne quísquam inveniat : íta probe in
    latebrís situmst.
édepol ne illic púlcram praedam agát, si quis illam
    invénerit
aúlam onustam aurí. verum id te quaéso ut pro-
    hibessís, Fides.
núnc lavabo, ut rém divinam fáciam, ne adfiném
    morer,   5
605 quín ubi accersát meam extemplo fíliam ducát
    domum.
víde, Fides, etiam átque etiam nunc, sálvam ut
    aulam abs te aúferam :

600. *indicassis:* see note on
v. 226.
602. *praedam agere* is originally a military phrase like the
Greek λεηλατεῖν.
603. The genitive *auri* after
onustam should be explained
after the analogy of *implere* (see
note on v. 544) and *aula auri
plena* 813. We might, however,
join *aulam auri* and consider
onustam as additional attribute.
But comp. v. 609. The ablative
onustam auro v. 804.—*prohibes-
sis = prohibevesis = prohibueris :*
for the formation comp. note
on v. 226 and the perfects *delevi
nevi flevi. prohibessit* Pseud. 14.
Lucretius has *avessis* iv 823.
605. *accersere* is so frequently found in the best mss. (for
Plautus see the examples collected by Gruter on Cas. iii 4,
10; for Caesar, Dinter's note on
B. G. i 31, 4) that it would be
very arbitrary to condemn this

form, because it is difficult to
explain. There certainly can be
no doubt that *arcessere* is a
genuine form : *ar* being another
form of the preposition *ad*
and *cesso* the intensive of *cio.*
Charisius iii (p. 227 P., 256 K.)
states '*accerso sicut arcesso. sed
interest quod arcessere est ac-
cusare, accersere autem vocare.*'
See also Diomedes i p. 375 P.
379 K. Prisc. xviii p. 1164 P.
This distinction between the two
forms does not hold good. The
form *accersere* was perhaps peculiar to the *sermo plebeius,* in
which case its frequent occurrence in Plautus should not
surprise us. Ritschl gives *accersere* in many passages, e.g.
Men. 729. 763. 770. 776. 875.
Most. 1044. 1093. See also an
able article on *arcesso* and *accerso* by Mr A. S. Wilkins, in the
New Journal of Philology vi
278—285.

tuaé fide concrédidi aurum, in tuó luco et fanó
situmst.

STR. di ínmortales, quód ego hunc hominem fácinus
audió loqui :
se aúlam onustam auri ábstrusisse hic íntus in fanó
Fide. 10

610 cáve tu illi fidélis quaeso pótius fueris quám mihi.
átque hic pater est, út ego opinor, huíus erus quam
méus amat.
íbo hinc intro, pérscrutabor fánum, si inveniam
úspiam
aúrum, dum hic est óccupatus. séd si repperero, ó
Fides,
múlsi congiálem plenam fáciam tibi fidéliam. 15
615 íd adeo tibi fáciam, verum ego míhi bibam, ubi *ita*
fécero. IV 3
Ev. nón temere est, quod córvos cantat míhi nunc
ab laevá manu :
sémul radebat pédibus terram et vóce crocibát sua.

607. For *fide* = *fidei* see Key,
L. G. § 88. Lucretius has *facie*,
Horace (Serm. I 3, 95) and
Terence (Andr. I 5, 61) have
fide, Livy (v 13, 5) *pernicie* as
datives.
609. The mss. read *fidei*,
whence *fide* should be written
at the end of the verse. This
is of course to be considered as
a contracted form of the genitive ; comp. Hor. Od. III 7, 4
constantis iuvenem fide with Mr
Wickham's note.
614. *fidelia* here ' a wine-
pot :' comp. Pers. v 183 *tu-
met alba fidelia vino.* Plautus
chooses this word on account of
the paronomasia with *Fides*.
616. The fears of the ever-
suspicious Euclio have been
awakened by an unlucky omen.

non temere est is justly explained by Calphurnius on Ter.
Haut. tim. IV 1, 7 as 'non sine
causa;' the same expression
occurs in Terence Eun. II 2,
60. Phorm. v 8, 8. Comp. Pl.
Bacch. 85. 920 ss. We learn
from Cic. de div. I 39, 85 that *a
dextra corvos, a sinistra cornix
facit ratum*, and this is confirmed by a Plautine passage
Asin. II 1, 12 *picus et cornix est
ab laeva, corvos porro ab dex-
tera: consuadent.* A raven on
the left was consequently an
unlucky omen. This should
not be confounded with the
expression *avi sinistra*, Pseud.
762 and Epid. I 2, 2, which
means a lucky omen.
617. In *semul* (for the form
see Ritschl Proll. XCVII) the final

cóntinuo meúm cor coepit ártem facere lúdicram
átque in pectus émicare : séd ego cesso cúrrere   IV 4
620 fóras *foras*, lumbríce, qui sub térra erepsistí modo,
quí modo nusquam cómparebas : núnc, quom com-
parés, peris.
égo hercle te, praestrígiator, míseris iam accipiám
modis.
STR. quaé te mala crux ágitat ?   quid tibi mécumst
conmercí, senex ?
quíd me adflictas, quíd me raptas, quá me causa
vérberas ?   5

l should be dropped : see. Introd. p. 36.—*crŏcire* occurs only
here; the long quantity of the
o has been unjustly suspected
on account of an erroneous reading in the late poem *de Philo-
mela*, where Burmann and Reifferscheid rightly read *crŏcitat
ĕt corvus* v. 28 (Suet. rell. p.
309), while former editors give
ĕt crŏcitat corvus. From old
glossaries I may mention *corvi
crocciunt* (Reiff. p. 249), *corvus
crocit* and *corvos craxare* (coax-
are?) *vel crocitare* ibid. p. 250,
and to Suetonius' *Pratum* Reifferscheid refers the notice *cor-
vorum crocitare* p. 250 (*crocant
croccant crocciunt grahant* several mss.). Comp. the Greek
κρώζειν, German *krächzen* and
krähen, English *to crow* and
croak.
618.   *artem facere ludicram*
'to dance,' comp. note on *ludius*
v. 399. Plautus has similar expressions Cist. II 3, 9 *cor salit*.
Cas. II 6, 9 *corculum adsultas-
cit metu*. ibid. 62 *cor lienosum
habeo : iam dudum salit*. Capt.
III 4, 104 *tu* (cor) *sussultas*. In
Greek we have the phrases καρ-

δία χορεύει (Soph.), ὀρχεῖται καρ-
δία φόβῳ (Aeschyl.), ἡ πήδησις
τῆς καρδίας (Plato and Plut.).
620.   On *fŏräs foräs* see
Introd. p. 38.
621.   Brix conjectures *peri*.
But the present *peris* stands em-
phatically in the sense of the
future *peribis*.
622.   *praestrĭgiator* is the
Plautine form of the word regis-
tered in our dictionaries as
praestigiator, as has been pointed out by A. Spengel on Truc.
I 2, 32. The word is derived
from *praestringere.—te miseris
accipiam modis* 'I shall treat
you miserably.' Comp. Ter. Ad.
II 1, 12 *indignis quom egomet
sim acceptus modis*.
623.   For the expression *mala crux* see Brix on Men. 707.
Comp. Bacch. 117 *quid tibi
conmercist cum dis damnosissu-
mis ?* and Rud. III 4, 20 *nihil
cum vestris legibus mi est con-
merci*. Terence says in the
same sense *quid tibi cum illa
rei est ?* Eun. IV 7, 34. The
other phrase occurs only in
Plautus.

625 Ev. vérberabilíssume, etiam rógitas? non fur, séd
trifur.

STR. quíd tibi subrupuí?   Ev. redde huc sis.   STR.
quíd tibi vis reddám?   Ev. rogas?

STR. níl equidem tibi ábstuli.   Ev. at illud quód
tibi abstulerás cedo.

écquid agis *tu*?   STR. quíd agam?   Ev. auferre nón
potes.   STR. quid vís tibi?

Ev. póne.   STR. id quidem pol té datare crédo con-
suetúm, senex.   10

630 Ev. póne hoc sis: aufér cavillam: nón ego nunc
nugás ago.

STR. quíd ego ponam? quín tu eloquere, quídquid
est, suo nómine.

nón hercle equidem quícquam sumpsi néc tetigi.

Ev. ostende húc manus.

STR. ém tibi.   Ev. ostende.   STR. éccas.   Ev. video.

age óstende etiam tértiam.

---

625. *verberabilissumus* (μασ-
τιγωσιμώτατος) is a comic superlative like *ipsissumus* Trin.
988, which is itself an imitation
of αὐτότατος Arist. Plut. 83.
Another superlative of the same
kind is *oculissumus* Curc. i 2,
28. *exclusissumus* Men. 695.
occisissumus Cas. iii 5, 52.

627. Euclio avoids the direct mention of the real object
of his search, lest he should be-
tray himself, in case Strobilus
should not be in possession of
the secret. There is a quibble
in the Latin here, which is however easily understood. Euclio
takes *tibi* as dat. eth., a turn
which cannot be rendered in
English. Similar jokes occur
Men. 645 and Capt. 862.

628. The phrase *ecquid agis*,
which is expressive of im-
patience, occurs also Cist. iii

12 in the same manner as here.

629. Euclio bids Strobilus
lay the pot down (*pone*), but
the slave purposely misunderstands him in construing an
obscenity upon the word *pone*
which may also be an adverb.
datare has here an obscene
sense in the same way as *dare*
Cas. ii 6, 10.

630. 'Scribitur fere in Plau-
tinis libris promiscue *hoc* et
huc.' GULIELMIUS, quaest. in
Aul. c. 4. The form *hoc = huc*
is well attested by grammarians and mss. alike.— *aufer cavillam:* comp. Capt. 960 *tandem
ista aufer* and Truc. iv 4, 8
aufer nugas. So Pers. 797,
iurgium hinc auferas. Comp.
also Ter. Phorm. 857, and
Phaedr. iii 6, 8.—*nugas ago*
recurs v. 643 below.

633. 'The archaic particle

STR. láruae hunc atque íntemperiae insániaeque
    agitánt senem.
635 fácisne iniuriám mihi an non?   Ev. quía non pendes,
    máxumam.   16
átque id quoque iam fíet, nisi fatére.   STR. quid
    fateár tibi?

em which in former editions
was usually replaced by the
more recent form *en*, is in
Plautus strongly recommended
by the best mss. and very frequently required by the metre,
e.g. Merc. ii 2, 82. Pseud. iii
2, 100. Poen. i 1, 79. Bacch.
ii 3, 40. iv 8, 29. Charisius
quotes *em* from an oration of C.
Gracchus and Poen. iii 4, 16.
hem, which in older mss. is but
rarely, in later ones frequently,
confounded with it, is of a
thoroughly pathetic nature and
serves for expressing joy, grief,
surprise and bewilderment.'
BRIX on Trin. 3.—On the words
ostende etiam tertiam Thornton
has the following note: ' This
has been censured as being too
extravagant and entirely out of
nature; but considering the
very ridiculous humour of the
Miser as drawn by our author,
it will not perhaps appear out
of character. Euclio talks in
the same strain of the cooks
being all of Geryon's race and
having six hands a piece. Molière, however, who has imitated
this scene, has not ventured
this seemingly absurd joke, as
undoubtedly he thought it
would appear too outré to a
modern audience; and our own
countrymen, Shádwell and
Fielding, have copied his ex-

ample, probably for the same
reason. But there is a direct
imitation of this whole passage
in the old play of Albumazar,
Act iii Scene 8, where *Trincalo*
(who is made to fancy himself
Antonio) questions *Ronca* about
his purse which the latter had
stolen from him:

Trin. O my purse;
    Dear master Ronca.
Ronc. What's your pleasure, sir?
Trin. Show me your hand.
Ronc. Here 'tis.
Trin. But where's the other?
Ronc. Why here.
Trin. But I mean where's your other
    hand?
Ronc. Think you me the giant with an
    hundred hands?
Trin. Give me your right.
Ronc. My right?
Trin. Your left.
Ronc. My left?
Trin. Now both.
Ronc. There's both, my dear Antonio.

634. *laruae hunc agitant*
'the Furies are upon him.'
Comp. Capt. iii 4, 66 *iam de-
liramenta loquitur, laruae sti-
mulant virum*. Hence, the phy-
sician in the Menaechmi v 4, 2
puts the question: *num larua-
tu's aut cerritus?*—For *intemperiae* we may refer to v. 71
above.—The plural *insaniae* is,
in all probability, confined to
the present passage.

635. *facisne* should be pronounced as *facin*, see Introd.
p. 31, 36. It appears to be gratuitous to write *facin*.

Ev. quíd abstulisti hinc? Str. dí me perdant, si
  égo tui quicquam ábstuli,
níve adeo abstulísse vellem.   Ev. ágedum, excute-
  dum pállium.
Str. túo arbitratu.   Ev. ne ínter tunicas hábeas.
  Str. tempta quá lubet.   20
640 Ev. váh, scelestus quám benigne, ut ne ábstulisse
  intellégam.
nóvi sucopháotias. age rúrsum ostende huc déx-
  teram.
Str. ém *tibi*.   Ev. nunc laévam ostende.   Str. quín
  equidem ambas prófero.
Ev. iám scrutari mítto: redde huc.   Str. quíd reddam?   Ev. a, nugás agis:
cérte habes.   Str. habeo égo?   quid habeo?   Ev.
  nón dico: audire éxpetis.   25
645 íd meum quidquíd habes, redde.   Str. insánis. per-
  scrutátus es
tuó arbitratu néque tui me quícquam invenistí
  penes.

---

637. For *quíd ábstulísti* see
Introd. p. 57.
638. Strobilus mutters these
words to himself. The sense
is *et di me perdant, si non
vellem me abstulisse.* Euclio is
not supposed to hear this.
639. *tunica* is the Latin for
the Greek χιτών. The plural
stands much in the same way
as Amph. i 1, 212. Men. 736.
803.—*temptare* has here its original sense 'to take hold of —,'
i.e. to search through —.
640. How liberally (*benigne*)
you allow me to feel every-
where!
643. *a* is the genuine spelling of the interjection, not *ah*,
as we learn from the best mss.

and the grammarian Probus.
See also Priscian p. 1024 P.
Marius Victorinus i p. 2475.
645. How little constant the
language in Plautus' time was
with regard to the deponent
and active forms, we see here
in a striking instance: 643 we
have *scrutari*, 645 *perscrutatus
es*, but 649 *perscrutavi*.
646. *penes* is rarely placed
after the word which it governs:
see Key, L. G. § 1349 where
Ter. Hec. iv 1, 20 is quoted.
The same collocation occurs
also Trin. 1146. Corssen con-
nects this preposition with
penu penus penitus, and says
that it originally meant 'in the
store-room.'

Ev. máne mane: quis illést qui hic intus álter
  tecum símul erat ?
périi hercle. ille intús nunc turbat : húnc si amitto,
  hinc ábierit.
póstremo hunc iam pérscrutavi. hic níhil habet : abi
  quó lubet.   30
650 STR. Iúppiter te díque perdant. Ev. haúd male
  egit grátias.
íbo intro atque illí socienno tuó iam interstringám
  gulam.
fúgin hinc ab oculís? abin an non ? STR. ábeo.
  Ev. cave sis *te videam.
STR. emórtuom ego me mávelim letó malo   IV 5
quam nón ego illi dém hodie insidiás seni.
655 nam hic íntus non audébit aurum abstrúdere :
credo écferet iam sécum et mutabít locum.
atát, foris crepuit. sénex eccum aurum ecfért foras. 5
tantísper huc ego ad iánuam concéssero.
Ev. Fidé censebam máxumam multó fidem :   IV 6
660 sed éa sublevit ós mihi paeníssume.

648. amittere, as Brix on
Capt. 36 rightly observes, has
in the latinity before Cicero frequently the sense of dimittere.
650. The words haud male
egit gratias are addressed to
the audience. (There is a confusion in the mss. as to the
distribution of these words between the two characters, but
I have now followed the ms. B.)
651. The form sociennus = so-
cius is attested by Nonius 172,
21.—interstringam: see Key, L.
G. § 1342, 1 e.
652. Hare compares a similar passage Cas. II 4, 23 abin
hinc ab oculis?—The termination of the line is corrupt in the
mss. : C. F. W. Müller conjec-

tures cave sis mi obviam. I have
thought of te intuam.
653. emortuos ' completely
dead : ' Key, L. G. § 1332 g.
654. For the hiatus dém
ho— see Introd. p. 69.
657. The syllables foris crepu
form a proceleusmatic : see
Introd. p. 31. Comp. fores cre-
puerunt Mil. gl. 410, concrepuit
ostium Men. 348, in Greek αἱ
θύραι ψοφοῦσιν, e.g. Lys. 1, 14.
659. For Fide as a genitive
see note on v. 609.
660. By way of explanation
of the phrase os alicui sublinere
(' to deceive, to cheat ') Nonius
p. 45, 21 says sublevit significat
' inlusit et pro ridiculo habuit,'
tractum a genere ludi quo dor-

ni súbvenisset córvos, periissém miser.
nimis hércle ego illum córvom ad me veniát velim
qui indícium fecit, út ego illic aliquíd boni   5
dicám—nam quod edit, tám duim quam pérduim.
665 nunc hóc ubi abstrudam, cógito solúm locum.
    Silváni lucus éxtra murumst ávius
    crebró salicto opplétus : ibi sumám locum.
    certúmst, Silvano pótius credam quám Fide.   10
    STR. eugae eúgae, di me sálvom et servatúm
        volunt.
670 iam ego illúc praecurram atque ínscendam aliquam
        in árborem,
    et índe observabo, aúrum ubi abstrudát senex.
    quamquam híc manere mé erus sese iússerat,
    certúmst malam rem pótius quaeram cúm lucro.   15

---

mientibus ora pinguntur. Gronovius observes that this ludi-
crous practice is mentioned by
Virgil, Ecl. vi 22 (Aegle) *san-*
guineis frontem moris et tempora
pingit, and by Petronius Sat.
22 (p. 23 Büch.) *cum Ascyltos...*
in somnum laberetur, illa...an-
cilla totam faciem eius fuligine
longa perfricuit et non sentientis
labra umerosque sopiti carboni-
bus pinxit. Gronovius quotes
the following instances of this
phrase in Plautus : Mil. gl. ii
5, 47. Merc. ii 4, 17. Capt.
iii 4, 123.—For *paenissume* see
note on 463.
  662. *illum corvom ad me ve-*
niat velim is a proleptic construction instead of *ille corvos*
ad me veniat velim.
  663. *illic = illice,* see Men.
304. 828. 842 in Ritschl's edition.
  664.·· *edit :* see Key, L. G.
§ 482.—*tam—quam* 'I might as
well give him as lose,' i. e. to

give and to lose would amount
to the same in this case.
  668. For the dative *Fide* see
note on v. 607.
  669. There are several Plautine passages where the two
words *fuge* (*fugae*) and *euge*
(*eugae*) have been erroneously
interchanged, e. g. Asin. 555
(= iii 2, 9) *B* has *eugae, J euge,*
but Bücheler justly emends
fugae (see Jahrb. für class. phil.
1863 p. 772). Again Most. 686
BCD have *Fuge* which Camerarius changed to *euge: A* gives
EUGAE and this form Ritschl
ought to have put into his text,
it being supported by good mss.
and evidenced by the metre,
notwithstanding the Greek εὖγε.
See e.g. Ter. And. ii 2, 8 (= 345
Fl.) *te ípsum quaero. eugaé, Cha-*
rine with Bentley's note. Fleckeisen has this spelling throughout his edition of Terence.
  672. For the hiatus *re mé*
er— see Introd. p. 69.

LYCONIDES. EVNOMIA. (VIRGO).   IV 7

LY. dixí tibi, mater, iúxta rem mecúm tenes
675 super Eúclionis fília: nunc te óbsecro
resecróque, mater, quód dudum obsecráveram :   4
fac méntionem cum ávonculo, matér mea.   3
EVN. scis túte facta vélle me quae tú velis :   5
et istúc confido a frátre me impetrássere,
680 et caúsa iustast, síquidem itast ut praédicas,
te eam cómpressisse vínolentum vírginem.
LY. egone út te advorsum méntiar, matér mea ?
VI. perií, mea nutrix, óbsecro te, uterúm dolet :   10
Iunó Lucina, tuám fidem. LY. em, matér mea,

674. *iuxta mecum* ' in the
same manner with myself.'
Comp. Mil. gl. 234 *scias iuxta
mecum mea consilia.* Pseud.
1161 (*nescio*) *iuxta cum ignaris-
sumis.* Sallust too says *iuxta
mecum omnes intellegitis* Cat. 58.
675. *super:* Key, L. G. § 1380 c.
676. *resecroque:* ' I implore
you again and again,' comp.
Persa 47 *obsecro resecroque te.*
In both passages this seems the
simplest explanation; the words
of Festus ' *resecrare est resol-
vere religione,*' which the editors since Pithoeus (Advers. i
10) connected with them, should
not be applied to them.
677. The construction *mentionem facere cum aliquo* occurs
again Cist. i 2, 15 and Persa
109.—For the pronunciation
aunculo see p. 84.
679. *impetrassere* is an old
infinit. fut. =*impetraturam esse.*
Comp. *reconciliassere* Capt. i 1,
65. In the same way Lucilius
has *depeculassere et deargentas-
sere.* See Zumpt, § 161.

682. *te advorsum* ' in your
face,' see Key, L. G. § 1307 b.
Comp. Poen. i 2, 188 *mendax
me advorsum siet.*
683. There are only two
other passages besides this
where the neuter *uterum* occurs instead of the masculine :
Turpil. 179 (Ribb. Com. p. 92)
*dispérii misera : úterum crucia-
túr mihi* (for the hiatus see
Introd. p. 67) a line which is
undoubtedly spoken by a girl
in the same situation as Euclio's
daughter. The other passage is
Afran. 346 *sedit uterum* (Ribb.
Com. p. 178).
684. ' *luna a lucendo nomi-
nata...eadem est enim Lucina.*
(see Max Müller's Lectures ii
p. 278) *itaque, ut apud Graecos
Dianam eamque Luciferam, sic
apud nostros Iunonem Lucinam
in pariendo invocant.*' Cicero
de nat. deor. ii 27, 68. Comp.
Ter. Andr. iii 1, 15 and Ad. iii
4, 41 *Iuno Lucina, fer opem,
serva me, obsecro* with the commentators and Preller, Röm.

685 tibi rém potiorem vídeo : clamat párturit.
    Eyn. i hac íntro mecum, gnáte mi, ad fratrém
        meum,
    ut istúc quod me oras ímpetratum ab eo aúferam. 15
    Ly. i, iám sequor te, mater. sed servóm meum
    Strobílum miror, úbi sit, quem ego me iússeram
690 hic ópperiri. quóm ego mecum cógito,
    si míhi dat operam, me ílli irasci iniúriumst.
    sed íbo intro, ubi de cápite meo sunt cómitia.   20

                    STROBILVS.   IV 8

Picí divitiis qui aúreos montís colunt,

Myth. p. 243. Donatus observes
on the line in the Andria '*nota
hoc versu totidem verbis uti omnes puerperas in comoediis, nec
alias* [perhaps *nec ullas*] *induci
loqui in proscaenio: nam haec
vox post scaenam tollitur.*'—
tuam fidem sc. *rogo, imploro:*
comp. Curc. 196 and the title
of Varro's satire Hercules, tuam
fidem p. 283 in the Bipontine
edition. For *vostram fidem* see
Westerhov on Ter. Andr. iv 3,
1, where Donatus observes that
in these elliptic expressions *fidem* means 'opem et auxilium.'
685. *rem* potiorem video *verbis*. Why shall I tell you of it
any longer ? my *words* are quite
superfluous, since the *fact*
speaks for itself.—For *tibi* see
Key, L. G. § 978.
689. *Strobilum miror ubi sit:*
prolepsis for *miror ubi Strobilus
sit*.
691. *iniurium* is an archaic
word, which was in later times
replaced by the adj. *iniustum* or
the subst. *iniuria*. It occurs
Cist. i 1, 105. Ter. Ad. i 2, 26

and ii 1, 51. Hec. ii 1, 14.
iniurius stands Andr. ii 3, 3.
Haut. tim. ii 3, 79. Curc. 65.
Epid. iv 1, 24. Rud. 1152.
692. The simile is easily understood. Comp. Pseud. 1232
and Truc. iv 3, 45 (=807 Geppert) where the word *comitia* is
used in a similar way. See also
v. 541.—*meo* should be pronounced as one syllable.
693. Ἔφη Ἀριστέης ... ὑπὲρ
Ἀριμασπῶν ... οἰκεῖν τοὺς χρυσο-
φύλακας γρῦπας Her. iv 13, who
mentions the same γρῦπας iii
116 and iv 27. According to
Nonius (152, 10) we should here
recognise a translation of this
Greek or rather Oriental (Preller, griech. Myth. 1, 158 first
ed.) fable ; but as the *picus* (i. e.
the woodpecker) holds a marked
position in old Italian mythology, and was believed to know
of hidden treasures (Preller,
Röm. Myth. p. 298), we are
rather inclined to think that
Plautus mixed the Greek *grypes*
and the tales told of their gold-
en treasures with the common

eos sólus supero. nám istos reges céteros
695 memoráre nolo, hóminum mendicábula.
ego sum ílle rex Philíppus. o lepidúm diem.
nam ut dúdum hinc abii, múlto illo advení prior,   5
multóque prius me cónlocavi in árborem,
indeque óbservabam, ubi aúrum abstrudebát senex.
700 ubi ille ábiit, ego me deórsum duco de árbore :
exfódio aulam auri plénam. inde exeo. *ílico*

beliefs current among his own
countrymen with regard to the
woodpecker. The *aurei montes*
of the *pici* appear only in this
one passage. I may venture to
draw the attention of my readers
to another passage in Plautus,
without myself deducing any
hasty conclusion from it: Stich.
24 *Persarum montis qui esse
aurei perhibentur*, a passage
which may be compared with
some lines from Varro's satire
'Ανθρωπουργία (p. 264 ed. Bip.)
*Persarum montes, non divitis
atria Crassi*.—For the form of
attraction noticeable in the present line, comp. note on v. 566,
and cf. also Ter. Eun. IV 3, 11
*Eunuchum quem dedisti nobis,
quas turbas dedit*.—*colunt* 'in-
habit :' see on v. 4.
   694. The joy in which Strobilus is makes his words somewhat incoherent. He says *reges
ceteros*, though he has not yet
mentioned the name of any
king whose wealth might be
compared to his. This has already been pointed out by Lambinus.—We may not think here
of *king* Picus (Preller, Röm.
Myth. p. 331 ss.) because we
have *Pici* in the plural.—*istos*
'those commonly admired.'
   695. Nonius is undoubtedly
wrong in using the word *mendi-*

catio for the explanation of
mendicabulum : the passage itself shows that we should translate 'beggarly fellows.' Appuleius has the same expression
in two passages, and in both he
applies it to persons.—For the
hiatus see Introd. p. 67. The
emendation *regum mendicabula*
('beggarly kinglets'), which is
found in Guyet's text, seems
due to Scipio Gentilis (whoever
that worthy may have been),
as appears from Taubmann's
note.
   696. *ille* 'the renowned.' See
note on v. 86.
   698. The construction *conlocare in aliquid* is not classic,
though by no means scarce.
See the dictionaries s. v. Men.
986 *in tabernam vasa et servos
conlocavi*. Plautus has also
ponere in aliquid, e. g. Trin.
739. Rud. IV 7, 11.
   699. For *indeque* see Introd.
p. 48.
   700. In *deorsum* the *e* is to
be elided before the *o :* see Introd. p. 65.
   701. The form *exfodio* occurs
again in the best mss. in Mil.
gl. 315. The common Plautine
form is *ecfodio* (v. 63). EXFO-
CIONT (i. e. *exfugiunt*) occurs in
the inscription on the so-called
'columna rostrata.' Comp. *ex-*

videó recipere sé senem : ille me haú videt.   10
nam ego déclinavi paúlu*lum* me extrá viam.
atát, eccum ipsum. íbo ut hoc condám domum.

EVCLIO.   IV 9

705 perii ínterii occidi ! quó curram ? quo nón curram ?
tene téne: quem quis ?
nescíó, nil video : caécus eo atque equidém quo eam
aut ubi sim aút qui sim,
nequeó cum animo certum ínvestigare. óbsecro vos
ego mi aúxilio
oro óbtestor, sitís et hominem demónstretis, qui eam
ábstulerit.   5
quid aís tu ? tibi credére certumst : nam essé bonum
e voltu cógnosco.   7
710 quid est quód ridetis ? novi omnis : scio fúres esse
hic cómpluris   8

ducier (*BC*) Truc. v 5, 16, *exmi-grasti* (*B*) Men. 822.

704. '*Atat* pro poëtae lubitu variat suum tonum : nunc *áttat*, nunc *atáttat*, nunc *atát :* quod postremum hoc loco placet.' Bentley on Ter. Andr. I 1, 98. The hiatus is justified by the punctuation.

705 ss. Molière's masterly imitation of this scene should be compared with Plautus, though it is difficult to decide which deserves the preference, the original or the imitation.— For *occidí* see Introd. p. 27. This quantity would not however occur in iambics or tro-chaics. Comp. *perdidí* v. 716. —For *tenĕ tenĕ* see Introd. p. 26.

706. For the hiatus *quo e—* see Introd. p. 69.

707. With the expression *cum animo investigare* comp. Plaut. Most. 702 *cogito cum meo animo.*

709. One of the French translators of Plautus thinks it 'uno malice très-fine' that En-clio is made to address the spec-tators as if the thief were among them. Tastes may of course differ on such points as this ; but it is difficult to believe that a modern audience would patiently submit to be called *thieves* by an actor. But the broad humour which reigns in the Plautine plays could safely venture to do this, especially as the poet might be certain that the bulk of his audience did not consist of a select company of refined taste, but of a bois-terous, noisy, and disorderly multitude. See the prologue to the Poenulus.

qui véstitu et creta óccultant sese átque sedent
   quasi sínt frugi.   6
hem, némon habet horum? óccidisti: díc igitur quis
   habét. nescis?   9
heu mé misere miserúm: perii: male pérditus
   pessume ornátus eo: 10
tantúm gemiti et malae maéstitiae hic dies mi
   óptulit et famem et paúperiem:
715 * perditissumus ego sum
omnium ín terra: nam quíd mihi opust vitá qui
   perdidi tántum auri
quod sédulo concustódivi: nunc égomet me de-
   fraúdavi
animúmque meum geniúmque meum: nunc érgo
   alii laetíficantur   15

711. *vestitu et creta=vestitu
cretato* (ἐν διὰ δυοῖν). There is
here an allusion to the more
elegant dress of wealthy citizens; it was common to cleanse
a white toga with chalk, comp.
Poen. 958; Plin. N. H. xxxv
17, 196 sq. We should also
observe the words *atque sedent*.
In Plautus' time ordinary spec-
tators used to stand, and only
'gentlemen' of rank and wealth
had their chairs brought into
the theatre : see Ritschl, Par.
218 and xx. Mommsen, Röm.
Gesch. i² 864. See Boltenstern
de rebus scaen. rom. (Stral-
sund, 1875) p. 26 sq. For *frugi*
see note on v. 579.
713. For *ōrnatus* see Introd. p.
56 sq. *ornare* has here a more
general sense ' badly furnished,'
i. e. 'I'm in a sorry plight'
(Hildy). Comp. a similar passage in Ter. Ad. ii 1, 22 *ornatus
esses ex tuis virtutibus* 'thou
shouldst be dealt with accord-

ing to thy merits.' See also
Capt. v 3, 19, *incedit huc ornatus haud ex suis virtutibus.*
   714. For *gemiti* see note on
83. *malae* should be considered
as two short syllables : see Introd. p. 23. *dies* forms only
one syllable, by way of synizesis, and the syllables *fam' et
pau* form together an anapaest,
et being pronounced as a mere *e*.
   718. *genium :* comp. Ter.
Phorm. i 1, 10 *suom defrudans
genium.* Lucilius used the same
expression, as we learn from
Nonius p. 117, 31. The contrary is *genio multa bona facere*
Persa 263.—*laetificare* occurs
even in Cicero, de nat. deor. ii
40, 102 *sol...terram laetificat.*
Comp. the analogous formations *magnificare* (Men. 371.
Rud. i 2, 43. Ter. Hec. ii 2, 18),
turpificare (Cic. de off. iii 19),
pacificare (Liv. Sall. Catullus),
and the deponent *causificor*
748.

meo málo et damno: pati néqueo.

LYCONIDES. EVCLIO.   IV 9 17

720 Ly. quínam homo hic ante aédis nostras éiulans
　　　　conquéritur maerens?
　átque hic quidemst, ut opínor, Euclio. óppido ego
　　　interií: palamst res.
　scít peperisse iam, út ego opinor, fíliam suam. núnc
　　　mi incertumst,
　ábeam an maneam, ádeam an fugiam—quíd ego
　　　agam, edepol néscio.　　　　　　　　　　　20
　Ev. quís homo hic loquitur? Ly. égo sum miser.
　Ev. immo égo sum et miser et pérditus, IV. 10
725 quoí tanta mala maéstitudoque óptigit. Ly. animó
　　　bono's.
　Ev. quo, óbsecro, pacto ésse possum? Ly. quía
　　　istuc facinus quód tuom
　sóllicitat animum, íd ego feci et fáteor. Ev. quid
　　　ego ex te aúdio?
　Ly. íd quod verumst. Ev. quíd ego de te cónmerui,
　　　adulescéns, mali,　　　　　　　　　　　　　5
　quam óbrem ita faceres méque meosque pérditum
　　　irĕs líberos?
730 Ly. dĕus impulsor míhi fuit: is me ád illam in-
　　　lexit. Ev. quó modo?
　Ly. fáteor me peccávisse et me cúlpam commeritúm
　　　scio:

719. For patī see Introd. p.
27.
720. The word eiulans de-
scribes Euclio's passionate and
effeminate wailing. Comp. Hor.
Epod. 10. 17 et illa non virilis
eiulatio and Cic. Tusc. ii 23,
55 ingemescere non numquam
viro concessum est idque raro,
eiulatus ne mulieri quidem.
728. Comp. Men. 490 quid

de te merui qua me causa per-
deres ?
730. Throughout the following passage the joke consists in
the regular misunderstanding
of the fem. pronouns, which
Euclio refers to his aula, while
Lyconides conceives him to be
speaking of his daughter.—For
fuit see Introd. p. 16.
731. The expression culpam

íd adeo te orátum advenio, ut ánimo aequo ig-
noscás mihi.

Ev. cúr id ausu̧'s fácere, ut id quod nón tuom esset
tángeres ?   10

Ly. quíd vis fieri ? fáctumst illud : fíeri infectum
nón potest.

735 deós credo voluísse. nam ni véllent, non fierét, scio.

Ev. át ego deos credó voluisse, ut ápud me te in
nervo énicem.

Ly. né istuc dixis.   Ev. quíd tibi ergo meám me
invito táctiost ?

Ly. quía vini vitio átque amoris féci.   Ev. homo
audacíssume,   15

cum ístacin te orátione huc ád me adire ausum,
ímpudens.

740 nám si istuc ius sít, ut tu istuc éxcusare póssies,

conmeritum justifies Brix's cor-
rection of v. 728. Comp. Capt.
II 3, 43 (=400). Ter. Phorm.
I 4, 29.

   733. *tangere* is very frequently used in the sense of
corrumpere filiam, e. g. Hor.
Serm. I 2, 54 *matronam nullam
ego tango*. Thus we have *tactio*
v. 737 with the same ambiguity.
Comp. a similar passage Pseud.
120 and 121 and the examples
given by Westerhov on Ter.
Eun. II 3, 81.

   734. *factum infectum fieri
non potest* is a principle of
common sense, and was therefore received among the max-
ims of Roman law. Comp. Try-
phonius l. 12 § 2 D. de captivis
(49, 15) *facti causae infactae
nulla constitutione fieri possunt*.
Pomponius l. 2 D. de rescind,
vend. (18, 5) *potest, dum res
integra est, conventione nostra
infecta fieri emtio...post pretium*

*solutum infectam emtionem fa-
cere non possumus*. We have
the same phrase Ter. Phorm.
v 9, 44 s. and Plaut. Truc. IV
2, 17.

   736. 'Nervum adpellamus
ferreum vinculum quo peues
impediuntur.' *Festus*. Comp.
Curc. v 3, 11. The instrument
was about the same as the
'stocks' formerly in ᵾse in
England.

   738. Comp. Ter. Ad. III 4,
24 *persuasit nox amor vinum
adulescentia*, where Westerhov
quotes Ovid, Amor. I 6, 59 *nox
et amor vinumque nihil modera-
bile suadent*. See 788.

   740. Compare Merc. v 4,
24 s. (=985 R.) *nam si istuc
ius sit, senecta aetate scortari
patres, Vbi loci siet res summa
puplica ?* where all the mss. and
old editions give *est*, but Ritschl
justly writes *sit*.

lúci claro déripiamus aúrum matronís palam :
póstid, si deprénsi simus, éxcusemus ébrios
nós fecisse, amóris causa. nímis vilest vinum átque
　amor,　　　　　　　　　　　　　　　　　　20
si ébrio atque amánti impune fácere quod lubeát
　licet.
745 Ly. quín tibi ultro súpplicatum vénio ob stultitiám
　meam.
Ev. nón mi homines placént qui quando mále fece-
　runt púrigant.
tu íllam scibas nón tuam esse : nón attactam
　opórtuit.

---

741. In this line we are indebted to Nonius for preserving the genuine phrase *luci claro*, which is generally obliterated in our mss.. Comp. Ter. Ad. v 3, 55 *cum primo luci*, where the Bembinus has *primo lucu*, while *prima luce* is found in recent mss. (see Bentley's note): Donatus, whose notes are here interpolated, has however a genuine remark on this passage *veteres masculino genere dicebant lucem.*—Plaut. Cist. II 1, 48 B gives *quom primo luci* and the mss. of Nonius give the same phrase in a line of Atta 468, 32 = Ribb. Com. p. 138. But in Cic. de off. III 31, 112 all the mss. give *cum prima luce.*— In a fable of Ennius rendered in prose by Gellius II 29 (Enn. ed. Vahlen p. 160) we have *primo luce*, which is the reading of the cod. Reg. of Gronovius, recent mss. having *prima luce.*— The phrase *luci claro* is quoted from Varro's Synephebus by Nonius 210; see Varro, Bip. ed. p. 309.—In general comp. Charisius p. 203 ed. Keil. *luci* (e.g. Men. 1006) should be con-

sidered as an adverb like *mani heri* (*mane here*) ; see Key, L. G. § 784. It shows clearly that these adverbs are originally ablatives, being construed with adj. and prepositions. Comp., moreover, the phrase *cum primo mane* in the Bell. Afr. c. 62. *cum luci simul* Stich. 364.

743. 'Love and wine are indeed extremely cheap things, if a drunken hot-brained youth be allowed to do anything without fear of punishment.' This is the plain sense of the passage, though it was not understood by Lambinus and the other commentators. Heinsius even conjectured *nimis utile*, which is against the metre.

747. For the construction comp. Ter. Haut. tim. II 3, 6 *non oportuit relictas*, IV 1, 22 *interemptam oportuit* 'you should have killed her.' Amph. II 2, 108 *comprecatam oportuit.* In such phrases Plautus commonly omits *esse :* see Mil. gl. 1336. Cist. II 3, 41. Truc. II 6, 29. Stich. 354.

162   AVLVLARIA.   [IV. 10. 25—38.

Ly. érgo quia sum tángere ausus, haúd causificor
    quín eam   25
égo habeam potíssumum. Ev. tun hábeas me invitó
    meam?
750 Ly. haú te invito póstulo: sed méam esse oportere
    árbitror.
quín tu iam inveniés, inquam, illam méam esse
    oportere, Eúclio.
Ev. nísi refers. Ly. quid tíbi ego referam? Ev.
    quód subrupuistí meum.
iám quidem hercle te ád praetorem rápiam et tibi
    scribám dicam.   30
Ly. súbrupui ego tuom? únde? aut quid id est?
    Ev. íta te amabit Iúppiter,
755 út tu nescis. Ly. nísi quidem tu míhi quid quaeras
    díxeris.
Ev. aúlam auri, inquam, té reposco, quám tu con-
    fessú's mihi
te ábstulisse. Ly. néque edepol ego díxi neque fecí.
    Ev. negas?
Ly. pérnego immo. nám neque ego aurum néque
    istaec aula quaé siet,   35
scío nec novi. Ev. illam éx Silvani lúco quam ab-
    stulerás, cedo.
760 í, refer: dimídiam tecum pótius partem dívidam.
tam étsi fur mihi és, molestus nón ero: i veró, refer.

750. oportere: according to
the laws of Athens. See 786 and
Ter. Andr. iv 4, 41. Ad. iii 4,
44. Phorm. ii 3, 68 ss.
    752. Euclio speaks ironically
' Of course you will be legitimate
possessor, unless you restore
the object.' Thus we need not
transpose the lines 752 and 753,
as Acidalius was inclined to do.
    753. Comp. Hor. Serm. i 9,
77 rapit in ius. Plautus Persa
745 s. Do. quid me in ius vocas ?

Sa. illi apud praetorem dicam,
sed ego in ius voco.—scribam
dicam : γράψομαι δίκην. Comp.
Ter. Phorm. i 2, 77. ii 2, 15.
iv 3, 63. Plaut. Poen. iii 6, 5
has subscribam dicam.
    758. immo: 'I don't only
deny it, but I obstinately deny
it.' The only other passage
where immo stands in the second place is Capt. ii 2, 104.
    759. For neque scio nec novi
see n. on v. 190.

Ly. sánus tu non és qui furem mé voces.   ego te,
Eúclio,
dé alia re réscivisse censuí, quod ad me áttinet.   40
námst res, quam ego tecum ótiose, si ótiumst, cupió
loqui.
765 Ev. díc bona fidé, tu id aurum nón subrupuistí?
Ly. bona.
Ev. néque scis quis *id* abstúlerit?   Ly. istuc quóque bona.   Ev. atqui sí scies,
quís *id* abstulerit, mi índicabis?   Ly. faciam.   Ev.
neque partém tibi
áb eo quoi sit índipisces, neque furem excipiés?
Ly. ita.   45
Ev. *quíd si* fallis?   Ly. túm me faciat quód volt
magnus Iúppiter.

763. For the hiatus *dé a—*
see Introd. p. 69.
   ib. quod should not be altered, though the construction
is somewhat loose and not in
accordance with strict grammar. Comp. Amph. ii 3, 11
*ego rem divinam intus faciam,
vota quae sunt.* Men. 120 *omnem rem, quicquid egi.*
   765. Hare compares Capt.
iv 2, 110 *dic bona fide tu mi
istaec verba dixisti?* : : *bona.*
In the present passage *bona*
means 'I tell you true that your
question would also be my answer' = *bona fide dico me aurum
non subrupuisse.'* Comp. the
next line where we should understand *istuc quoque bona* (*fide
dico me nescire*).
   768. The active form of the
verb *indipisces* occurs here and
Asin. ii 2, 13, the deponent
Trin. 224. Rud. v 2, 28. Epid.
iii 4, 15: see Brix on Trin. 224.
In later writers we generally

find *adipiscor*, though *indipis-
cor* occurs in Lucretius, Livy,
Gellius and Appuleius.—*furem
excipere* = *f. recipere.*   Gronovius compares Cic. de imp. Cn.
Pomp. 9, 23 *hunc in illa fuga
Tigranes rex excepit.*—*ita* 'yes:'
comp. Ter. Andr. v 2, 8. Key,
L. G. § 1451 c. It is properly
a curtailed sentence: *ita aio.*
   769. The present *fallis* is
here given by all our mss.
Comp. however Amph. i 1, 235,
So. *quid si falles?*   Me. *tum
Mercurius Sosiae iratus siet.*
But in another passage we have
the present, Amph. iii 2, 52 *id
ego si fallo, tum te, summe Iuppiter, Quaeso Amphitruoni ut
semper iratus sies.*   In this passage *fallo* means *falsum dico*
('to deceive'), and the same
sense would explain the present
line.—For the construction *me
faciat* (abl.) see Key, L. G.
§ 1003.

770 Ev. sát habeo. age nunc, lóquere, quid vis. Ly. sí
me novistí minus,
génere quo sim gnátus, hic mihi ést Megadorus
aúnculus.
méus fuit pater *hínc* Antimachus, égo vocor Lycónides :
máter est Eunómia. Ev. novi génus. nunc quid
vis ? íd volo   50
nóscere. Ly. filiam éx te tu habes?   Ev. ímmo
eccillam *meaé* domi.
775 Ly. eám tu despondísti, opinor, Mégadoro. Ev. omnem rém tenes.
Ly. ís me nunc renúntiare répudium iussít tibi.
Ev. répudium rebús paratis, éxornatis núptiis ?
út illum di inmortáles omnes deaéque quantumst
pérduint,   55
quém propter hodie aúri tantum pérdidi infelíx,
miser.
780 Ly. bóno animo es, benedíce : nunc quae rés tibi et
gnataé tuae
béne feliciúérque vortat : íta di faxint, ínquito.
Ev. íta di faciant. Ly. ét mihi ita di fáciant. audi
núnciam.
quí homo culpam admísit in se, núllust tam parví
preti,   60

---

770. *Antiqui pro 'sufficit'*
'*sat habeo*' *dicebant.* Donatus
on Ter. Andr. ii 1, 35. Westerhov in his note gives the
following examples : Andr. iv
2, 22. Eun. ii 2, 32. Haut.
tim. iv 3, 70. Plaut. Most. iii
1, 125.—For *quid vis* (=*quid
velis*) see note on v. 63. It
would also be possible to write
loquere: quid vis ?
771. For *qui* see Key, L. G.
§ 312.—For *aúnculus* see intro-
ductory note on the prologue.

776. *repudiumrenuntiare*'vel
remittere est cum desponsa pac-
taque futurum matrimonium
dirimere.' Gronov. Comp. the
commentators on Ter. Phorm.
iv 3, 72 and v 7, 35.
778. Comp. Pseud. 37 *at te
di deaeque, quantumst* : : *ser-
vassint quidem.*—For *perduint*
see 664.
781. See v. 147.
783. For the hiatus *quí ho*—
see Introd. p. 69. Translate:
' There is no evil-doer so bad

quóm pudeat, quin púriget se. núnc te optestor,
    Eúclio,
785 út si quid ego ergá te imprudens péccavi aut gnatám
    tuam,
    út mi ignoscas, eámque uxorem míhi des, ut legés
    iubent.
    égo me iniuriám fecisse fíliae fateór tuae
    Céreris vigiliís, per vinum atque ímpulsu adules-
        céntiae.   65
    Ev. eí mihi, quod ego fácinus ex ted aúdio. LY. cur
        éiulas?
790 quém ego avom fecí iam ut esses fíliai núptiis.
    nám tua gnata péperit decumo ménse post : nume-
        rúm cape.
    eá re repudiúm remisit aúnculus causá mea.
    í intro, exquaere, sítne ita ut ego praédico. Ev.
    perii óppido.   70
    íta mihi ad malúm malae res plúrumae se adglú-
        tinant.

that, in case he should feel a
sense of shame, he would not
excuse himself.'
    785. *erga* of unfriendly do-
ing is very rare. See Key, L. G.
§ 1334 c. *peccare in aliquem* is
the phrase used by Ter. Ad. iv
7, 7.
    790. For the construction
avom feci ut esses see note on
v. 440.
    791. Gellius has a whole
chapter on the question πόσος ὁ
τῆς τῶν ἀνθρώπων κυήσεως χρόνος
iii 16 where he says *multa
opinio est eaque iam pro vero
recepta, postquam mulieris ute-
rus conceperit semen, gigni hominem septimo rarenter, numquam octavo, saepe nono, saepius
numero decimo mense.* In the

comic writers we generally find
therefore the tenth month: see
Westerhov on Ter. Ad. iii 4,
29. The ten months are of
course lunar months. So also
Verg. Ecl. iv 61 *matri longa
decem tulerunt fastidia menses.*
    793. In *intro* the first syl-
lable is shortened, see note on
448 ; we should therefore pronounce *i* ĭntro (for the hiatus
see Introd. p. 69), not *i* ĭntro
(compare Ritschl's and Fleckeisen's editions with regard to
Stich. 396).—The form *exquae-
re* is here given by Priscian and
the later mss., comp. Stich. 107
where all our mss. give *exquae-
situm*, and Capt. ii 2, 43 *ex-
quaesivero.* Comp. also Merc.
633 *requaereres,*

795 íbo intro, ut quid huíus ver*um* sít sciam.　Ly. iam
　　té sequor.
haec própemodum iam esse ín vado salútis res
　　vidétur.
nunc sérvom esse ubi dicám meum Strobílum, non
　　repério.
nisi étiam hic opperiár tamen paulísper, postea
　　íntro　　　　　　　　　　　　　　　　　　　　　75
hunc súbsequar. nunc ínterim spatium eí dabo ex-
　　quiréndi
800 meum fáctum ex gnatae pédisequa nutríce anu : ea
　　rem nóvit.

STROBILVS. LYCONIDES.　　　V. 1

Str. di ínmortales, quíbus et quantis mé donatis
　　gaúdiis.
quádrilibrem aulam onústam auro habeo : quís mest
　　hominum dítior ?
quís me Athenis núnc magis quisquamst hómo quoi
　　di sint própitii ?
Ly. cérto enim ego vocem híc loquentis módo m*i*
　　audire vísus sum.　Str. hem,

795. For the expression *quid
huius sit* see Ter. Eun. iv 3, 10.
iv 7, 34. Haut. tim. ii 2, 8.
iv 4, 21.
　796. *in vado salutis* 'in the
haven of safety.' Comp. Ter.
Andr. v 2, 4 *omnis res est iam
in vado,* on which passage Donatus observes ' proverbiale, *in
vado,* in tuto, in securitate.
nam ut in profundo periculum
est, ita in vado securitas est.'
　801. The phrase *donare gaudiis* has its parallels in the expressions *donare salute* (Tibull.)
and *donare honoribus* (Stat.).

　802. For the transposition
onustam auro comp. 603 and
609.
　803. As far as the pleonastic construction is concerned,
Brix justly compares Most. 256
*vah, quid illa pote peius quic-
quam muliere memorarier?* as
the line should be read according to the mss.
　804. Comp. Ter. Eun. iii 2,
1 *audire vocem visa sum modo
militis.* Plaut. Cist. ii 3, 1 *audire vocem visa sum ante aedis
modo.* For the construction
comp. Mil. gl. 389 *arguere in*

805 érumne ego aspició meum ?
   LY. vídeo ego hunc servóm meum ?   5
   STR. ípsus est. LY. haud álius est. STR. con-
     grédiar. LY. contollám gradum.
   crédo ego illum, út iussi, eampse adisse anum, huíus
     nutricem vírginis.
   STR. quín ego illi me ínvenisse dícam hanc praedam
     atque éloquar.
       *   *   *   *   *   *   *
   ígitur orabo, út manu me emíttat : ibo atque élo-
     quar.
810 répperi ... LY. quid répperisti ?   STR. nón quod
     pueri clámitant   10
   ín faba se répperisse. LY. iámne autem, ut solés,
     deludis ?
   STR. ére, mane, eloquár : iam ausculta. LY. age
     érgo, loquere. STR. répperi hodie,
   ére, divitias nímias. LY. ubinam ? STR. quádri-
     librem, inquam, aulam aúri plenam.
   LY. quód ego facinus aúdio ex te ? STR. Eúclioni
     huic séni subrupui.
815 LY. úbi id est aurum ? STR. in árca apud me.
   núnc volo me emittí manu.   15

---

*somnis me meus mihi familiaris
visust.*
  806. For *ipsus* see note on
v. 354.
  810. The right explanation of
this passage was first given by
Lambinus. Gronovius explains
it as follows ' servus significans
non parvam rem neque levem
repperisse se, negat inventum
sibi nihil maius quam quod
pueri clamitant se repperisse
in faba, nempe vermiculum
quem *Midam* vocant : eum enim
pueri in fabis quaerere sole-
bant, quique inveniebat inde

exultare ac velut triumphum
agere.' He compares Curc. 586
*in tritico facillume vel quingen-
tos curculiones pro uno faxo
reperies.*
  811. Comp. Bacch. 203 *iamne
ut soles,* and Poen. v 7, 39 where
Spengel (' T. Maccius Plautus,'
p. 16) justly introduces the same
phrase, as Acidalius had done
before in Truc. III 2, 27 (=683
G.).
  814. For the hiatus see Introd. p. 67.—The *i* in *seni* is
shortened : see Introd. p. 23.

Ly. égone te emittám manu,
scélerum cumulatíssume?
Str. ábi, ere; scio quam rém geras:
lépide hercle animum tuóm temptavi: iám ut eri-
    peres, ádparabas:
quíd faceres, si répperissem? Ly. nón potes pro-
    básse nugas.
820 í, redde aurum. Str. réddam ego aurum? Ly. rédde,
    ut huic reddátur. Str. unde?   20
Ly. quód modo fassu's ésse in arca. Str. sóleo
    hercle ego garríre nugas.
íta loquor.   *   *   *   *
Ly. át scin quo modó? Str. vel hercle me énica:
    numquam hínc feres
á me   *   *   *   *
Ly. ut ádmemordi hominem . . . . . .
        *   *   *   *   *

816. For the genitive *scele-*
rum see Key, L. G. §§ 931, 941.
Caecilius has *ineptitudinis cu-*
mulatus v. 61 (p. 37 Ribb.).
817. *abi* 'varium habet
usum, estque vel formula lau-
dandi, ut Ad. iv 2, 25 *abi, vi-*
rum te iudico [Eun. i 2, 74.
Plaut. Asin. iii 3, 114], vel con-
temnendi, uti Ad. ii 2, 12. Eun.
iv 3, 9.' Westerhov on Ad. ii
2, 12. This expression is quite
equivalent to the English 'get
off.'
818. *lepide* 'cunningly,' v.
493.—For the hiatus *iám ut* see
Introd. p. 69.
819. For the perfect infinitive
probasse see Key, L. G. § 1256.

822. Comp. Amph. iv 2, 1.
Am. *ego sum.* Me. *quid, ego*
sum? Am. *ita loquor.*
823. *vel* is in the comic
writers frequently employed to
enforce an imperative; comp.
Ter. Phorm. 140 sqq. And.
679 sq. Pl. Rud. 549 sq. 1401.
Bacch. 902. Pseud. 120.
824. The perfect *memordi*
occurs also in Laberius (28 and
50) and Atta (6). In Poen. v 2,
114 (=1062) Geppert has justly
edited *memordit* on the authority of the mss. *BC*, while former editions give *momordit.* Cf.
also Schuchardt on Vulgar Latin
ii 212.

ACTVS V.

*   *   *   *   *

825 Ev.   néc noctu nec diú quietus úmquam er̆am :
       nunc dórmiam
          *   *   *   *
       ego écfodiebam ín die denós scrobes.
          *   *   *   *

Ly.   qui mi hólera cruda pónunt, *etiam* alléc duint.
          *   *   *   *

825. These words were probably spoken by Euclio after he had bestowed his treasure upon his son-in-law (see Arg. II 9) and had thus divested himself of all future cares. *Now* he hopes to sleep quietly, while formerly he had no rest by day or night—very much like Mozart's Leporello !

826. This may possibly have been a proverbial expression denoting a care-worn and anxious life. If so, it would likewise seem to have occurred in that speech of Euclio's to which we have ascribed the preceding fragment.

827. Lyconides receives Euclio's daughter (*holera cruda*) and the dowry (*allec*, properly 'the sauce'). This is, however, a mere guess.

W. P.

METRA HVIVS FABVLAE HAEC SVNT

— 471 ad 578 iambici senarii
— 579 ad 652 trochaici septenarii
— 653 ad 704 iambici senarii
— 705 ad 714 anapaestici octonarii
— 715 versus corruptus, ut videtur
— 716 ad 718 anapaestici octonarii
— 719 anapaesticus dimeter catalecticus
— 720 ad 722 trochaici octonarii
— 723 ad 795 trochaici septenarii
— 796 ad 800 iambici septenarii
— 801 ad 804 trochaici septenarii
— 805 A et 805 B trochaicae tetrapodiae catalecticae
— 806 ad 810 trochaici septenarii
— 811 ad 814 trochaici octonarii
— 815 trochaicus septenarius
— 816 ad 817 trochaicae tetrapodiae catalecticae
— 818 ad 821 trochaici octonarii
— 822 A versus trochaicus mutilus
— 822 B trochaicus septenarius
— 823 versus trochaicus mutilus
— 824 versus iambicus mutilus
— 825 trochaicus septenarius
— 826 aut iambicus senarius aut (versus initio deperdito)
   trochaicus septenarius
— 827 iambicus senarius

ADDENDA

Note on v. 353. Quintilian i 7, 9 derives *abstemius* from *abstinentia temeti*.

Note on v. 419. Even Cicero says *magis malle* Tusc. i 31, 76. Constructions of this kind occur also in Appuleius.

Note on v. 443. *Pipulus* occurs also in Fronto, ep. ad Anton. imp. 1, 3.

Note on v. 451. For *fissum* comp. also Cic. de n. deor. iii 6, 14. de divin. ii 13, 32. 14, 34.

Note on v. 505. *Patagiarius* occurs also Doni Inscript. cl. No. 78.

Note on v. 529 read λόγου instead of λόγους, and comp. also Theophrast., Char. 8 δοκῶ μοί σε εὐωχήσειν καινῶν λόγων.

LATIN TEXTS AND COMMENTARIES

the Ayer Company collection

Butler, H.E. and M. Cary, editors. **M. Tulli Ciceronis De Provinciis Consularibus Oratio Ad Senatum.** 1924

Camps, W.A., editor. **Propertius Elegies Book IV.** 1965

Dilke, O.A.W., editor. **Statius Achilleid.** 1954

Dougan, Thomas Wilson and Robert Mitchell Henry, editors. **M. Tulli Ciceronis Tusculanarum Libri Quinque.** Two vols. in one. 1905/1934

Duckworth, George E., editor. **T. Macci Plauti Epidicus.** 1940

Enk, P.J., editor. **Plauti Mercator.** Two vols. in one. 1932

Enk, P.J., editor. **Plauti Truculentus.** Two vols. in one. 1953

Getty, R.J., editor. **M. Annaei Lucani De Bello Civili Liber I.** 1940

Gibb, John and William Montgomery, editors. **The Confessions of Augustine.** 1927

Gildersleeve, Basil L., editor. **The Satires of A. Persius Flaccus.** 1903

Holder, Alfred, editor. **Pomponi Porfyrionis Commentum in Horatium Flaccum.** 1894

Holmes, T. Rice, editor. **C. Iuli Caesaris De Bello Gallico.** Seven vols. in one. 1914

Lindsay, W.M., editor. **The Captivi of Plautus.** 1900

Magnus, Hugo, editor. **P. Ovidi Nasonis Metamorphoseon Libri XV.** 1914

Mayor, John E.B., editor. **Thirteen Satires of Juvenal.** Two vols. in one. 1877/1878

Mooney, George W., editor. **C. Suetoni Tranquilli De Vita Caesarum Libri VII-VIII.** 1930

Nisbet, Robert G., editor. **M. Tulli Ciceronis De Domo Sua Ad Pontifices Oratio.** 1939

Pease, Arthur Stanley, editor. **M. Tulli Ciceronis De Divinatione.** Two vols. in one. 1920/1923

Pease, Arthur Stanley, editor. **M. Tulli Ciceronis De Natura Deorum.** Two vols. 1955/1958

Rostagni, Augusto, editor. **Suetonio De Poetis E Biografi Minori.** 1944

Sandys, John Edwin, editor. **M. Tulli Ciceronis Ad M. Brutum Orator.** 1885

Shipp, G.P., editor. **P. Terenti Afri Andria.** 1960

Shuckburgh, Evelyn S., editor. **C. Suetoni Tranquilli Divus Augustus.** 1896

Smith, Kirby Flower, editor. **The Elegies of Albius Tibullus.** 1913

Sonnenschein, Edward A., editor. **T. Macci Plauti Rudens.** 1891

Spengel, Leonardus and Andreas Spengel, editors. **M. Terenti Varronis De Lingua Latina Libri.** 1885

Sturtevant, Edgar H., et al., editors. **T. Macci Plauti Pseudolus.** 1932

Suetonius. **Suetonius on the Life of Tiberius: C. Suetonii Tranquilli Vita Tiberii,** edited by Mary Johnstone Du Four *and* C. Suetoni Tranquilli **Vita Tiberi—C.** 24-C.40, edited by Joannes Renier Rietra. Two vols. in one. 1941/1928

Wagner, Wilhelm, editor. **T. Macci Plauti Aulularia.** 1876

Wilkins, Augustus S., editor. **M. Tulli Ciceronis De Oratore.** Three vols. in one. 1895/1890/1892